PORTFOLIO THEORY AND THE
DEMAND FOR MONEY

Also by Neil Thompson

MACROECONOMICS (*with David Demery, Nigel W. Duck,*
Michael T. Sumner and R. Leighton Thomas)

Portfolio Theory and the Demand for Money

Neil Thompson
Lecturer in Economics
University of Salford

First published in Great Britain 1993 by
THE MACMILLAN PRESS LTD
Houndmills, Basingstoke, Hampshire RG21 2XS
and London
Companies and representatives
throughout the world

A catalogue record for this book is available
from the British Library.

ISBN 0–333–57260–2

First published in the United States of America 1993 by
Scholarly and Reference Division,
ST. MARTIN'S PRESS, INC.,
175 Fifth Avenue,
New York, N.Y. 10010

ISBN 0–312–09580–5

Library of Congress Cataloging-in-Publication Data
Thompson, Neil, 1953–
Portfolio theory and the demand for money / Neil Thompson.
p.   cm.
Includes bibliographical references and index.
ISBN 0–312–09580–5
1. Portfolio management.   2. Demand for money.
HG4529.5.T48   1993
332.6—dc20   92–44661
                                               CIP

Printed and bound in Great Britain by
Biddles Ltd, Guildford and King's Lynn

8   7   6   5   4   3   2
02 01 00 99 98 97 96

To my parents

Contents

The Line 10,000

List of Figures

Govt. Securities.

Preface

This book is concerned with the theoretical and empirical analysis of asset demand functions, with particular reference to the demand for money. A basic knowledge of macroeconomics and econometric theory is assumed, with the coverage of the book aimed primarily at final-year undergraduate and graduate students in economics. The demand for money function is arguably the most researched relationship in the whole of empirical macroeconomics: few economic relations have received so much attention from empirical investigators, and yet yielded so many contradictory results. Once regarded as a central pillar of macroeconomics, it is now widely viewed to be one of its weakest relations. This, in turn, has considerable implications for the conduct of monetary policy.

The empirical relationship between the stock of money and its key demand determinants first appeared to break down in the early 1970s and a major theme of this book is to consider the various possible explanations for the observed instability and predictive failure in the estimated relation. The different empirical approaches to the analysis of money demand are analysed in detail, with consideration given to the use of new econometric techniques, such as cointegration and error-correction modelling. In this respect, the aim of the book is to bridge the gap between the traditional textbook treatment of the demand for money and the journal literature. In practice, of course, the demand for money is merely one part of a much-wider portfolio choice problem, involving decisions about other financial and real assets. Some consideration is given to these other allocation decisions, particularly the demand for government bonds and the determination of bank advances. Much of the current work on the empirical modelling of asset demand functions is carried out by the large macro model-building groups, and in this respect the work of the Treasury is described in detail.

The overall framework of the book can be summarised as follows. Chapter 1 is devoted to a brief introduction to the portfolio choice problem. Chapters 2, 3 and 4 look at some alternative theoretical approaches to the asset allocation decision; these involve mean–variance analysis, transactions and precautionary motives and general demand theory. Models of asset demand, which have utilised these different approaches, are considered in each case. Empirical work on the demand for financial assets is dominated by studies of money demand. This work, ranging from the traditional restricted distributed lag models to the more recent focus on monetary disequilibrium and the role of money as a buffer stock, is reviewed in Chapters 5, 6 and 7. Considerably fewer studies have analysed the demand for other assets, but in Chapters 8 and 9 we discuss the empirical modelling of bank lending equations and the private sector's demand for government bonds. The more complete multi-asset models are considered in Chapter 10. The form of the general portfolio model is described, together with the findings of empirical studies of asset allocation within the private and banking sectors. Finally, in Chapter 11, we make some concluding comments about the modelling of monetary aggregates and other financial assets. The policy implications of our findings are also discussed.

The preparation of this book has occupied a considerable amount of my time in recent years and some words of thanks are due to those who have helped me in this task. I owe a particular debt of gratitude to George Zis for the time he spent reading an earlier version of the manuscript. Acknowledgements are also due to Rob Simmons, Roger Smyth and Leighton Thomas for their advice on specific issues, and to Derek Carline, Tony Sampson and Bob Ward for their encouragement and help throughout the final tedious stages of preparation. Finally, I must express my thanks to Shirley Woolley who has typed and corrected different versions of the manuscript over the preparation period. Needless to say, any remaining errors and omissions are entirely my own responsibility.

NEIL THOMPSON

Acknowledgement: The author and publishers wish to thank Harper & Row for permission to use Figures 3.3 and 3.4, adapted from *The Demand for Money: Theories, Evidence and Problems* (3rd edn, 1985), pp. 65–6, by D. E. W. Laidler.

1 An Introduction to Portfolio Analysis

Portfolio analysis is concerned with the development of theoretical models designed to analyse the factors affecting the financial assets held by economic agents, together with the empirical testing of these models. The agents may be individuals and firms, in which case we are concerned with the way in which private sector wealth is allocated between different assets, or alternatively financial institutions where the deposits of customers are allocated among competing assets so as to satisfy the balance sheet identity. Such an approach to asset choice decisions has its roots in early studies of the demand for money. In his formulation of the speculative demand for money, Keynes analysed the way in which individuals allocate their given wealth between interest-bearing bonds and money in the form of cash balances which earns no pecuniary return. The choice is based upon the expected holding-period return on bonds, which not only depends upon the interest income, but also upon expectations about movements in the market rate of interest and hence the price of bonds; these expectations will, in turn, be based on what is perceived to be the 'normal' rate of interest. If market rates are low, below the 'normal' rate, and therefore expected to rise over the holding period, a capital loss is to be expected on bond holding; individuals will sell bonds and hold their entire portfolio in cash, as long as the interest income from bond holding is not enough to offset this expected capital loss. On the other hand, if market rates are high, above the 'normal' rate, and expected to fall over the holding period, individuals will expect capital gains from bond holding; they will accordingly transfer their wealth from cash to bonds.

Several criticisms can be levelled at the model. The theory is based upon the view that expectations are regressive, whereas in practice they are often extrapolative in the short run; that is, a fall in interest rates produces the initial expectation of an even greater fall over the holding period. Also, the model implies that the individual wealth holder cannot maintain a diversified portfolio; at any given time, the individual holds his wealth either entirely in bonds or entirely in cash. Only at one interest rate, termed the 'critical' rate, which is below the 'normal' rate, is it the case that the expected capital loss from bond holding is equal to the interest gain, so that the individual is indifferent between holding bonds or cash. This implies that there will be a discontinuity in the individual's demand for money function at this 'critical' rate of interest; above the 'critical' rate, all wealth is held in bonds, while at interest rates below this rate only cash is held. However, because it is assumed individuals do not all have the same expectations, the 'critical' rate at which switching occurs between bonds and cash will vary among individuals, so that at the aggregate level it is possible to obtain the traditional downward-sloping continuous relationship between the market interest rate and the demand for money. At very low rates of interest, with nobody expecting the rate to fall further, the demand for money balances may become infinite, giving rise to the phenomenon of the liquidity trap.

The mean–variance model of Tobin (1958) enables both portfolio diversification and the downward-sloping relationship, between the demand for money and the rate of interest, to be explained at the individual level. Again the investor has to allocate his wealth between bonds and cash. However, whereas in Keynes' speculative demand model, it is assumed that each individual has definite expectations about movements in interest rates, which may or may not be correct, in Tobin's model it is assumed that he knows only the probability distribution of returns from holding bonds. In this sense, it can be argued that the model owes more to the precautionary element of Keynes' theory of the demand for money, which is based on uncertainty, rather than the speculative element where expectations are held with certainty.[1] Tobin assumes that wealth holders are uncertain as to the likely magnitude and direction of interest rate movements, and therefore also the return on bonds. Holding bonds offers higher potential returns than cash, but also the risk of capital losses if bond prices fall. The individual has therefore to allocate his wealth between safe, but zero-earning cash, and bonds, which offer a potentially higher return, but greater uncertainty. Expected returns, measured by the mean of the probability distribution of returns from the portfolio, and risk, proxied by the variance or standard deviation of the distribution, are therefore crucial in determining portfolio allocation within this mean–variance approach.

Tobin's original model, like that of Keynes, is based upon a two-asset choice set involving cash and bonds. Tobin (1965) extended the model to more than two assets, while Friedman (1956) reformulated the Quantity Theory of Money as a theory of the demand for money, based upon a portfolio choice decision involving not only cash and bonds, but also equities and real goods. Relative rates of return on these assets are seen as being crucial in determining the demand for the different assets. Friedman's analysis owed much to the work of the early Cambridge economists such as Marshall and Pigou. Within a transactions-orientated model, in which holdings of money balances vary in response to nominal income, the view of the Cambridge approach was that substitution between money and other assets would occur as a result of changes in relative yields and overall wealth. The principles of portfolio choice, involving cash and bonds, have also been extended to the transactions demand for money through the inventory–theoretic models of Baumol (1952) and Tobin (1956). In these models, the demand for transactions balances is shown to depend upon brokerage fees and the interest return on bonds. The brokerage costs of moving between the two assets may justify the holding of cash, even though bonds offer an interest yield.

Since these pioneering studies, based upon the demand for money, analysis of the asset allocation decision process has been developed in several ways, both at the theoretical and empirical level. Major developments have included the formal statement of the multi-asset portfolio choice problem by Brainard and Tobin (1968) and the extension of the model to incorporate the analysis of financial institutions, in studies such as Parkin *et al.* (1970). These developments and other extensions to the basic models are considered in later chapters. In addition, the findings of empirical studies of asset choice behaviour are analysed in detail, with a particular emphasis placed upon the demand for money function. First of all, however, we consider in more detail some alternative theoretical approaches to the asset allocation decision; these involve mean–variance analysis, transactions and precautionary motives and general demand theory.

2 The Mean–Variance Approach

The mean–variance, or risk–return, approach to portfolio analysis is based upon the premise that the investor in allocating his wealth between different assets takes into account, not only the returns expected from alternative portfolio combinations, but also the risk attached to each such holding. This risk is usually assumed to arise out of uncertainty over future asset prices, and can occur in any asset where the expected holding period is less than the term to maturity. Stocks and shares fall into such a category because prices vary according to market conditions, with the risk of capital losses potentially high. However, even the returns from interest-paying capital-certain money deposits may involve an element of uncertainty over the holding period, if the interest rate is subject to market variability. In formal terms, the mean–variance approach assumes that the investor maximises the expected utility obtainable from his portfolio holding, expressed in terms of expected return and risk, subject to the restriction imposed by his budget constraint. Expected return is measured by the mean of the probability distribution of portfolio returns and risk by the standard deviation or variance of the distribution, which provides a measure of the dispersion of possible returns around the mean value. A large standard deviation implies a high probability of big deviations from expected returns, both positive and negative. Such an approach to portfolio analysis stems from Markowitz's (1952, 1959) studies of efficient portfolio selection and Tobin's (1958) paper on liquidity preference.

The investor's attitude to risk is fundamental to the mean–variance model and before considering the approach in detail, we will consider the form of the individual's utility function under different assumptions about risk. If the investor is risk-averse, so that he does not obtain satisfaction from risk-taking, the functional relationship linking utility to wealth or returns (π) for the individual will be concave to the horizontal axis, as illustrated in Figure 2.1. The slope of the utility function, which represents the marginal utility of wealth, decreases as returns rise. This implies that the certainty of a given return is preferred to a gamble offering an equivalent expected return: in Figure 2.1, the

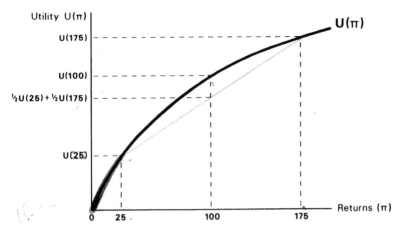

Figure 2.1   Utility function of a risk-averse individual

utility obtained from the certainty of £100 is greater than the expected utility obtainable from the gamble offering equal probabilities of either £25 or £175. A fifty–fifty chance of either no return or £200 would provide an even lower expected utility. Alternatively, individuals may display other attitudes towards risk. For example, investors who are indifferent between the certainty of a given amount and the gamble offering an equivalent expected return are said to be risk-neutral; such an individual's utility function can be represented by a straight line from the origin. Finally, the individual who expects to achieve more utility from the gamble has a utility function which is convex to the horizontal axis, as illustrated in Figure 2.2. A fifty–fifty chance of either £25 or £175 is preferred to the certainty of £100. The marginal utility of wealth, as represented by the slope of the utility function, increases as returns rise and the investor is termed a risk-lover.

Based on the properties of the utility function, Arrow (1965) and Pratt (1964) developed a formula which gives some indication of the individual's attitude towards risk. Their measure of absolute risk aversion, RA_A, is defined as

$$RA_A = -\frac{U''(\pi)}{U'(\pi)} \tag{2.1}$$

where $U'(\pi)$ and $U''(\pi)$ are, respectively, the first- and second-order derivatives of the utility function. The derivative $U'(\pi)$ is always positive, no matter the individual's preferences, but $U''(\pi)$ is either

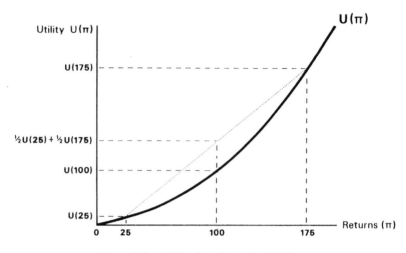

Figure 2.2   Utility function of a risk-lover

negative, zero or positive, according to whether the individual is risk-averse, risk-neutral or risk-loving. Accordingly, the value of RA_A is positive for the risk-averse individual, zero for the risk-neutral investor and negative for the lover of risk. The greater the positive (negative) value of RA_A, the greater the degree of risk aversion (enjoyment).

TOBIN'S MODEL OF LIQUIDITY PREFERENCE

Tobin (1958) considers the possible strategies for these different types of investor in his two-asset mean–variance model of liquidity preference. The problem facing the individual is to allocate wealth between a safe asset, which is taken to be cash, and a risky asset, namely bonds. Cash has a fixed nominal capital value, but offers no monetary return, while the return on bonds, over the holding period, is made up of an interest component which is known and an uncertain element representing capital gains and losses. As in Keynes' speculative demand model, the risk in holding bonds therefore arises from the possibility of capital value changes if bond prices fall. However, whereas Keynes' model assumes that the individual has definite expectations about the capital gain or loss likely from bond holding at each rate of interest, Tobin's model assumes that the probability distribution of capital gains and losses is independent of the current interest rate. At any time, an equal probability is attached to a fall in the price of a bond as to a rise in its price, so that the expected capital gain is zero; the expected return from bond holding is merely equal to the rate of interest.

We will assume that the proportion of the portfolio held in cash is given by X_1 and the proportion in bonds by X_2, so that X_1 and X_2 add up to unity. The actual return on the portfolio, over the holding period, depends upon the proportion held in bonds, the interest income and the capital gain or loss element of the return on bonds. In notational form, we can write

$$\pi = X_2(r + g)$$

where π is the actual portfolio return per unit of wealth over the period, r is the interest rate and g is the capital gain. Because the expected value of capital gains is zero, the expected return on the portfolio is given by the product of the interest rate and the proportion held in bonds. We can write

$$E(\pi) = \mu_\pi = X_2 r \qquad (2.2)$$

where E is the expectations operator, such that $E(\pi) = \mu_\pi$ is the expected portfolio return. The variance of returns, σ_π^2, is given by the expression

$$\sigma_\pi^2 = E[\pi - \mu_\pi]^2 = E[X_2 g]^2 = X_2^2 \sigma_g^2$$

where σ_g^2 is the variance of the distribution of capital gains and losses, which is equal to the variance of the price of bonds. Tobin measures risk by the standard deviation of portfolio returns (the square root of the variance) which can be written as

$$\sigma_\pi = X_2 \sigma_g \qquad (2.3)$$

where σ_g is the standard deviation of capital gains and losses. By substituting equation (2.2) into (2.3), and rearranging, it can be shown that

$$\mu_\pi = \left[\frac{r}{\sigma_g}\right] \sigma_\pi$$

Given that r and σ_g are both greater than zero, it must follow that expected return is positively related to risk. If all wealth is held in cash, the portfolio offers zero risk but zero return; such a combination is represented by the origin, point O, in Figure 2.3.

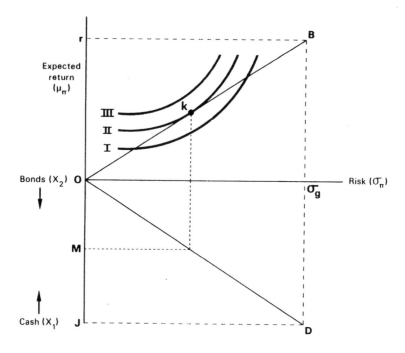

Figure 2.3   The equilibrium portfolio for a risk-averse individual

At the other extreme, if all wealth is held in bonds, the portfolio offers maximum risk, σ_g, but also the highest expected return, equal to r. This combination is represented by point B in Figure 2.3. The other combinations of risk and expected return available to the individual are represented by the opportunity locus, OB, which joins the two extreme positions. The line OD in the lower half of Figure 2.3 enables us to reveal the exact distribution of the portfolio between bonds and cash for all risk–return combinations. In addition to the cash-only portfolio at point O, and the bonds-only portfolio, represented by point D in the lower segment, the composition of diversified portfolios can also now be determined. This is made possible if a line is drawn from any point on the risk–return opportunity locus OB, to the point directly below it on the diagonal line OD; the distance from the risk axis to the diagonal in each case indicates the proportion of the portfolio held in bonds, and since total wealth is given by the distance OJ, the difference represents the proportion of the portfolio held as cash. We can see that the risk and expected return associated with any portfolio combination is directly related to the proportion of the portfolio held in bonds.

In order to determine the portfolio actually held by the investor, we must take account of the individual's preferences between risk and expected return, as represented by the indifference map. Each indifference curve shows the different combinations of risk and expected return which have the same utility for the investor. The precise shape of the curves will depend upon the investor's attitude towards risk. The indifference curves of a risk-averse individual are positively sloped: in order to accept increased risk, he needs to be compensated in the form of an increase in expected return. Moreover, the curves are convex to the risk axis, as illustrated in Figure 2.3, so that the investor needs ever-increasing increments to expected returns, in order to accept equal extra elements of risk. Utility increases as we move upwards and to the left along the indifference map, with curve III offering a higher level of utility than curve II, and the latter a higher level of utility than curve I. The equilibrium risk–return combination is represented by the tangency point, k, between the opportunity locus OB and indifference curve II. As illustrated here, a risk-averse individual is normally a diversifier; the proportion OM of his total wealth is held in bonds and the remainder, represented by MJ, is held in cash. If the individual is risk-neutral, the indifference curves will be a set of horizontal straight lines, as illustrated in Figure 2.4. The optimal

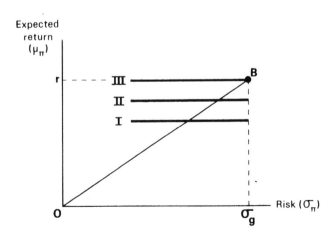

Figure 2.4   The equilibrium portfolio for a risk-neutral individual

solution is represented by the bonds-only portfolio at point *B*, which offers the highest expected return. Finally, investors may be risk-lovers, in which case their indifference curves are everywhere negatively sloped and concave to the risk axis, as illustrated in Figure 2.5. Such individuals are willing to accept a smaller expected return, if risk, and with it the chance of capital gain, increases. They put all their wealth into bonds, so as to enjoy maximum risk, and the optimal position is again at point *B*.

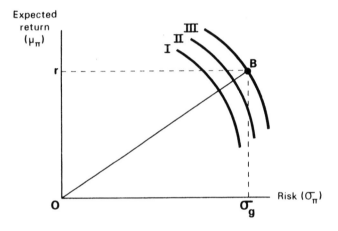

Figure 2.5   The equilibrium portfolio for a risk-lover

Assuming typical risk-averse behaviour, Tobin's model can be used to derive a relationship between the rate of interest and the demand for money. The effect of an increase in the rate of interest, from r_1 to r_2 in Figure 2.6, is to increase the expected return from bonds over the holding period; consequently, the investor allocating his wealth is now faced with a new opportunity locus, represented by the line *OE*. A new equilibrium is established at point *f*, on indifference curve III, with the investor holding a portfolio which involves more risk than previously, but also a higher expected return. The proportion of the portfolio held in bonds has increased from *OM* to *ON*, while the proportion in cash balances has fallen from *JM* to *JN*; the increase in the rate of interest has caused a fall in the demand for money. However, this result is not necessarily universal; it depends crucially upon the direction and relative magnitude of the income and substitution effects of the interest

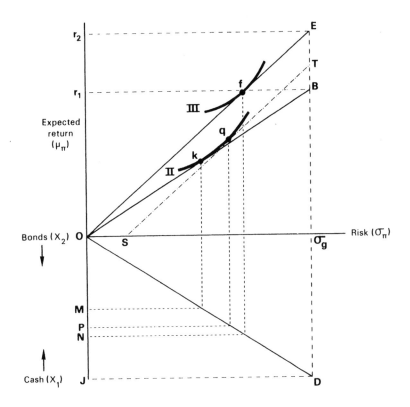

Figure 2.6   The effect of an increase in the rate of interest

rate change. The substitution effect of an increase in the interest rate always leads to an increase in bond holding, as the greater interest return available from bonds increases the opportunity cost of holding cash and encourages individuals to substitute risk for security. The income effect of a rise in the interest rate is ambiguous because it gives the individual the opportunity to have the same expected portfolio return for less risk or to enjoy more of both; it can therefore lead either to an increase or a decrease in the demand for bonds depending upon the nature of the individual's preferences between risk and expected return. Some individuals will prefer to divide largely in favour of security; others will divide largely in favour of expected return, while yet others will divide fairly evenly. In Figure 2.6, the income and substitution effects are isolated by drawing a new opportunity line *ST*,

which is parallel to *OE*, and tangential to indifference curve II at point
q. The substitution effect is represented by the move from point *k* to
point *q* and the distance *MP* in the lower half of the diagram, while the
income effect is represented by the move from point *q* to point *f* and the
distance *PN*. In this case, the income effect reinforces the substitution
effect, increasing the demand for bonds and indicating that the investor
regards security as an inferior good and is willing to accept more risk as
the expected return from bond holding increases. On the other hand, if
security is viewed as a normal good, the income effect will lead to a
decrease in bond holding as the increase in the interest rate allows the
investor to lower his risk exposure. If this is the case, and the
magnitude of the response is larger than that of the substitution
effect, the overall effect of the increase in the interest rate will be an
increase in the proportion of the portfolio held in cash balances. The
investor prefers greater security to the higher expected return now
available.[1]

Tobin's framework can also be used to analyse the effect of a change
in the risk attached to bond holding. The effect of an increase in
'riskiness' is illustrated in Figure 2.7 for a typical risk-averse individual.
The opportunity locus of risk–return combinations moves from *OB* to
OC, with the maximum bond holding now involving the same expected
return as before, but greater risk (σ_{g2}). A new equilibrium is established
at point *z* on indifference curve I, with the investor in this case holding
a portfolio offering a lower expected return and more risk than the
initial position at point *k* on indifference curve II. The combination of
cash and bonds implied by the new equilibrium can be determined from
the diagonal *OA* in the lower half of the diagram; the proportion of the
portfolio held in cash is represented by *JQ* and the proportion in bonds
by *OQ*. The extra risk attached to bond holding has increased the
proportion of the portfolio held in cash balances by *MQ* compared to
the initial equilibrium position, illustrating the negative relationship
that is to be expected between risk and the demand for bonds. In
Tobin's model, the division of wealth between cash and bonds
therefore depends upon the interest rate and the risk attached to
bond holding, as represented by the standard deviation of the
probability distribution of capital gains and losses. However, in order
to obtain explicit functional forms for the demands for cash and bonds,
more specific assumptions must be made about the form of the
investor's utility function, as we shall see later in this chapter.

Tobin's analysis explains the presence of non-interest-bearing money
in the investor's portfolio in terms of the uncertain returns involved in

13

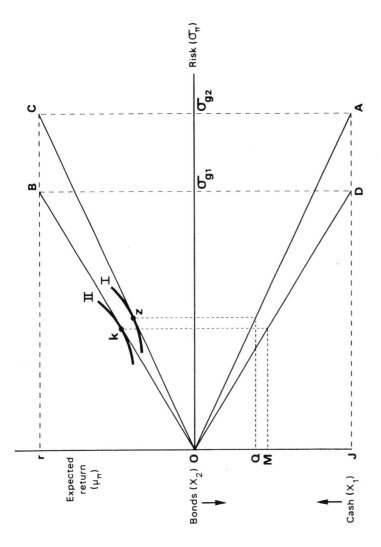

Figure 2.7 The effect of an increase in 'riskiness'

the holding of other assets. However, the use of such a model to explain cash holdings poses conceptual problems because, in practice, bank and building society deposit accounts may exist which pay a fixed known rate of interest over the holding period and so dominate non-interest-bearing money as a safe asset. Fortunately, Tobin's framework can easily be amended to analyse the choice between a fixed-interest-earning asset with a constant nominal value and an interest-earning asset with an uncertain, but possibly higher, future capital value. The opportunity locus of risk–return combinations available to the investor merely rotates about point *B* in Figure 2.3, so that it meets the vertical axis at the positive fixed rate of interest, rather than at the origin. Within such a framework, the mean–variance model can be used to explain the demand for fixed-interest-bearing money balances. In addition, there are many other types of bank and building society account which provide capital-certainty, but are formally subject to uncertain returns, because they bear a rate of interest which may vary over the holding period. Such assets, which display only interest-risk in the context of the mean–variance model, are also likely to dominate cash in the investor's portfolio.[2]

PORTFOLIO CHOICE WITH TWO RISKY ASSETS

Following Tobin (1965), we can develop the mean–variance model to consider the choice between two risky assets. For illustrative purposes, it will be assumed that the investor has to allocate wealth between two assets, where the return on each involves both a certain interest payment and an uncertain element, representing capital gains and losses. We will also relax the assumption that expected capital gains are zero. This means that the expected return on each risky asset may incorporate an expected capital gain element as well as the interest payment, while the variance of returns is now based upon the distribution of capital gains around a non-zero expected value. The actual portfolio return, per unit of wealth over the holding period, can be written as

$$\pi = X_1(r_1 + g_1) + X_2(r_2 + g_2)$$

where X_1 and X_2 represent the proportion of wealth invested in each asset, r_1 and r_2 refer to the respective interest rates, and g_1 and g_2 represent the actual capital gains accruing in each case. Assuming a non-zero expected capital gain, the expected return on the portfolio can be written as

$$\mu_\pi = X_1\mu_1 + X_2\mu_2 \tag{2.4}$$

where $\mu_1 = r_1 + g_1^e$ is the expected return on the first asset and $\mu_2 = r_2 + g_2^e$ is the expected return on the second asset, with g_1^e and g_2^e representing the capital gain or loss expected in each case over the holding period. The variance of total portfolio returns is given by the expression

$$\begin{aligned}\sigma_\pi^2 &= E[\pi - \mu_\pi]^2 = E[X_1(g_1 - g_1^e) + X_2(g_2 - g_2^e)]^2 \\ &= X_1^2\sigma_1^2 + X_2^2\sigma_2^2 + 2X_1X_2\sigma_{12}\end{aligned} \tag{2.5}$$

where σ_1^2 and σ_2^2 represent the variance of returns on each asset, and σ_{12} is the covariance of returns between the two assets. This covariance can be related to the correlation coefficient between the returns on the two assets, with $\sigma_{12} = \rho_{12}\sigma_1\sigma_2$ where ρ_{12} is the correlation coefficient. Substituting this relation into equation (2.5), we can show

$$\sigma_\pi^2 = X_1^2\sigma_1^2 + X_2^2\sigma_2^2 + 2X_1X_2\rho_{12}\sigma_1\sigma_2 \tag{2.6}$$

From equation (2.6), it is obvious that the variance of the overall portfolio return, and hence the opportunity locus of risk–return combinations available to the investor, from different combinations of the two assets, is dependent upon the extent to which the returns on the two assets are correlated.

In Figure 2.8, we examine some of the different possibilities under the assumption that the risk and expected return associated with the second asset is greater than that perceived for the first asset. For consistency with our earlier diagrams, the standard deviation of the distribution of portfolio returns is used to measure risk on the horizontal axis. If the returns on the two assets are independent, so that $\rho_{12} = 0$, the risk–return opportunity locus facing the individual will be a curve, represented by *LMN* in Figure 2.8. Point *L* represents a portfolio in which all wealth is held in the minimum-risk asset, while a portfolio comprising only the more risky asset is illustrated by point *N*. Points along the frontier between *L*, *M* and *N* represent different combinations of the two assets, and in all cases diversification leads to an overall portfolio risk smaller than the weighted average of the separate risks on the two assets, as represented by the straight line

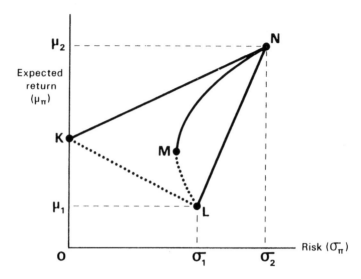

Figure 2.8   Risk–return combinations for two risky assets

joining L and N. The minimum-risk portfolio is not at L, but at point M; it is a diversified portfolio, with the two assets held in inverse proportion to the variance of their respective returns.[3] However, not all portfolios lying along the opportunity locus are efficient and the risk-averse individual will only choose combinations between M and N; points between L and M are not efficient because other portfolios offer greater expected return for no more risk.

When the returns on the two assets are not independent, but negatively correlated, the overall variance (risk) of the portfolio is further reduced and the gains from diversification become more marked. In the extreme case of perfect negative correlation, the returns on the two assets always change inversely by the same proportion; the opportunity locus, linking risk and expected return, is now given by LKN in Figure 2.8, although only portfolios represented by points between K and N are efficient for the risk-averse individual. At point K, it is now possible to avoid risk entirely by complete hedging, with the two assets held in inverse proportion to the standard deviation of their respective returns.[4] In contrast, positive correlation between the returns on the two assets reduces, and in the extreme case eliminates, the possibility of reducing risk by diversification. In practice, the returns obtainable on different securities tend to be positively correlated, as they are all influenced by the same economic and political factors. When all returns move in the same direction by identical proportions, they are said to be perfectly positively correlated; in this case, the opportunity locus facing the investor is given by the straight line *LN* in Figure 2.8. All portfolio combinations are now efficient. For minimum risk, at point *L*, all wealth must be held in the lower risk asset, while the maximum-risk portfolio, at point *N*, is composed entirely of the more risky asset. In this case, the risk of any other combination is simply a weighted average of the risks attached to these two extreme positions, with the weights equal to the portfolio shares of the two assets. Imperfect correlations between the rates of return on the two assets, whether positive or negative, give rise to opportunity loci lying between the two extreme examples illustrated in Figure 2.8; in each of these intermediate cases, the opportunity locus will be curvilinear. For each possible frontier, the combination of risk and expected return chosen by the investor will, of course, ultimately depend upon his preferences, as indicated by the indifference map.

GENERAL RESULTS AND OTHER EXTENSIONS

Tobin (1965) also extends his basic model to include choices involving three or more assets. Some general results emerge from his analysis. Firstly, whereas with only two basic assets the available portfolios all lie along either a straight line or a single curve, with three or more assets the available opportunities cover an area. However, the efficient frontier for the risk-averse individual is still either a line or a curve concave from below, or in special cases a single point. Secondly, the minimum-risk combination is generally a diversified portfolio; the exceptions occur when there is a riskless asset or when there are high positive correlations among asset returns. Thirdly, the maximum-risk combination is always an undiversified portfolio, concentrated on the asset of highest risk. Finally, if one of the assets is riskless, only one permutation of the different risky assets will be mixed with the riskless asset. To illustrate this point, we can consider the case of an investor choosing between two risky assets and a safe interest-earning asset. The efficient frontier of portfolio combinations for the two risky assets is given by the curve *PR* in Figure 2.9, while point *F* represents the portfolio in which all wealth is held in the safe asset, with return equal to *r*. The set of optimum portfolios for the three assets together will lie along a line from *F* to the point of tangency with the curve *PR*,

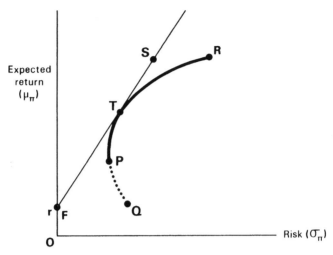

Figure 2.9   The separation theorem and 'borrowing' and 'lending' portfolios

represented by point *T*. Each point along *FT* represents some combination of the safe asset and the particular risky-asset mix represented by point *T*, so that the two risky assets are always held in the same proportion no matter the overall portfolio chosen. Generalising to any number of assets, we can state that the composition of the bundle of risky assets is a separate issue, unrelated to the problem of dividing wealth between the bundle of risky assets and the riskless asset. This result is known as the separation theorem. Of course, between *T* and *R*, the riskless asset no longer forms part of the efficient portfolio, and the exposure to risk and expected return is varied by combining the two risky assets in ever-changing proportions.

This framework was used by Sharpe (1964) and Lintner (1965) to analyse the situation in which the investor engages in both 'borrowing' and 'lending'. In order to do this, it is necessary to assume that the safe asset is money in the form of fixed-interest bank deposits, which can be viewed as a loan from the individual investor to the banking system. Consequently, combinations of the safe asset and the risky-asset mix lying along *FT*, in Figure 2.9, can be termed 'lending' portfolios. It is also assumed that the investor can supplement his existing wealth, by borrowing money at the same rate of interest which he earns on the safe asset. Using this borrowed money, he is able to increase his holdings of risky assets, so that 'borrowing' portfolios, which involve higher expected returns but greater risk, can now be considered by extending the line *FT* beyond point *T*. In all cases, holdings of the risky assets are maintained in the same fixed proportions as dictated by the separation theorem. The further we move to the right of *T*, to points such as *S* and beyond, the more borrowed money is being invested in this bundle of risky assets. These 'borrowing' portfolios clearly dominate the section of the efficient frontier between *T* and *R*, in which variations in the risky-asset mix are possible. The decision on whether to hold a 'lending' or a 'borrowing' portfolio will, of course, ultimately depend upon the investor's preferences between risk and expected return. The above analysis makes the unrealistic assumption that borrowing and lending rates are identical. However, it is possible to relax this assumption and make the borrowing rate, r_b, greater than the lending rate, r_a. The effect of making this distinction is shown in Figure 2.10. The efficient frontier, represented by *GWVZ*, now consists of three distinct, but connected, segments. Between *G* and *W*, the optimal portfolios all involve 'lending' in combination with the mix of risky assets denoted by point *W*. From *V* to *Z* and beyond, 'borrowing' portfolios are efficient; various amounts of borrowing are combined with the risky-asset portfolio combination represented by point *V*. Finally, between *W* and *V*, points on the risky-asset efficient frontier are dominant, with the risky assets combined in ever-changing proportions.

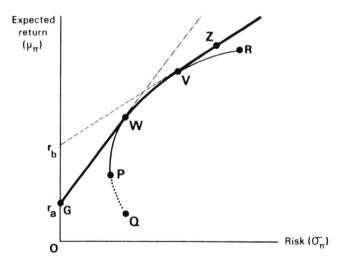

Figure 2.10   The efficient frontier with different 'borrowing' and 'lending' rates

The asset choice decisions considered above are all formulated in terms of nominal returns. Buse (1975) develops an alternative two-asset model, involving a safe and a risky asset, in which the investor is concerned with the mean and variance of real returns. In an inflationary environment, an asset with a known monetary return will not offer a safe real rate of return, unless the future course of inflation is also known with certainty. Expected real returns on the portfolio depend upon the expected rate of inflation, as well as the expected nominal returns on the two assets, while the variance of real returns is dependent upon the variance of nominal returns on the risky asset, the variance of the inflation rate and the covariance between the rate of inflation and the return on the risky asset. In the case of bonds, this covariance is likely to be negative, since a rise in the rate of inflation will normally exert upward pressure on nominal interest rates, inducing a capital loss on bond holdings.

ISSUES IN MEAN–VARIANCE ANALYSIS

Considerable criticism has been levelled at the mean–variance approach, much of it concerned with the restrictive nature of the analysis. Markowitz (1959) and Hicks (1967) both question the validity of using the standard deviation or variance of returns as a surrogate for risk, and suggest that other measures of dispersion should be considered, either instead of, or in addition to, this variable. One such additional measure is the skewness of the distribution. Because the mean–variance approach considers only the first two moments of the probability distribution of returns, factors such as skewness, which is representable by the third moment, are explicitly assumed not to affect the overall portfolio choice. However, the variance provides a symmetric measure of dispersion about the mean and is, for example, likely to underestimate the true risk involved in the portfolio decision, if the distribution of returns is negatively skewed, so that investors are faced with the possibility, albeit small, of large losses. Similarly, in the case of a positively skewed distribution, where there is a small probability of much higher returns, the variance will tend to overestimate the risk involved.[5] Even if the distribution of returns is symmetric about the mean, it is quite conceivable that the typical investor, in his aversion to capital loss, will give a greater weight in his utility function to possible negative outcomes, rather than to possible positive ones with the same probability of occurrence. The variance of returns cannot be used to capture such an effect, but a measure of risk, such as the semi-variance, which takes into account only below-mean returns would satisfy such criteria. Another alternative measure is the mean absolute deviation of returns, which lays less emphasis on larger deviations from the mean than does the variance. Unfortunately, these other measures have drawbacks themselves and have failed to gain popularity.[6] For both simplicity and convenience, there are therefore strong grounds for employing the variance or standard deviation as the risk surrogate.

In order to restrict the analysis to the first two moments, one of two limiting assumptions must be made. Either it must be assumed that the probability distribution of the uncertain returns from an investment can be described by the normal distribution, or alternatively that the utility function of the investor is quadratic in returns. In the first case, if the distribution of returns follows the symmetric normal distribution, a knowledge of the mean and variance is all that is required to describe the entire probability distribution. The validity of this assumption can be criticised, with progressive taxation, limited liability company organisation and hedging behaviour all able to change otherwise symmetric distributions of returns into skewed ones in net returns.[7] Of course, under the extreme assumption that the returns on the various assets are independent of one another, the possible returns on a large portfolio consisting of many different kinds of assets will approximate a normal distribution.[8]

Many studies, including Parkin *et al.* (1970), Sharpe (1973) and Friedman and Roley (1979), have justified the use of mean–variance models by invoking this normality assumption. The use of this method of justifying the approach places no constraints on the form of the utility function, but it is common to postulate a relation which is negative exponential in portfolio returns of the form

$$U(\pi) = a - ce^{-s\pi} \tag{2.7}$$

where e is the exponent, the parameter a can take any value, and the parameters c and s are both greater than zero. By the Arrow–Pratt formula, given in relation (2.1), such a utility function implies a coefficient of absolute risk aversion which is independent of the level of returns and equal to the parameter s. The investor is assumed to maximise the expected value of the utility function in (2.7) which, given the normality assumption, is equivalent to the use of the objective function

$$Z = \mu_\pi - \frac{s}{2}\sigma_\pi^2 \tag{2.8}$$

in which the maximand responds positively to expected returns and negatively to the variance of returns.[9]

Assuming the investor has to allocate wealth between two assets where the return on each is uncertain, we can use the expressions in (2.4) and (2.5), to substitute for μ_π and σ_π^2 in equation (2.8), to obtain the relation

$$Z = X_1\mu_1 + X_2\mu_2 - \frac{s}{2}(X_1^2\sigma_1^2 + X_2^2\sigma_2^2 + 2X_1X_2\sigma_{12}) \tag{2.9}$$

In matrix notation, equation (2.9) can be rewritten as

$$Z = X'\mu - \frac{s}{2}X'\sum X \tag{2.10}$$

where X is a vector of asset shares, μ is a vector of expected asset returns and $\sum$ is the variance–covariance matrix of returns. The maximisation of this function, subject to the budget constraint that the sum of portfolio shares equals unity, leads to a demand system in which asset holdings, as a proportion of wealth, depend upon the risk aversion parameter, the variances and covariances of asset returns and the expected holding period returns on each asset. For the objective function given in equation (2.9), it can be shown that the asset demand functions will take the form

$$X_1 = \frac{\sigma_2^2 - \sigma_{12}}{\sigma_1^2 + \sigma_2^2 - 2\sigma_{12}} + \frac{(\mu_1 - \mu_2)}{s(\sigma_1^2 + \sigma_2^2 - 2\sigma_{12})}$$

$$X_2 = \frac{\sigma_1^2 - \sigma_{12}}{\sigma_1^2 + \sigma_2^2 - 2\sigma_{12}} - \frac{(\mu_1 - \mu_2)}{s(\sigma_1^2 + \sigma_2^2 - 2\sigma_{12})} \tag{2.11}$$

For empirical purposes, it is difficult to quantify most of these terms and, in practice, to facilitate the estimation of such equations, the investors' views about the variances and covariances of asset returns, and the risk aversion parameter, are normally assumed to be constant over time.[10] The portfolio shares then become linear functions of the expected rates of return on the two assets, with the estimated coefficients dependent upon the variance–covariance terms and the risk aversion parameter. Furthermore, the cross rate response coefficients are identical in each equation, so that the effect upon asset one, of a change in the expected return on asset two, is equal to the effect upon asset two, of a change in the expected return on asset one; this property follows from the symmetry of the variance–covariance matrix of asset returns. If the variances and covariances of returns do not remain constant over time, instability may be introduced into the coefficients of the estimated demand function. In particular, according to the Lucas (1976) critique, regime changes relating to the policy stance of the authorities in the financial markets, may alter agents' expectations about the variability of rates of return and so create instability in the estimated relationship.[11] We shall return to the stability issue as it affects the demand for money in Chapters 5 and 6, while the properties of portfolio demand systems are considered in more detail in Chapter 10.

As an alternative to normally distributed asset returns, the mean–variance approach can also be justified if it is assumed that the utility function of the investor is quadratic in portfolio returns. Such a utility function can be written as

$$U(\pi) = a + k\pi - c\pi^2 \tag{2.12}$$

where the parameter a can take any value, $k > 0$ and the value of c depends upon the individual's attitude towards risk. For the risk-averse individual, the utility function must be concave, implying $c > 0$, while for the risk-lover who has a convex utility function, we have $c < 0$. The investor is assumed to maximise the expected value of the utility function given in equation (2.12), which we can write as

$$E(U) = a + kE(\pi) - cE(\pi^2)$$

where E is the expectations operator. Given $E(\pi^2) = \sigma_\pi^2 + (\mu_\pi)^2$, this maximand can also be written in the form

$$E(U) = a + k\mu_\pi - c\sigma_\pi^2 - c(\mu_\pi)^2 \tag{2.13}$$

in which expected utility is related positively to the term in expected return and negatively to the variance of returns. A similar utility function is used by Courakis (1974) in a mean–variance model of bank behaviour. However, this way of justifying the mean–variance approach also has drawbacks. Quadratic utility functions are only relevant over a limited range: for the risk-averse individual, the utility function given in equation (2.12) requires that $\pi < k/2c$, if the marginal utility of returns is to be positive.[12] By the Arrow–Pratt formula, given in relation (2.1), the utility function exhibits increasing absolute risk aversion over this limited range; that is, the value taken by the Arrow-Pratt measure increases as returns rise, so that the individual becomes more averse to constant additive risks. Also, the reduced form demand equations, obtained from quadratic utility functions, are non-linear and less tractable empirically than those arising from negative exponential utility functions, in which returns are assumed to be normally distributed. For the two-asset model discussed above, substitution for μ_π and σ_π^2 in equation (2.13), using the expressions given in (2.4) and (2.5), leads to the objective function

$$E(U) = a + k(X_1\mu_1 + X_2\mu_2) - c(X_1^2\sigma_1^2 + X_2^2\sigma_2^2 + 2X_1X_2\sigma_{12})$$
$$- c(X_1\mu_1 + X_2\mu_2)^2$$

Maximising this function, subject to the budget constraint, results in complex asset demand equations, which contain extra non-linear composite variables in rates of return and variance and covariance terms, in addition to the variables included in the equations in (2.11).

3 Transactions and Precautionary Demand Models

Mean–variance models are most applicable to asset choice decisions where returns are truly stochastic. When applied to the study of capital-certain assets, the approach is suspect. In particular, when the variances and covariances of the rates of return are small, a mean–variance model implies that most wealth will enter the asset with the highest yield. The diversification of holdings among relatively low risk-low return assets can often only be explained in terms of transactions and liquidation costs, and many studies have considered the portfolio choice problem largely in terms of such factors. This alternative treatment of the demand for money and other assets is often termed the inventory–theoretic approach, because of its similarity to the more general analysis of the demand for inventories; it emanates from the preliminary work of Baumol (1952) and Tobin (1956) on the transactions demand for money. Although these models were developed independently, their conclusions are very similar. In each case, the demand for transactions balances arises from the non-synchronisation of income receipts and expenditures, both of which are perfectly foreseen, and the brokerage costs involved in transferring funds between non-interest-bearing money and interest-earning financial assets, which provide the alternative temporary store of value. The models are important because they attribute a role to the rate of interest in the transactions demand function, a relationship which was ignored by Keynes.

THE BASIC INVENTORY MODEL

Baumol's approach is slightly easier to follow and it is this model which we shall concentrate on analysing. In its simplest form, the expenditure of the individual is financed out of accumulated wealth, from periodic sales of bonds or other short-term interest-earning assets. The transactor must decide upon the number of such sales and the amount encashed each time; and hence his demand for cash balances over the transactions period. This is done in such a way as to minimise the costs involved in managing the portfolio. These comprise the opportunity cost of holding cash, as measured by the interest foregone on such holdings, and the transactions cost, or brokerage fee, incurred each time bonds are exchanged for cash. The latter is defined to include the time and effort involved in making a transfer, as well as any pecuniary charge levied on the actual transaction itself. Each transfer of funds is taken to be equally spaced in time and of an identical amount, equal to *K*. Assuming that expenditure is evenly spread over the transactions period, and money holdings are run down to zero before the next transfer is made, the time profile of transactions balances will follow a saw-tooth pattern, as illustrated in Figure 3.1, with average holdings

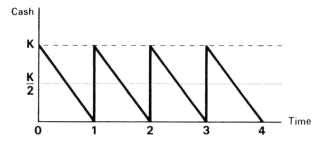

Figure 3.1   The time profile of cash holdings in the Baumol model

equal to *K*/2. Furthermore, the number of such transfers that can take place is *T*/*K*, where *T* is the volume of expenditure. Consequently, the interest cost of holding money is *rK*/2, where *r* represents the rate of interest payable on bonds, while the brokerage cost is *bT*/*K*, where *b* is the fixed brokerage fee. The total cost, *C*, of holding money over the period is the sum of these two separate components, so that we can write

$$C = \frac{bT}{K} + \frac{rK}{2}$$

Minimising this cost, with respect to *K*, enables us to derive the square root formula for the size of the optimal withdrawal, namely

$$K = \sqrt{\frac{2bT}{r}}$$

The average cash balance, or demand for money over the period, is therefore given by the equation

$$M = \frac{K}{2} = \sqrt{\frac{bT}{2r}}$$

Holdings of transactions balances are positively related to the square root of the volume of expenditure, which for simplicity we can equate with income, and inversely related to the square root of the rate of interest. Money demand elasticity values for income and interest rates of $\frac{1}{2}$ and $-\frac{1}{2}$, respectively, are therefore predicted by the model. The former value implies that there are economies of scale in individual money holdings. It follows that, at the aggregate level, the demand for money will be a function of the distribution of incomes, such that the greater the inequality in the income distribution, the lower will be the aggregate demand. The model also implies homogeneity of degree one in the price level: a once and for all doubling of all prices will double the brokerage fee and the value of transactions, and with the interest rate unchanged, this will double the demand for money in nominal terms.

Extensions and Criticisms

Several modifications to this basic model have been considered, involving different assumptions about the form of transfer costs and payment patterns. The brokerage fee can, for example, be redefined so that it involves, in addition to the fixed cost element, a variable transfer cost related to the size of the withdrawal. Under this assumption, Baumol shows that the optimal withdrawal size, and ensuing average cash balance, are identical to those obtained from the basic model. Another common approach is to assume that the stream of expenditure is financed, not from accumulated asset stocks, but out of periodic income payments. In such a form, the model more closely mirrors the behavioural patterns of households, who receive weekly or monthly income payments and then have to decide upon the time profile of their cash or current account balances, in the light of their regular, predictable expenditure requirements over the period. Expenditure is assumed to exhaust income received in each period, and the analysis now involves the additional brokerage cost of switching a proportion of income into bonds, or other interest-earning assets, at the beginning of the period.[1] Initially, expenditure is financed out of retained cash balances, and then later by bond encashment as in the basic model.[2] The optimum withdrawal size remains the same as in the basic model, but the size of the average cash balance is now also dependent upon the quantity of cash initially retained for expenditure, which itself varies according to the nature of the brokerage costs of investing and withdrawing funds. Brunner and Meltzer (1967) show that the average money holding in this case is given by the equation

$$M = \sqrt{\frac{bT}{2r}}\left[1 + \frac{K_d + K_w}{r}\right] + \frac{T}{2}\left[\frac{K_d + K_w}{r}\right]^2$$

where K_d is the variable cost of buying bonds and K_w is the variable cost of encashing bonds. Only when these variable costs are zero is it the case that the average cash balance and ensuing elasticity values are the same as those in the basic model. For the general case, Ahmad (1977) and Brunner and Meltzer have shown that the income and interest elasticities are no longer constant. The income elasticity tends to unity, implying that there are no economies of scale in the use of money, unless the fixed brokerage cost of encashment is large or the level of transactions is small. Only as transactions fall towards zero is it the case that the elasticity value approaches $\frac{1}{2}$, which is the result obtained from the simple Baumol model for all values of transactions. The interest elasticity has a limiting value of -2, as the fixed brokerage cost tends to zero or the level of transactions increases towards infinity.

Other studies have considered additional amendments to the inventory model. A notable development has centred around the notion of the value of time, in which the costs of cash withdrawals are defined to include an explicit time (foregone earnings) component. Under this assumption, it can again be shown that the standard elasticity predictions are no longer necessarily valid. For example, if the brokerage fee is entirely a time cost and if the value of time is proportional to income, then the elasticity of money demand with respect to income will be unity ($\frac{1}{2}$ from transactions and $\frac{1}{2}$ from the brokerage fee). Economies of scale are only realised if transactions costs rise at a slower rate than income. Karni (1973, 1974) develops an inventory model, in which the brokerage costs of cash withdrawals depend partly upon a foregone earnings component, related to wage payments. A distinction is also drawn between labour income (hours worked multiplied by the real wage) and other income, with the model producing a demand function in which money holdings depend upon non-labour income, hours worked, the real wage rate and the interest rate. The wage rate is shown to have a positive effect upon money demand. The model predicts a small negative interest elasticity and a labour-income elasticity of the demand for money which is higher than the other-income elasticity. More general transactions demand models, incorporating the value of time hypothesis, are developed by Dutton and Gramm (1973) and Dowd (1990a). These models utilise the work of Saving (1971), in which individuals are assumed to allocate their time between leisure, work and transactions (consumption) activities. Utility is obtained from the consumption of goods and leisure, with money held because it saves transactions time, in comparison to the use of barter, and therefore allows an increase in leisure activities. In each case, the demand for money is shown to depend upon a scale variable and the interest rate, as well as the value of time, which is again proxied by the real wage rate.

Sprenkle (1966) considers the possibility that transactions balances earn a positive rate of interest. The demand for money is now related to the differential between the bond rate and the return on money, with the income and interest elasticities dependent upon the extent to which the own rate responds to changes in both transactions volumes and the bond (market) rate. The Baumol model implicitly assumes that an infinite cost is involved in running short of cash, but this is not the case if agents can draw upon overdraft facilities or use credit cards to finance transactions. Amending the model to allow for such borrowing possibilities, it can be shown that the optimal money holding is lower than that implied by the basic model.[3] The standard inventory–theoretic framework assumes that money is exchanged for goods in infinitesimal amounts at a uniform rate throughout the transactions period. Attention is focused upon the transactions costs of exchanging bonds for money, to the exclusion of any consideration of the costs involved in exchanging money for goods. When a non-zero cost is attached to purchases of commodities, the infinite number of shopping trips, implicitly assumed in the Baumol model, become sub-optimal. Individuals will now make only a finite number of shopping trips to purchase goods and in between will hold inventories of commodities. Such a rationale underlies the models of Feige and Parkin (1971) and Santomero (1974), who extend the choice set of the inventory frame-work to include commodities as well as bonds and money.[4] In addition to the usual variables, the demand for money is shown to depend upon the brokerage costs involved in purchasing goods. The greater are these transactions costs, the less frequently shopping trips are made and the higher is the average level of commodity inventories maintained, so lowering the average money balance. Only when the cost of shopping trips is zero is it the case that money demand is at the level suggested by the standard inventory model. In Santomero's model, the demand for money also depends upon the yield on consumption goods, which is related to the expected rate of inflation, after allowing for storage and depreciation costs. As the expected inflation rate rises, it becomes optimal to hold larger commodity inventories and reduce average money balances. This is accomplished by increasing the quantity of goods purchased and reducing the frequency of commodity purchase trips within any given payments period.[5] In a general equilibrium version of the Baumol model, Romer (1986) shows that the interest rate affects money holdings, not only by influencing the frequency of cash withdrawals, but also through wealth effects and by its influence upon the pattern of consumer spending between transfers. These additional factors, not considered in the basic model, have potentially important implications for the overall interest elasticity of the demand for money.

From these different model variants, it is apparent that the precise square root formula and specific elasticity predictions of the Baumol model are not universal and only hold under a particular set of restrictive assumptions. Relaxing these assumptions leads to more complex relationships between money holdings, interest rates and transactions volumes. However, in all cases, the demand for money balances is crucially dependent upon the existence of a positive brokerage fee. Without any form of transactions cost, individuals will perfectly synchronise bond sales with purchases of goods, so that money will never be held.

The inventory–theoretic model is most applicable to the analysis of personal sector transactions balances, since most households receive regular known lump-sum income payments. However, as we have seen, the basic model overlooks many of the important institutional features of the monetary system which influence the demand for transactions balances. Sprenkle (1969) has pointed out that the frequency of income receipts over the planning interval is likely to be important in determining whether or not it is profitable to undertake switches between money and bonds. The greater the frequency of receipts for a given total income, the less is the likelihood of such optimising behaviour taking place. Also, transactions costs may be so high, relative to the rate of interest, that such optimising behaviour is uneconomic for all but high income households. For many individuals, it is optimal to retain all income in cash or current account balances, so that the average money balance becomes $T/2$, with the income and interest elasticities equal to unity and zero respectively.[6] Firms are more likely to be in a position to command balances of a size that will make cash management profitable, but it is doubtful whether a model involving certainty in the timing of receipts and payments is appropriate to any analysis of the firm's cash management problem. In any case, cash receipts within firms occur continuously and are likely to be decentralised among the different branches of the organisation, making optimal cash management more difficult. Sprenkle (1969, 1972) provides a detailed critique of the applicability of the inventory model of transactions demand to large firms.[7]

TARGET-THRESHOLD MODELS

A model of the cash management behaviour of firms is developed by Miller and Orr (1966, 1968) and Orr (1970). Several features of the model follow the basic Baumol approach: the firm must choose between holding zero-yielding money or interest-earning bonds, and transfers between the two assets involve brokerage costs. However, cash flows are assumed to be stochastic; balances fluctuate irregularly, building up when operating receipts exceed expenditure and falling off when the reverse is true. Also, a target-threshold approach is adopted, so that money holdings are not adjusted at regular predictable intervals as in the Baumol model; instead the fund manager attempts to keep the level of balances within certain permissible bounds, and only if one of these thresholds is reached does a portfolio transfer take place in order to restore the balance to some intermediate target or return point. Money balances are replenished when they fall to the lower threshold value, while balances are transferred to higher-yielding assets when holdings reach the upper threshold value. The agent's desired money holding is therefore not a single-valued function of the usual choice arguments, but consists of a band of acceptable holdings, whose upper and lower limits change in response to movements in interest rates, income variance and transfer costs. Actual money balances held at any time depend upon the target and threshold values, and the prevailing inflows and outflows of cash. In the Miller–Orr model, the lower bound for cash balances is taken to be zero, so that the firm has to select values for the upper bound and the intermediate return point, so as to minimise the expected transfer and interest costs of managing money holdings over the decision period. The objective function, C, can be written as

$$C = b\rho(T) + rM \qquad (3.1)$$

where b is the brokerage cost per transfer, $\rho(T)$ is a measure of the probability or expected number of transfers in the period, r is the yield on the alternative asset and M is the average or expected money balance over the period.

The form of the optimal cash management policy depends upon the precise assumptions of the model, particularly the form of the probability distribution of cash flows and the nature of the brokerage costs involved in transferring funds between interest-earning assets and money. The monitoring of money balances is implicitly assumed to be continuous and costless.[8] In the simplest version of the model, an equal probability is attached to net cash inflows, increasing or decreasing by an amount m in any period, and with t transactions in every period, changes in the cash balance follow a binomial distribution with mean zero and variance equal to $m^2 t$. Assuming a fixed brokerage cost per transfer, the solution for the optimal return point, z, is shown to be

$$z = \left[\frac{3bm^2 t}{4r}\right]^{1/3}$$

with the optimal upper bound, given by $h = 3z$. Given the lower bound is zero, the average cash balance emerging from this behaviour is equal to $(h+z)/3$. Appropriate substitution for h and z leads to an expression for the demand for money of the form

$$M = \frac{4}{3}\left[\frac{3bm^2 t}{4r}\right]^{1/3}$$

These results indicate that the optimal return point is not half-way between the bounds, but only one-third of the way to the upper bound. This is because the expected transfer cost is a symmetric function of the distance of the return point from the bounds, while the interest foregone is an increasing function of the average size of cash balance held. The time profile of cash balances arising from such a policy rule will look something like that illustrated in Figure 3.2. As with the Baumol transactions model, the demand for money depends upon the relative transfer and interest costs, with the interest elasticity here equal to $-\frac{1}{3}$. However, whereas in the Baumol model, it is the level of

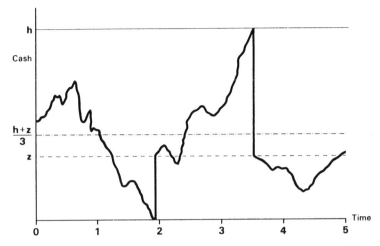

Figure 3.2 Cash balance management in the Miller–Orr model

transactions which are important, with uncertain payments the demand for money is related to the variance of cash flows, m^2t, which is in effect a measure of the lack of synchronisation between cash receipts and payments. The income elasticity predictions obtained from the model are dependent upon the way in which increases in incomes bring about changes in the frequency of transactions, t, as compared to changes in their average size or value, m. If the size remains constant as incomes rise, but frequency increases, the elasticity value is equal to $\frac{1}{3}$, while if transactions frequency remains constant, but the value of all transactions increases in proportion to incomes, then the income elasticity is equal to $\frac{2}{3}$. As in the Baumol model, the nominal demand for money is homogeneous of degree one in prices: doubling all prices increases both the value of transactions (with an elasticity of $\frac{2}{3}$) and the brokerage fee (with an elasticity of $\frac{1}{3}$) and so leads to a doubling of the quantity of money demanded.[9]

Studies by Akerlof (1979) and Akerlof and Milbourne (1980) have also looked at the elasticity values implied by particular target-threshold models. Akerlof's model of bank account money holdings is based on that of Miller and Orr. Receipts and expenditure follow a binomial distribution, with the probability of a cash inflow assumed different to that of a cash outflow. The model is shown to imply a zero income elasticity of the demand for money, as increased spending merely speeds up payments around the system. Akerlof and Milbourne develop a target-threshold model of household behaviour, which takes account of lump-sum payments. In its simplest form, the model assumes lump-sum receipts of Y per period, with spending of E at a constant rate during the period. Money balances accumulate through savings, S, which are determined as the difference between Y and E. When money holdings reach the threshold level, h, they are returned to E, so that balances fall to zero by the next receipt date. The process of accumulation is then repeated. The average money balance is shown to depend upon the threshold level and the level of savings. Akerlof and Milbourne introduce uncertainty into their model by allowing for the possibility of stochastic outflows, occasioned by additional durable good purchases. When these lump-sum purchases are small, they can be financed out of existing money balances, so that their effect is merely to alter the time profile of money holdings. Alternatively, if the purchase is large, in the sense of being greater than h, funds must be transferred from elsewhere in the portfolio, in order to finance the transaction. The Akerlof and Milbourne models predict a near-zero and possibly negative income elasticity; higher income levels imply that the threshold is reached more quickly, so that money balances are returned to E more frequently, resulting in an increase in the velocity of circulation (the ratio of income or transactions to the stock of money).[10]

In the models discussed above, no justification is given for the particular target-threshold rules which form the basis of the cash management problem; instead the models concentrate on determining optimal parameter values once particular rules are followed. The former issue is considered by Milbourne (1983a) who develops the form of the general optimal rule for money holding under uncertain payment flows. This is chosen so as to minimise the sum of the transfer and holding costs of the current period and the discounted expected costs of future periods resulting from this period's decision. Holding costs are defined by Milbourne to comprise the interest costs of maintaining a cash surplus and the costs of credit or other penalty costs of being short of cash. The costs of transfer are assumed to consist of a fixed amount and a component dependent upon the size of the transfer, which also varies according to whether the transfer is from cash to short-term assets or vice versa. The general form of the optimal solution is shown to be a two target–two threshold system, which involves upper and lower targets as well as upper and lower threshold values. In practice, this means that if the cash balance falls below the lower threshold, it is optimal to re-set it to a lower target level, while if it rises above the upper threshold, it is desirable to re-set it to the higher target level. Only when there are no variable transfer costs are the two targets the same. When this is the case, and in addition the lower threshold level is zero, the optimal rule reduces to that stated in the Miller–Orr and Akerlof models. When there are no fixed transfer costs (so that small transfers are not excessively penalised) the optimal rule reduces to that used by Eppen and Fama (1969), in which the threshold and target values are identical at both the upper and lower levels. Milbourne asserts that even the deterministic models of Baumol and Tobin can be viewed as special cases of the general two target–two threshold model, in which the lower threshold is zero, and the upper threshold and upper and lower target values are all identical and equal to the optimal withdrawal size.

PRECAUTIONARY DEMAND MODELS

Once uncertainty over the timing of income and expenditure flows is introduced into the transactions demand framework, it becomes difficult to distinguish between transactions and precautionary motives for holding money.[11] Whalen (1966) considers the firm's cash management problem in a similar analytical framework to that adopted by Miller and Orr, but interprets it as a model of precautionary money holdings. In this case, transfers take place if net payments per period, S (payments minus receipts) exceed money holdings, M, rather than when upper or lower bounds for money are reached. The brokerage or transfer costs now represent a penalty for illiquidity and involve the cost of selling interest-bearing assets at short notice. As well as time and inconvenience, these costs may involve interest penalties or even capital losses, if less liquid assets have to be sold. For simplicity, it is assumed that the cost of illiquidity does not depend upon the size of the cash deficiency.[12] Whalen's results depend upon the particular assumptions made about the individual transactor's behaviour. For the simplest case, assuming extreme risk-averse behaviour, it is shown that the probability of S exceeding M, over the decision period, has a maximum value equal to σ^2/M^2, where σ^2 is the variance of the distribution of net payments.[13] Substituting this value for $\rho(T)$ in relation (3.1), the expected total cost function becomes

$$C = b\left[\frac{\sigma^2}{M^2}\right] + rM \qquad (3.2)$$

The agent must therefore weigh the probability of being caught short of funds, and the associated costs of such illiquidity, against the certain loss of income from holding cash. As precautionary cash balances increase, the expected cost of illiquidity tends to diminish, while the opportunity cost of holding cash increases. Minimisation of the cost function in (3.2), with respect to M, produces a demand function for optimal precautionary balances of the form

$$M = \left[\frac{2\sigma^2 b}{r}\right]^{1/3}$$

with holdings positively related to the variance of the distribution of net payments and the cost of illiquidity, and negatively related to the opportunity cost interest rate. Although no scale variable is included in the function, as in the Miller–Orr model, an increase in income is linked to the demand for money through its relationship with the variance term, with the actual relationship dependent upon the form of the net payments distribution. When a normal distribution is assumed, it can be shown that the income elasticity of the demand for money will vary between $\frac{1}{3}$, when incomes rise due to the increased frequency of receipts and payments with values remaining constant, and $\frac{2}{3}$, when the value of each receipt increases with the frequency kept constant. This result is identical to that obtained from the Miller–Orr model, and the same is true of the interest rate elasticity value of $-\frac{1}{3}$ and the implied price elasticity of unity.

An alternative model of the precautionary demand for money is developed by Laidler (1985); this follows a similar approach to that used by Weinrobe (1972). The individual is assumed to have information on the probability distribution of cash shortfalls and surpluses arising from his income receipts and expenditure payments. In Figure 3.3, the cash surplus or shortfall, S, is assumed to follow a normal distribution, with the horizontal axis measuring the difference between cash inflows and outflows in any period, and the vertical axis showing the proportion of periods, on average, in which a discrepancy of a particular size will occur. The distribution is symmetrical about zero, indicating that equality between expenditure and income is a more likely outcome than any specific positive or negative discrepancy, while an excess of receipts over expenditure of a given amount occurs just as frequently as an excess of expenditure over receipts of the same magnitude. Also, the larger is the size of a particular discrepancy, in either direction, the less frequently it occurs. A demand function for

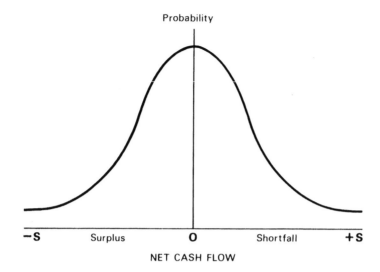

Figure 3.3   The probability distribution of cash flows

precautionary balances can be derived directly from the portion of the curve that lies to the right of point *O* in Figure 3.3. Laidler considers an individual who begins each period holding a precautionary balance equal to £*M* in money. In those periods in which his income is greater than his expenditure, or falls short of his expenditure by less than *M*, the individual does not have to alter his existing portfolio. However, in periods when expenditure is greater than income by more than *M*, the individual must sell bonds, or other interest-earning assets, in order to meet the shortfall, incurring brokerage costs in the process.

Assuming that *C*(*M*) is the expected brokerage-cost outlay associated with holding £*M* in precautionary balances over the period, we can write

$$C(M) = \rho(S > M)b \tag{3.3}$$

where *b* is the fixed brokerage fee per transaction and $\rho(S > M)$ is the probability or proportion of periods in which the shortfall, *S*, of income below expenditure, will exceed *M*. If the individual adds £1 to his money holdings, we can write the new expected brokerage-fee outlay as

$$C(M + 1) = \rho(S > M + 1)b \tag{3.4}$$

The expected saving in brokerage fees, resulting from the extra £1, is obtained by subtracting (3.4) from (3.3) to yield

$$C(M) - C(M + 1) = \rho(M + 1 > S > M)b$$

Adding an extra £1 to money balances, therefore, saves the individual, on average per period, the brokerage fee times the proportion of periods in which the amount of cash required, to meet the shortfall of income below expenditure, falls between M and $(M + 1)$. In other words, the marginal saving from the $(M + 1)$th pound is determined by multiplying the probability of a shortfall of just $£(M + 1)$ by the constant brokerage fee. Because the probability of a shortfall of a given amount is inversely related to the size of the discrepancy, the marginal savings from extra balances are a declining function of the quantity of money held. The curve MB, in Figure 3.4, relates these marginal savings to money holdings; it is simply the right-hand portion of the probability distribution in Figure 3.3, with the probability variable on the vertical axis multiplied by the constant brokerage fee. This saving must be balanced against the cost of foregone interest, which is incurred in holding the extra money balance. Assuming a constant rate of interest, r_0, the marginal cost per pound of money holdings is represented by the horizontal line MC in Figure 3.4. The point at which the curve MB, crosses the line MC, determines the level of

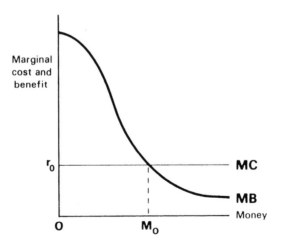

Figure 3.4   The demand for precautionary balances

precautionary balances, M_0, at which the marginal benefits obtained, in terms of saved brokerage fees, is just equal to the marginal costs incurred. In effect, MB represents the demand curve for precautionary balances. From Figure 3.4, it is obvious that an increase in the interest rate will move MC upwards and therefore lower the demand for precautionary balances, while an increase in the brokerage fee causes the MB curve to move to the right, increasing the demand for money at each interest rate. It is also possible to show that changes in income and expenditure patterns, which alter the dispersion of the distribution of cash surpluses and shortfalls, may also affect the demand for money. Finally, we can note that the model predicts that the demand for nominal money balances will vary in proportion to the price level. A doubling of all prices will cause a proportionate increase in the value of income receipts and expenditure payments, and in the size of the brokerage fee, which will in turn result in a doubling of the nominal quantity of money demanded.

Gray and Parkin (1973) develop a model based upon optimal precautionary behaviour, in order to explain portfolio diversification among capital-certain financial assets. Even among assets which are risk-free, differences exist in respective yields and liquidity; and it is these factors which are utilised in the model to provide the rationale for diversification. It is assumed the portfolio of assets is reviewed at regular intervals, but that stochastic cash requirements, between portfolio review dates, force the liquidation of assets. The order in which this occurs depends upon the liquidation costs of the respective assets: the cheapest (lowest expected liquidation costs) are disposed of first and the most costly last. The model is used to determine the optimal asset choice in the light of these differences in liquidation costs, as well as interest rates. The objective function is defined in terms of profit, π, per period where

$$\pi = \sum_{j=1}^{n} r_j X_j - \sum_{j=1}^{n} C_j X_j^\dagger$$

and r_j is the interest rate on the jth asset which is known with certainty, X_j is the quantity of the jth asset initially held, C_j represents the liquidation costs (principally brokerage fees) of the jth asset and $X_j^\dagger$ is the quantity of the jth asset liquidated. The expected value of this objective function is maximised, subject to the constraint that the sum of asset holdings equals portfolio wealth. The solution enables optimal values for the initial asset allocations to be derived.

The precise form of the asset demand functions depends upon the assumptions made about the probability distribution of cash requirements, but certain general comments can be made. Ranking assets according to their liquidation costs, which is equivalent to ranking by yield if there are no dominated assets, the demand for each asset is shown to depend upon its own yield and the yields of the two adjacent assets in the liquidity spectrum. In addition, the demand for the *n*th asset, with the highest liquidation costs, depends upon wealth, which is the scale variable of the portfolio. The other asset demand functions are independent of wealth, so that all wealth increases go into this least liquid asset. Finally, demand for the first and *n*th assets also depends upon the parameters of the probability distribution of cash requirements. In each case, liquidation costs do not enter the demand equation as separate variables, but influence only the parameters of the system. The simplest demand system is obtained when it is assumed that cash requirements follow the uniform distribution. The resulting asset equations are linear in rates of return, with positive own rate response coefficients and negative and symmetric adjacent rate coefficients. This implies that all assets are substitutes for their neighbours in the liquidity spectrum. The upper limit of the probability distribution of cash requirements influences the demand for the first and *n*th assets; an increase in this bound leads to a straight substitution out of the last asset and into the first, most liquid asset. Such a model is adopted by Barrett *et al.* (1975) in their study of the demand for capital-certain financial assets by the personal sector. In this study, the parameters of the distribution of cash requirements are related to the sum of the level of consumer expenditure and tax payments, while asset liquidation costs are assumed to differ between individuals, so that each asset has the potential to be ranked as the *n*th asset in some portfolios. Aggregation across holders therefore implies demand equations for each asset, which will normally contain the set of all interest rates and the wealth variable.

Sprenkle and Miller (1980) extend the precautionary demand model by introducing the possibility that unexpected cash drains can be met, not only by liquidating short-term assets, but also by utilising bank overdraft facilities.[14] No brokerage fees exist and the individual or firm has to balance the costs of holding excess money balances, with the cost of resorting to an overdraft if cash shortages arise. The return on cash is zero, so that the opportunity cost of holding excess balances is equal to r_b, the market rate of return on short-term liquid assets. The opportunity cost of running an overdraft is $(r_c - r_b)$, where r_c is the cost of the overdraft.[15] Agents are assumed to choose their desired cash holdings so as to minimise the sum of these costs. The model predicts that optimal cash holdings are likely to be negative, so that it is desirable to utilise overdraft facilities. The nature of the model makes it difficult to derive explicit demand functions, but by assuming a normal distribution for the net cash drain, it can be shown that optimal cash holdings depend upon relative interest rates and the standard deviation of the distribution, which measures the uncertainty of receipts and payments. Short-term investments and borrowings decrease, and holdings of cash increase, when either the overdraft rate rises or the short rate falls. Furthermore, cash holdings decrease and borrowings increase if both interest rates rise by the same amount. Consequently, the model predicts that a rise in the general level of interest rates will decrease the demand for cash, while increasing both borrowings and short-term investments.[16] Variants to the model are also considered, involving loan limits and penalty costs for being overdrawn over the limit. If the penalty cost of being overdrawn falls, the average cash holding declines.

4 Mixed Models and the General Utility Approach

Both the risk–return and transactions cost approaches to portfolio analysis concentrate on particular themes as the basis for asset diversification. This may be deemed to be unduly restrictive; in practice, portfolio holders choose from a large set of assets, with characteristics which can often neither be solely represented by mean-variance space nor differences in liquidity and associated transactions costs. A more theoretically consistent solution lies in the formulation of mixed models, which combine elements of both approaches. However, this type of approach is likely to result in demand functions which are not empirically tractable and consequently there have been few attempts to develop such models. Exceptions are the models of Buiter and Armstrong (1978) and Spencer (1984). Buiter and Armstrong utilise the Baumol inventory–theoretic model of money demand, but assume an uncertain return on the bond. The demand for money is shown to depend upon a mixture of transactions and risk–return variables; the former consisting of income and the brokerage fee, and the latter the expected return and the standard deviation of the return on the risky asset. The expected return on the whole portfolio, μ_π, is given by the relationship

$$\mu_\pi = \left[\frac{Y - K}{2}\right]\mu_B - b\left[\frac{Y}{K}\right]$$

where Y is income, K is the amount of cash withdrawn at each transfer, $(Y - K)/2$ is the average bond holding, b is the fixed cost per withdrawal and μ_B represents the expected rate of return on bonds, which includes the expected capital gain. The standard deviation of the return on the portfolio, σ_π, is given by the formula

$$\sigma_\pi = \left[\frac{Y - K}{2}\right]\sigma_B$$

where σ_B is the standard deviation of the return on bonds. It is shown that a typical risk-averse individual, with indifference curves which are

42

convex to the risk axis, will always hold more money balances than that implied by the maximum expected return solution, which is optimal in the basic risk-neutral Baumol model. The comparative static properties of the model indicate that, once considerations of risk are introduced, the transactions demand for money balances may have an income elasticity greater than unity. Only when the agent's objective is solely the maximisation of the expected portfolio return, is it the case that the income elasticity of the demand for transactions balances is equal to $\frac{1}{2}$, as in the pure Baumol model.

Spencer (1984) develops a model of UK bank behaviour, which explicitly allows for uncertainty in both asset prices and transactions flows. Banks are assumed to be risk-averse and attempt to maximise expected utility, in terms of the mean and variance of returns, but must also keep precautionary balances, in cash and reserve assets, in order to guard against outflows of funds. If the balances kept are insufficient to cope with deposit withdrawals during the decision period, the bank is faced with penalty costs and unplanned sales of other investments may have to take place. Spencer's model is not a true mixed model, as the same set of explanatory variables is not used in each demand equation. Precautionary factors, based on uncertain deposit flows, influence only a subset of the choice assets, namely cash and reserve assets, while risk–return considerations are the dominant influence upon the other portfolio allocation decisions. However, the different demand equations are estimated together in one system and the model stops short of imposing a full separability structure on the decision framework; a practice which is common in large-scale macro model building. For example, in the Treasury model, the imposition of a separability structure on the decision framework of many of the financial sectors allows the allocation process to become a series of sub-decisions, each determined by a specific set of factors which are consistent with some particular theory of asset allocation. Such an approach effectively lessens the need for a 'super' model of portfolio allocation.

THE GENERAL UTILITY APPROACH

The need to develop more general theories of asset diversification, which are less dependent upon a particular set of factors to the total exclusion of all other influences, underlies the use of traditional demand theory in portfolio modelling. In the analysis of consumer demand, utility functions displaying positive first-order derivatives and negative second-order derivatives, so as to indicate diminishing marginal utility, are maximised subject to a budget constraint, to give demand functions for goods in terms of income and prices. The same approach can be applied to a portfolio of assets, since an asset holder gains utility from stocks of assets, just as a consumer derives utility from his consumption of real goods. The pioneering Cambridge models of the demand for money, based upon the work of Marshall and Pigou, were developed using such an approach.[1] These models assume that money is held because of the convenience derived from it by individuals. It is universally acceptable in exchange for goods, so that the demand for money balances depends upon expenditure requirements. Moreover, if prices increase by a certain proportion, the quantity of money an individual has to hold, in order to achieve the same convenience as before, also has to increase by the same proportion. The demand for nominal balances therefore varies exactly in proportion to the price level. In addition to expenditure variables, wider portfolio choice considerations, based upon factors such as wealth and opportunity cost measures of the rates of return on other assets, are viewed as other potentially important influences on the demand for money. However, the analysis was never really formalised and the approach says little about the nature of the relationships that are likely to prevail among these variables.

Friedman's Model

The general utility approach was further developed by Friedman (1956) in his restatement of the Quantity Theory of Money. As with the Cambridge approach, no explicit utility function is posited, but it is assumed that utility is derived from interest yields and the flow of non-pecuniary services provided by money and each of the other assets available to the wealth holder. These other assets include bonds, equities and real goods. Money is unique among these assets because it offers the individual a degree of convenience, security and liquidity. Wealth is taken to be the scale variable and is defined by Friedman to include not only the aggregate stocks of all physical and financial assets, but human wealth as well; that is, the present discounted value of the income-earning capacity embodied in an individual's ability to produce. It represents the skill and expertise gained by individuals through education or from performing a particular job over a period of time. Friedman introduces the concept of permanent income as the maximum amount a consumer can spend while still maintaining his total wealth intact. It is therefore the rate of return on wealth, or alternatively the level of income, which if received in perpetuity, has a discounted present value exactly equal to wealth. We can write $W = Y^p/r$ where W is wealth, Y^p is permanent income and r is the market rate of interest. Although Friedman formulates the model primarily as a theory of the demand for money, all assets, whether real or financial, are treated as substitutes. In each case, demand is dependent upon relative rates of return, wealth, the ratio of human to non-human wealth and the holder's tastes and preferences. The higher the ratio of human to non-human wealth, the greater is the demand for money to compensate for the lack of marketability of human wealth.

The rates of return on each of the assets are defined in detail by Friedman. Money yields a return in kind, owing to the services that are derived from balances held. In particular, such balances provide a readily available source of purchasing power. However, as in general utility theory, holdings of money display a diminishing marginal rate of substitution with respect to other assets; the more money that is held, the less valuable, relative to the services of other assets, do those flowing from money become. This implicit yield on money holdings will depend upon movements in the price level. If the price level rises, the purchasing power of nominal money balances decreases and the return on money holdings can be said to have fallen. If the price level falls, the reverse is true and the yield on money balances rises. A constant flow of services is only obtained if nominal money holdings are varied in line with changes in the price level. Following Keynes' speculative demand model and Tobin's mean–variance approach, the return on bonds is composed of two elements: the interest payment received with certainty by the bond holder and any capital gain or loss resulting from a rise, or fall, in the price of the bond. Friedman defines an equity as an asset which provides the wealth holder with a stream of income of constant real amount. The nominal return on an equity therefore includes an adjustment for the change in the general price level, as well as a constant nominal income payment and a component, analogous to the capital gain or loss adjustment on bonds, which takes account of any change in the nominal price of the equity. It is assumed that real goods yield an income in kind by providing a flow of services of constant real value to their owners. The nominal yield on real goods is therefore defined to include an adjustment for changes in the price level, as well as a term representing the real yield.

Unlike many of the theories analysed in Chapters 2 and 3, Friedman's model does not lead to a precise demand equation, but by bringing all the variables together, a general functional form can be specified for the demand of money. Few testable restrictions are generated by the model, although Friedman argues that homogeneity of degree one in the price level should be imposed upon the function, with the dependent variable becoming real money balances. A simplified functional form for the demand for money can be written as

$$M/P = f(\mu_B, \mu_E, \dot{P}^e, Y^p, h, u)$$

where M represents money holdings, P is the price level, μ_B is the expected rate of return on bonds, μ_E is the expected rate of return on equities, $\dot{P}^e$ is the expected rate of inflation which is used to proxy the return on real goods, h is the ratio of human to non-human wealth and u represents tastes and preferences.

Other Demand Theory Models

We conclude this chapter with a brief mention of some other models of asset choice behaviour, which have been developed from a general utility approach. Barr and Cuthbertson (1990, 1991) apply the principles of demand theory to the analysis of the demand for liquid assets by the personal sector. Decisions concerning the allocation of these assets are assumed to be separable from other decisions involving non-liquid financial and real assets. Utility depends upon the expected (one period ahead) real value of all the liquid assets held. The model assumes a 'characteristics' approach, in which different assets are perceived to offer distinct liquidity services to agents planning transactions in goods and services. For example, notes and coin offer liquidity services for transactions involving the purchase of items such as a bar of chocolate or bus ticket, while chequing accounts are more useful for transactions involving higher-value purchases. Other types of monetary asset, such as non-chequing accounts or time deposits, offer lower levels of liquidity and brokerage costs may have to be incurred before they can be converted to forms of money suitable for the financing of transactions. Assets are also assumed to differ in terms of their other characteristics, such as the probability of default and the indemnity offered in the case of theft. However, because these different characteristics are difficult to quantify empirically, the model leads to equations in which the demand for each asset depends upon a vector of real prices (rates of return) and total real wealth held in liquid assets.

Dutkowsky and Foote (1988) develop an integrated model of consumption and money demand, in an environment of uncertainty, under the assumption that individuals form expectations rationally. Utility in each period is derived from current real consumption and the exchange services provided by real money balances. In this respect, money holdings generate utility by facilitating consumption, while also providing income in their interest-earning form. Bonds only provide income and give utility only by financing future consumption opportunities. Each period, the individual allocates his available income to present-period consumption and holdings of money and bonds. The model predicts that real money holdings are dependent upon previous-period holdings, one-period ahead forecasts of future bond and money interest rates, past expectations of current rates, unanticipated changes in income and unanticipated current interest rates (through a windfall effect on income). Expected changes in income play no role in determining money demand. Grice and Bennett (1984) also specify a model of the demand for money, in which the individual maximises a utility function defined over present and future values of consumption expenditure and money holdings. A budget constraint is specified for each period, in which money holdings and consumption expenditure are constrained by wealth, income and borrowing levels. The solution of the multi-period problem leads to a functional form, relating the current demand for money to rates of return, current and expected income and gross wealth.

Keating (1985) formulates a model of asset choice, based upon a modified mean–variance framework. Utility depends not only on total portfolio return, but also on the quantity of each asset held. Agents are assumed to maximise an objective function of the form

$$Z = X'\mu - \frac{s}{2}X'\Omega X \qquad (4.1)$$

where X is a vector of asset holdings, μ is a vector of expected asset yields, s is a scalar coefficient of risk aversion and Ω is a matrix which is obtained from the summation of two other matrices. The first of these is a variance–covariance matrix of returns in which some rows and columns may contain only zeros, while the second matrix has entries representing the effect of other factors causing declining marginal utility from asset holdings. The form given in equation (4.1) is similar to the mean–variance objective function specified in equation (2.10), but in this case the interpretation given to the matrix Ω means that it is theoretically consistent to use the model to explain choices among non-risky assets. Finally, we can note that the general utility approach has been applied to the analysis of bank behaviour in studies such as Aigner and Bryan (1971) and Aigner (1973). Banks are assumed to act so as to maximise a utility function defined over certain short-run decision variables. The utility derivable from an asset (or the disutility from a liability) is composed of two elements; the nominal rate of return (cost) on the asset (liability) and a subjective component reflecting non-quantifiable factors. No explicit allowance is made for uncertainty at a theoretical level in the model. Nevertheless, risk factors and liquidity concerns, based upon uncertainty regarding future deposit movements and loan demands, may all be considered as part of the subjective returns variable.

5 The Empirical Demand for Money Function

The empirical relationship which has received most attention in the modelling of private sector financial behaviour is the demand for money function. Over the years, there has been a plethora of studies on the aggregate demand for money functions of both the UK and US, and it is arguably the most estimated relationship in the whole of empirical macroeconomics. The majority of these studies have not been primarily concerned with testing, at the aggregate level, the empirical validity of the alternative micro theories of money demand discussed in earlier chapters. This is partly because total money holdings are not readily separable into their different transactions, precautionary and risk–return elements, a degree of disaggregation which is required for the satisfactory testing of most of these theories. Also, variables such as the risk attached to bond holding, the level of brokerage costs and the variance of net receipts, which are crucial to the testing of particular theories, are by their very nature, difficult to measure in any satisfactory way for empirical purposes. These data limitations have meant that most empirical studies have been concerned with finding a stable aggregate time-series relationship, between money holdings and a few key determining variables, such as the rate of interest and the level of income or wealth.[1] Knowledge of the existence and form of such a relationship is important for policy purposes: the more stable is the aggregate money demand function, the easier it is to predict the effect of a given increase in the quantity of money upon interest rates, the price level and total expenditure. A stable demand for money function should also allow the authorities to control the money stock, via the manipulation of interest rates.

The traditional approach in empirical studies has always been to estimate money demand functions in isolation, with little consideration given to the possible existence of a separate supply function for money. Such an approach is based upon the belief that the aggregate money stock is demand determined, so that supply merely adjusts to demand. Only a very few studies, such as Teigen (1964) and Brunner and Meltzer (1964), have actually attempted to analyse the demand for money in a simultaneous system, involving a supply function as well.

These early studies, both of which used US data, tended to indicate that explicit consideration of the supply function made little difference to the 'demand' estimates obtained, so that the potential problem of simultaneous equations bias could be ignored. Indeed, it became the accepted orthodoxy to dismiss the possible existence of an independent supply function when modelling the money market. Such an assumption has the effect of considerably simplifying the specification and estimation of the key money market equations, and was largely uncontroversial in the 1950s and 1960s, when the stock of money could reasonably be taken to be demand determined. However, analysis of the money market has become more complicated over the past two decades, as separate supply influences on the stock of money have increased in importance.[2] In recent years, investigators have also begun to question the view that the money market always clears to equate demand and supply, so that it is no longer automatically correct to assume that the stock of money in any period represents an 'equilibrium' observation on the demand curve. Much of the recent work on the demand for money has therefore been concerned with the notion of 'disequilibrium money' and the mechanisms by which market clearing can be achieved, if demand and supply fall out of line. Associated with this view of money market adjustment is the idea that money fulfils the role of a buffer stock in the individual's portfolio. We shall return to these issues in Chapter 7, but first we consider the form of the basic equations used in most empirical demand for money studies and the main results that have been obtained with respect to the role of particular variables in the specification.

THE LONG-RUN MONEY DEMAND EQUATION

Real income or wealth, the rate of interest and the price level have traditionally been viewed to be the principal determinants of the empirical demand for money function. The long-run or steady-state demand for money can therefore be represented by the relation

$$M = \gamma + \alpha R + \beta Y + \delta P + \varepsilon \tag{5.1}$$

where M represents the stock of money balances, defined in either a narrow or broad sense, R is the opportunity cost of holding money, as represented by the interest rate or rate of return on an appropriate alternative asset, Y is some measure of real income or wealth which acts as the scale or constraint variable, and P is the price level. The disturbance term, represented by ε, captures the effect of all other influences upon M, while γ, α, β and δ are the parameters of the equation. Many variants of the basic form, given in equation (5.1), can be used in empirical work. For example, it is possible to combine the terms in real income and prices to form a single term in nominal income. A more common restriction involves the imposition of the property of homogeneity of degree one in prices on the estimated relationship, so that the doubling of the price level results in the same proportionate increase in nominal money holdings. Such a restriction implies that agents are concerned with the real purchasing power of money balances and is implicit in several of the models discussed in earlier chapters. It results in a demand function in which the dependent variable is written in terms of real money balances, that is the nominal quantity of money deflated by the price level. It is also possible to impose income homogeneity upon the estimated relationship, so that the demand for real money balances is proportional to real income. In this case, the dependent variable becomes the ratio of money to nominal income. The inverse of this ratio is the velocity of circulation and is an approximate measure of the frequency of use of each unit of money in the economy. It is also common practice in empirical studies to transform the model into logarithmic form. Such an approach produces an equation in which the coefficient estimates can be interpreted to be elasticity values.

The concept of stability requires the demand for money relation to be highly predictable in a statistical sense, as measured by the overall goodness of fit statistics, the precision of the estimated coefficients and the ability of the equation to forecast accurately out of the sample period. In relation to equation (5.1), this means that given values of R, Y and P should always result in the same, or at least very similar, values for M. This requires, not only that the parameters of the equation should remain relatively constant over time, but also that the variance of the disturbance term should be small. If the second condition does not hold, large changes in ε can lead to large variations in M, even for constant values of R, Y and P. This may imply that other variables are important influences upon the demand for money, and if this is the case, these variables should be included explicitly in equation (5.1) as additional regressor terms. Such variables could include the 'riskiness' of bond holdings, which is an important factor in Tobin's mean–variance model, the brokerage fee which is given a role in transactions and precautionary demand models, or the expected rate of inflation which is used as a measure of the rate of return on real goods in Friedman's model. As more forms of money become interest-bearing, it may also be necessary to take account of the own rate of return on money itself. Normally, however, a stable demand function will have relatively few arguments; a relationship which requires for its explanation a knowledge of a large number of variables is, in effect, not predictable.

THE SHORT-RUN EQUATION

Early empirical studies, such as those by Meltzer (1963) for the US, and Kavanagh and Walters (1966) and Laidler (1971) for the UK, suggested that stable long-run aggregate relationships could be isolated between the quantity of money and real income or wealth, the rate of interest and the price level. These studies used long sample periods of annual time-series data, which abstract from short-term influences. However, when investigators estimated the same equations, using quarterly data over shorter time periods, it was often only possible to isolate a well-determined relationship when a lagged dependent variable was included in the specification. Models of short-run dynamic behaviour, involving both adjustment and expectational effects, were therefore developed in order to explain the presence of the lagged dependent variable in the estimated equation. Soon it became the accepted orthodoxy to specify and estimate these restricted-lag partial adjustment and permanent income (adaptive expectations) models. In recent years, more general distributed lag representations of the short-run function have also become popular with empirical investigators. We will now consider, in more detail, these different approaches to the modelling of the short-run function.

The Partial Adjustment Model

The presence of a lagged dependent variable, in the short-run money demand function, is most frequently justified in terms of a partial adjustment model of money demand, in which actual holdings adjust slowly towards desired balances. In order to develop such a model, we will assume that the desired long-run demand for money function, in real terms at time t, takes the constant elasticity form

$$\tilde{M}_t^* = k R_t^\alpha Y_t^\beta \varepsilon_t \qquad (5.2)$$

where k is an arbitrary parameter and the asterisk is used to denote a desired value. The inflection above the money stock variable is used to denote a real value, with $\tilde{M} = M/P$. Rewriting equation (5.2) in logarithmic form, using lower case letters to denote log variables, we obtain the linear long-run relationship

$$\tilde{m}_t^* = \gamma + \alpha r_t + \beta y_t + v_t \tag{5.3}$$

where $\tilde{m} = (m - p) = \log \tilde{M}$, $\gamma = \log k$ and $v_t = \log \varepsilon_t$. The essence of the partial adjustment model is that actual balances held, in any time period, may not necessarily equal desired long-run holdings, as given by equation (5.3). This situation arises because of inertia, habit persistence and transaction and information costs, both pecuniary and non-pecuniary. It therefore becomes necessary to specify some form of short-run adjustment mechanism, by which actual balances move towards desired holdings. The simple partial adjustment mechanism, proposed by Chow (1966), assumes that the change in money holdings, between two periods, is a constant fraction of the discrepancy between desired balances in the current period and actual holdings in the previous period. In logarithmic form, we can write this mechanism as

$$\tilde{m}_t - \tilde{m}_{t-1} = \theta(\tilde{m}_t^* - \tilde{m}_{t-1}) \tag{5.4}$$

where θ is the adjustment parameter, which takes a value between zero and unity.

Feige (1967) derives the relation, given in (5.4), from the hypothesis that individuals choose their money holdings so as to minimise the cost function

$$QC = \Psi(\tilde{m}_t - \tilde{m}_t^*)^2 + \omega(\tilde{m}_t - \tilde{m}_{t-1})^2 \tag{5.5}$$

The first term in this expression represents the disequilibrium costs of money holdings, which vary in proportion to the square of the difference between actual and desired real balances, with Ψ equal to the cost per unit of disequilibrium. The second term represents the adjustment costs of moving towards equilibrium, which vary in proportion to the square of the change in actual real balances held, with ω equal to the cost per unit of adjustment. The quadratic form of each of these terms implies symmetric costs in each case. In reality, this may be unrealistic; for example, the disequilibrium cost of being below the equilibrium position might be greater than that of being above the desired holding. Similarly, the adjustment costs of increasing money holdings may be greater than those of reducing balances held.[3]

Substituting equation (5.3) into (5.4), we can derive a relationship for short-run real money holdings, at time t, of the form

$$\tilde{m}_t = b_0 + b_1 r_t + b_2 y_t + (1 - \theta)\tilde{m}_{t-1} + u_t \tag{5.6}$$

where $b_0 = \theta\gamma$, $b_1 = \theta\alpha$, $b_2 = \theta\beta$ and $u_t = \theta v_t$.[4] The model therefore predicts a role for the lagged dependent variable in the estimated money demand equation, with the coefficient on this variable allowing an estimate of the adjustment coefficient to be derived. The b values represent short-run or impact coefficients, and given that the equation is specified in log-linear form, they provide estimates of the short-run elasticities. They indicate the percentage effect, upon the demand for money, of a 1 per cent change in an explanatory variable, in the time period in which the change takes place. From the coefficient estimates of equation (5.6), it is also possible to derive the (implied) parameters of the long-run demand function; in this form, they indicate the long-run elasticity values and measure the percentage effect, upon money holdings, of a 1 per cent change in an explanatory variable, when all adjustment is complete.

The adjustment cost formulation of the short-run demand for money function has been widely used in empirical studies because of its simplicity; see, for example, Goodhart and Crockett (1970), Laidler and Parkin (1970) and Artis and Lewis (1976). Nevertheless, criticisms can be levelled at the model. For example, it imposes the same geometric lagged response in money holdings to a change in any of the independent variables. This is a highly restrictive lagged response; in reality, it might be expected that the adjustment over time in money holdings would be different if the change in desired demand was caused by a change in the interest rate, rather than in income.[5] A more specific criticism arises because the adjustment mechanism in equation (5.4) is specified in real terms: agents are assumed to adjust their real balances slowly over time, in response to changes in income and the rate of interest. However, because prices are exogenous for the individual agent, he must vary his holdings of nominal balances in order to attain a given level of real balances. By implication, when the price level changes, nominal balances must be adjusted fully and instantaneously to keep real balances constant. This can be seen more clearly if we rearrange the adjustment mechanism in (5.4), so as to obtain the relation

$$m_t - m_{t-1} = \theta(\tilde{m}_t^* - \tilde{m}_{t-1}) + \Delta p_t$$

in which the symbol Δ is used to denote the first-difference operator and the coefficient on the price change term is unity.

The requirement of instantaneous adjustment to price level changes would seem to contradict the slower adjustment of money balances that occurs with respect to changes in income and the interest rate. Accordingly, it could be argued that a more appropriate adjustment formulation is one cast in terms of nominal, rather than real balances, with the relation in (5.4) replaced by the mechanism

$$m_t - m_{t-1} = \theta(m_t^* - m_{t-1}) \tag{5.7}$$

Assuming that price homogeneity is still imposed upon the desired long-run relation, as given by equation (5.3), we can show that the short-run demand equation will now take the form

$$\tilde{m}_t = b_0 + b_1 r_t + b_2 y_t + (1 - \theta)(m_{t-1} - p_t) + u_t \tag{5.8}$$

with $b_0 = \theta\gamma$, $b_1 = \theta\alpha$, $b_2 = \theta\beta$ and $u_t = \theta v_t$. This does not represent the same form as equation (5.6), where $\tilde{m}_{t-1}$ represents lagged nominal balances deflated by the lagged price level. In equation (5.8), deflation is by the current price level, which implies a lagged response to price level variations that is identical to the adjustment to changes in income and the interest rate. This can be seen more clearly if we rewrite equation (5.8), with nominal money balances as the dependent variable. We obtain the relation

$$m_t = b_0 + b_1 r_t + b_2 y_t + \theta p_t + (1 - \theta)m_{t-1} + u_t \tag{5.9}$$

which clearly illustrates the lagged response of nominal balances to price level variations.

Despite the intuitive appeal of this model, equations such as (5.8) have not been widely used by UK empirical investigators. A notable exception is Hacche (1974) who estimates an equation for real money balances, which is based upon a nominal partial adjustment model. In addition, Goodhart and Crockett (1970) estimate a short-run model of money demand, based upon a nominal partial adjustment mechanism and a long-run demand function for nominal balances, in which long-run price homogeneity is not imposed. For the US, a whole series of studies, such as Goldfeld (1976), Hafer and Hein (1980), Spencer

(1985), Hwang (1985), Serletis (1987a) and MacKinnon and Milbourne (1988), have found that short-run equations for real money balances, which are based upon a nominal partial adjustment model, are statistically superior to those involving real partial adjustment. The nominal adjustment specification is also favoured in a multi-country study by Fair (1987) which compares the two approaches.

More general comments can be made about the incorporation of adjustment factors into long-run models of the demand for money. In the standard partial adjustment model, the agent is assumed to undertake a two-stage decision process. First, he determines the desired level of money balances and then he makes an independent decision concerning the speed of adjustment towards this long-run desired position. Ideally, it would be desirable to have a theory that deals with the simultaneous determination of the desired path of money balances and the speed of adjustment. Unfortunately, such models tend to be less tractable for estimation purposes.[6] In the basic inventory and target-threshold models discussed in Chapter 3, costs of adjustment, in the form of the lump-sum brokerage fee, are implicitly taken into account in the determination of the optimal rule for money holdings. In target-threshold models, monitoring is continuous and the target and threshold values are changed immediately in response to variations in factors such as interest rates, transfer costs and the variance of cash flows. Nevertheless, actual money holdings are autoregressive, since transfers to target or return point holdings are made only when a threshold is reached. The idea of continuous partial adjustment towards desired money holdings would therefore appear to be inconsistent with such lump-sum adjustment cost models. The dynamics of the Baumol (1952) and Miller–Orr (1966) models are analysed by Chant (1976), Milbourne *et al.* (1983) and Smith (1986). Chant shows that, at the aggregate level, the adjustment patterns implied by these models are complex, with possible asymmetries existing between upward and downward adjustments of cash balances, and different adjustments occurring according to the independent variable which changes to institute the desired variation in optimal balances. It is argued that the derived lag structures do not, in most cases, conform to the simple distributed lag pattern used in the majority of empirical work. Milbourne *et al.* and Smith argue that target-threshold models can lead to a process of gradual adjustment in money holdings at the aggregate level, with an adjustment speed which is variable. This is the case because individual agents adjust their portfolios at different times, so that shocks to money holdings, arising from the uncertain flows of payments and receipts, can persist for some time, if some agents have just acted when a shock occurs. In this way, the existence of lump-sum transfer costs, at the individual level, can be reconciled with the presence of a lagged dependent variable in the equation for aggregate short-run money holdings.

Adaptive Expectations and Permanent Income

The presence of a lagged dependent variable in the demand for money function can also be justified by making use of the adaptive expectations hypothesis. The theories outlined in earlier chapters illustrate the role played by expectations in determining the demand for financial assets. Expectations about income, relative yields and other variables, such as the rate of inflation, are all potentially important influences upon the demand for money. A long-run demand function for real balances, incorporating expectational variables, and specified in terms of logarithms, can be written in the form

$$\tilde{m}_t = \gamma + \alpha r_t^e + \beta y_t^e + v_t \qquad (5.10)$$

where r^e and y^e refer to the expected values of the interest rate and real income respectively. The adaptive expectations hypothesis, in which expectations in each period are revised according to previous forecasting errors, provides one of the simplest methods of generating values for these variables. Assuming an identical expectations formation mechanism for each explanatory variable, we can write

$$r_t^e - r_{t-1}^e = \lambda(r_t - r_{t-1}^e) \quad \text{and} \quad y_t^e - y_{t-1}^e = \lambda(y_t - y_{t-1}^e) \qquad (5.11)$$

where λ is the expectations coefficient. The mechanisms given in (5.11) imply that interest rate and income expectations are revised according to the difference between current actual values and the expectations of the previous period. The extent of this revision depends upon the expectations coefficient, which takes a value between zero and unity; if $\lambda = 0$, expectations are never revised, while if $\lambda = 1$, expected and actual values are identical. The formulations in (5.11) can be shown to be equivalent to the expressions

$$r_t^e = \lambda \sum_{j=0}^{\infty} (1 - \lambda)^j r_{t-j} \quad \text{and} \quad y_t^e = \lambda \sum_{j=0}^{\infty} (1 - \lambda)^j y_{t-j} \qquad (5.12)$$

The adaptive expectations hypothesis, therefore, implies that the expected value for each variable is an average of current and past actual values, with geometrically declining weights.

Substituting the relations given in (5.11) into equation (5.10), and applying the Koyck transformation, produces the short-run equation

$$\tilde{m}_t = b_0 + b_1 r_t + b_2 y_t + (1 - \lambda)\tilde{m}_{t-1} + u_t$$

where $b_0 = \lambda\gamma$, $b_1 = \lambda\alpha$ and $b_2 = \lambda\beta$. The model therefore predicts a role for the lagged dependent variable in the estimated money demand equation, with the coefficient on the lagged money term allowing an estimate of the expectations parameter to be derived. From the other coefficient estimates, the (implied) parameters of the structural long-run relation, given in equation (5.10), can also be obtained. The form of the short-run equation resulting from this model is almost identical to that produced by the real partial adjustment model in equation (5.6). The only difference lies in the error term, with the adaptive expectations formulation producing a moving average error in which $u_t = v_t - (1 - \lambda)v_{t-1}$.

A related model, which also produces a similar reduced form, is the simple empirical representation of Friedman's model of the demand for money, in which money holdings depend upon the interest rate and permanent income. In this case, the long-run demand function for real balances can be written as

$$\tilde{m}_t = \gamma + \alpha r_t + \beta y_t^p + v_t \tag{5.13}$$

where y_t^p represents permanent real income, which is generated using the adaptive expectations hypothesis, as given in (5.11). This, in turn, implies that permanent income can be expressed, as in (5.12), as a geometric distributed lag of current and past actual values of real income. Substituting for permanent income in equation (5.13), and applying the Koyck transformation, yields the short-run relation

$$\tilde{m}_t = b_0 + b_1 r_t + b_2 r_{t-1} + b_3 y_t + (1 - \lambda)\tilde{m}_{t-1} + u_t \tag{5.14}$$

where $b_0 = \lambda\gamma$, $b_1 = \alpha$, $b_2 = -(1 - \lambda)\alpha$, $b_3 = \lambda\beta$ and $u_t = v_t - (1 - \lambda)v_{t-1}$. This equation is tested using quarterly UK data by Laidler and Parkin (1970). Again, the lagged dependent variable appears in the estimated equation and although the model also introduces an additional term in the lagged interest rate, the similarity of equation (5.14) with the other short-run equations already derived is evident.[7]

The comparability between the empirical representation of the partial adjustment and adaptive expectations (permanent income) models creates a problem for the investigator who wishes to test the validity of the different hypotheses. Feige (1967) attempts to solve this problem by developing a model which involves both the partial adjustment of actual to desired balances and the use of permanent income as the scale variable. The three-equation structural model assumes that the level of long-run desired money balances is given by the equation

$$\tilde{m}_t^* = \gamma + \alpha r_t + \beta y_t^p + v_t$$

with permanent income generated as before and the adjustment mechanism specified as in relation (5.4). Algebraic manipulation of the model yields a short-run equation of the form

$$\tilde{m}_t = b_0 + b_1 r_t + b_2 r_{t-1} + b_3 y_t + (2 - \theta - \lambda)\tilde{m}_{t-1}$$
$$- (1 - \theta)(1 - \lambda)\tilde{m}_{t-2} + u_t \qquad (5.15)$$

with $b_0 = \theta \lambda \gamma$, $b_1 = \theta \alpha$, $b_2 = -\theta(1 - \lambda)\alpha$, $b_3 = \theta \lambda \beta$ and $u_t = \theta v_t - \theta(1 - \lambda)v_{t-1}$.[8] Using this model, an attempt can be made to isolate the relative importance of the adjustment and permanent income parameters, and therefore the possible rationale for the inclusion of lagged variables in demand for money equations.[9] Feige estimated his model using annual US data and variants of the model have also been applied to quarterly US data by Thornton (1982), and to quarterly UK data by Laidler and Parkin (1970) and Coghlan (1978).

More General Dynamic Models

The models outlined above all lead to short-run demand for money equations which include lagged dependent variables. The lags are justified in terms of adjustment costs or expectations generating mechanisms. However, in each case, the lagged response of money balances, to changes in the independent variables of the demand for money function, is constrained at the outset to take a particular geometric form. More flexible lag responses can be allowed and have been incorporated into demand for money functions in recent years in the search for stable relationships. One alternative procedure involves the specification of short-run equations which involve a large number of lagged terms in the independent variables. Such an equation can be represented in logarithmic form by the general relation

$$m_t = b_0 + \sum_{j=0}^{n} b_{1j} r_{t-j} + \sum_{j=0}^{n} b_{2j} y_{t-j} + \sum_{j=0}^{n} b_{3j} p_{t-j} + u_t \qquad (5.16)$$

where n represents the number of lagged terms to be considered for each variable. Again, these extra lagged variables can be justified in terms of either expectational or adjustment effects. In order to make the specification as general as possible, equation (5.16) is specified with nominal money balances as the dependent variable, and current and lagged price level variables included as additional regressor terms. This general distributed lag approach has the advantage of allowing a flexible and distinct response in the dependent variable to changes in each of the independent variables; the form of the lagged response is unrestricted in each case, being determined by the data rather than imposed at the outset, as in the partial adjustment and adaptive expectations models. One disadvantage of the procedure is that it can require the estimation of a large number of parameters; this has the effect of reducing the degrees of freedom available with a small number of observations.

Most empiricists using this approach tend to estimate short-run equations which allow for lags in both the dependent and independent variables. The general form of such an equation can be written as

$$m_t = b_0 + \sum_{j=0}^{n} b_{1j} r_{t-j} + \sum_{j=0}^{n} b_{2j} y_{t-j} + \sum_{j=0}^{n} b_{3j} p_{t-j} + \sum_{j=1}^{n} b_{4j} m_{t-j} + u_t \quad (5.17)$$

By testing different versions of equation (5.17) against the data, it is possible to impose restrictions upon the coefficients in the short-run demand for money function, so as to simplify its empirical form. The 'testing-down' procedures adopted here may involve, not only the removal of insignificant variables from the general specification, but also some rearrangement or 'reparameterisation' of the function, so that it includes 'differenced' terms as well as the original 'levels' variables. The resulting preferred equation should have a 'sensible' economic interpretation, with the 'levels' terms providing information on the long-run equilibrium properties of the relation and the 'differenced' variables modelling the short-run dynamics around the static equilibrium position.[10]

This 'general to specific' approach often gives rise to what is termed an error-correction or error-feedback relation. Such an equation incorporates a corrective mechanism, by which previous disequilibria in the relationship between the level of money balances and the level of one or more of the determining variables are permitted to affect the current change in money holdings. In this way, an allowance can be made for any short-run divergence in money balances from the long-run target holding. Any short-run demand for money equation can be reparameterised to incorporate an error-correction mechanism. In order to illustrate the empirical form of such a mechanism, we begin with a relatively simple short-run equation for real money balances of the form

$$\tilde{m}_t = b_0 + b_1 r_t + b_2 y_t + b_3 y_{t-1} + b_4 \tilde{m}_{t-1} + u_t \tag{5.18}$$

where all variables are defined in terms of logarithmic values. Subtracting $\tilde{m}_{t-1}$ from both sides of (5.18), and reparameterising the resulting equation, produces the relation

$$\Delta \tilde{m}_t = b_0 + b_1 r_t + b_2 \Delta y_t + (b_2 + b_3) y_{t-1} - (1 - b_4) \tilde{m}_{t-1} + u_t \tag{5.19}$$

where Δ is the first-difference operator, so that $\Delta \tilde{m}_t = \tilde{m}_t - \tilde{m}_{t-1}$ and $\Delta y_t = y_t - y_{t-1}$. Because it is expressed in logarithmic form, the dependent variable in equation (5.19) represents the proportionate change in real money holdings, with the Δy term representing the proportionate change in real income.[11]

Further reparameterisation of (5.19) produces an error-correction equation of the form

$$\Delta \tilde{m}_t = b_0 + b_1 r_t + b_2 \Delta y_t - (1 - b_4)[\tilde{m}_{t-1} - \beta y_{t-1}] + u_t \tag{5.20}$$

where $\beta = (b_2 + b_3)/(1 - b_4)$. The term in square brackets in equation (5.20) represents the error-correction mechanism; it measures the previous-period or short-term disequilibrium error in the long-run relationship between the level of real money holdings and the level of one or more of the determining variables, in this case real income. The parameter β is the long-run elasticity of money demand with respect to income; in many error-correction models its value is constrained to be equal to unity, implying a long-run proportionate relationship between money holdings and income.[12] A negatively-signed coefficient is attached to the error-correction term, indicating that the lower (higher) are money holdings in the previous period, in relation to their equilibrium value with respect to income, the greater (smaller) will be the current-period rise in balances held. In this way, total money holdings are corrected for the previous-period disequilibrium error. In addition to the error-correction variable, equation (5.20) implies that the growth in real money balances is dependent upon a constant term, the interest rate and the growth in income.

This reformulation of equation (5.18) is not unique and it is possible to further reparameterise equation (5.20), so as to incorporate the interest rate variable within the error-correction term. In this case, we obtain an error-correction equation of the form

$$\Delta \tilde{m}_t = b_0 + b_1 \Delta r_t + b_2 \Delta y_t - (1 - b_4)[\tilde{m}_{t-1} - \alpha r_{t-1} - \beta y_{t-1}] + u_t \quad (5.21)$$

where $\alpha = b_1/(1 - b_4)$. The term in square brackets is the error-correction mechanism for this formulation, with α representing the long-run elasticity of money demand with respect to the interest rate. In this case, the error-correction term captures all of the relationships, among the levels of the variables, which are deemed to be important in determining the demand for money in equation (5.18); it can therefore be assumed to provide a sufficient characterisation of the long-run steady-state demand for money for our particular example. This will not be the case if any of the restrictions which are imposed upon the term, such as price or income homogeneity, do not hold; or if key variables, such as the interest rate, are omitted from the term; or if there are different lags linking the levels of the variables within the mechanism. In these cases, additional 'levels' terms, in the offending variables which contribute to the long-run solution, are likely to appear in the short-run equation. This is evident in equation (5.20), where the interest rate variable is excluded from the error-correction term, but appears elsewhere in the relation.

A recent development has linked the notion of an error-correction mechanism to the concept of cointegration. A vector of economic variables is said to be cointegrated if an equilibrium relationship can be established statistically between the variables. While the error-correction term imposes a particular equilibrium relationship upon the long-run form of the model, cointegration analysis is designed to search for, and verify, the existence of such a relationship, before it is embodied within the short-run dynamic specification. Cointegration analysis can therefore be used to determine the nature of the error-correction mechanism. The techniques employed involve a consideration of the stationarity properties of the data; cointegration requires that the separate trended series are stationary only after differencing, while a particular linear combination of their levels is stationary. Therefore, even though the individual series may be subject to upward or downward shifts over time, this requirement means there is a particular linear combination of the different series that is non-divergent over time, and which therefore represents a potential equilibrium relationship between the variables.[13] The approach is designed to eliminate the possibility of spurious links being established between variables, that is associations which are based solely upon correlated trends, rather than upon any underlying economic relationship. Proponents of the approach argue that the concept of a stable underlying long-run money demand function can only have a valid empirical representation if the monetary aggregate and the vector of determining variables are cointegrated. If this is not the case, it is argued that money and the determining variables cannot be assumed to move together over time in some equilibrium relationship.

Cointegration analysis in conjunction with error-correction modelling can be viewed as a two-stage process. However, before any estimation can be undertaken, the stationarity properties of the data must be examined; only if the data, or some transformation of it, is stationary in differences is it appropriate to apply the procedures for estimating cointegrating relationships. If stationarity can be established, the first stage is to use the data to estimate an equation linking the different variables. The residuals from this equation, which represent a particular linear combination of these variables, must also display stationarity before the estimated function can be viewed to be a cointegrating regression. If a cointegrating relation is confirmed between money and a vector of determining variables, the residuals from the regression are assumed to be estimates of the disequilibrium errors, that is measures of the short-run deviations of money demand from the long-run equilibrium level. The lagged value of these residuals can be used to represent the error-correction term, so facilitating the second stage of the process which involves the estimation of the short-run equation. 'General to specific' techniques may be employed at this stage, involving a consideration of the current and lagged difference terms in the dependent and determining variables.[14] It is important to note that cointegration analysis only provides information on the properties of the long-run steady-state relation. It tells us nothing about the precise form and lag structure of the short-run equation, and other modelling procedures must be adopted to estimate such equations. However, if no cointegrating relationship can be established between the variables, further analysis based upon the approach becomes invalid.[15]

The methodology behind 'general to specific' modelling techniques is described by Hendry *et al.* (1984) and Gilbert (1986), while the basic principles of cointegration analysis are described in Granger (1986) and Engle and Granger (1987), and related to the demand for money in Boughton (1991a and 1991b) and Cuthbertson *et al.* (1992). More general dynamic modelling techniques have been used, with varying degrees of sophistication, in a number of empirical demand for money studies, such as Price (1972), Coghlan (1978), Hendry and Mizon (1978), Grice and Bennett (1984), Hendry (1979, 1985), Taylor (1987), Hall *et al.* (1990) and Hendry and Ericsson (1991b). The ultimate objective of the general distributed lag approach, in whatever form it takes, is to obtain a short-run equation which provides an adequate explanation of the data within the sample period, and exhibits good statistical properties including parameter stability and forecasts well outside the data period used for estimation. The preferred equation should also be consistent with some plausible static long-run demand for money relationship. However, because the procedures use very general and unrestricted lag structures to proxy both lagged adjustment and the formation of expectations, it is not possible to identify the separate expectations and adjustment effects, and the estimated short-run coefficients may reflect either or both types of response. Thus, for example, the terms in the lagged change in prices, used by Hendry (1979) to proxy the expected rate of inflation, could equally well represent the adjustment process by which money balances respond to price level changes, or indeed some combination of the two effects. The 'general to specific' modelling approach can therefore be criticised for being a purely 'data-mining' exercise, which often fails to distinguish between competing economic hypotheses. The 'testing-down' procedures employed are also necessarily inexact and the investigator has to use his own judgement throughout. Because of this subjective element, it is perfectly possible for two researchers to come up with different preferred models, even when they are each using an identical data set.

CHOICE OF VARIABLE

Whichever type of modelling approach is adopted, the empirical investigator has also to make a decision on the set of variables to include in the estimated demand for money equation and, given this, the precise definitions to be used in each case. The dependent variable can either be defined in narrow or broad terms; in UK empirical studies, the most commonly-used narrow definition of the money stock is $M1$, comprising notes and coin in circulation with the public and private sector sight deposits with the banks, while $M3$ and sterling $M3$, which include private sector time deposits and certificates of deposit, in addition to the items in $M1$, have been the most frequently used broad definitions of money.[16] Personal sector retail deposits have traditionally dominated the $M1$ aggregate, although the 1980s witnessed a sharp rise in interest-bearing sight deposits, many of which were wholesale in nature. The broader money measures contain significant corporate holdings, many of them wholesale deposits.[17] In recent years, empirical work has also begun to use the very narrow $M0$ aggregate, which comprises notes and coin in circulation with the public, banks' till money and bankers' balances at the Bank of England. The broadly-defined $M4$ aggregate, which includes private sector holdings of building society shares and deposits in addition to the items in $M3$ has, as yet, been subjected to little empirical analysis. The same is true of the $M5$ aggregate, which in addition to the items in $M4$, includes private sector holdings of 'money-like' liquid assets, such as bank bills, Treasury bills, local authority deposits, certificates of tax deposit and certain national savings instruments. In US studies, most empirical work is carried out using either the narrow $M1$ definition of the money stock or a broader $M2$ aggregate, which also includes small savings deposits at commercial banks.

The choice among alternative rates of return, as measures of the opportunity cost of holding money, has traditionally been between a short-term rate of interest, such as the Treasury bill or local authority rate, and a long-term rate such as the yield on consols. Attempts have also been made to take account of the rates of return on both equities and international capital funds. The scale or constraint variable normally reduces to a choice between a narrow income measure and a broader wealth concept which may be associated with permanent income. The respective choices, over the most appropriate money, interest rate and scale variables to use in the estimated relationship, may not be independent. For example, the specification of money demand functions for broad money might be expected to reflect the factors which affect wide portfolio choice decisions, where wealth is the likely scale variable and long-term rates of interest may be judged to be the most appropriate opportunity cost measure. In such a demand function, it may also be reasonable to include a measure of the own rate of return on money, as represented, for example, by the rate on bank time deposits. In contrast, the demand for narrow money is more likely to be associated with transactions or precautionary needs, so that narrow income measures of the scale variable and short-term rates on closely competing assets are possibly more appropriate explanatory variables than broad definitions of wealth and long rates of return on less liquid assets.

THE MAIN EMPIRICAL FINDINGS

We will now briefly consider the main empirical findings on the key explanatory variables in the demand for money function, before going on to discuss the evidence on the overall stability of the relationship in more detail in Chapter 6. For reasons of brevity, we concentrate our discussion on the main findings of UK and US studies. There is also a considerable amount of evidence on the money demand equations of other countries and an increasing tendency in empirical work is to apply a particular money demand function to data from several economies, so that a more general test of the model's empirical validity can be made. Examples of studies which adopt such an approach are Carr and Darby (1981), Fair (1987) and Boughton (1991a).

The Price Level

Many of the theoretical models, considered in earlier chapters, predict that the long-run demand for nominal balances is homogeneous of degree one in the price level. Early empirical studies, such as Chow (1966) and Laidler (1971), suggested that this was also a valid assumption at the empirical level, so that it became the tradition in empirical work to impose the restriction of a unitary price elasticity at the outset, by specifying the function in real terms, with real money balances as the dependent variable. Later studies by Coghlan (1978) and Courakis (1978), based on UK data, questioned the validity of the restriction. In a demand function for $M1$, which involves a more flexible lag structure, Coghlan finds a value of approximately 0.7 for the long-run price elasticity. More recently, Boughton (1991a) has also doubted the validity of imposing price homogeneity upon the long-run money demand function. In a five-country study (including the UK and US) which employs cointegration analysis and 'general to specific' modelling procedures, Boughton obtains values for the long-run price elasticity which are significantly less than unity in many cases. For four of the five countries, the estimated price elasticity is much closer to unity for narrow money than for the broad aggregate; the exception is the US where the reverse is true. However, in another study which applies cointegration techniques to the long-run demand function, Hall *et al.* (1990) find general support for the homogeneity assumption for UK data on both narrow and broad money. Other studies which consider the homogeneity issue, using US data, such as Spencer (1985), Goldfeld and Sichel (1987) and MacKinnon and Milbourne (1988), are also unable to reject the restriction of a long-run price elasticity of unity.[18]

Rate of Return Variables

A more established result is the significance of the interest rate variable, which is used to measure the opportunity cost of holding money. The magnitude of the effect varies considerably between studies, although most findings imply a long-run interest elasticity less than unity in absolute value, and often considerably lower. While the values obtained are not noticeably dependent upon the definition of money used, it seems that higher elasticity values are often associated with the use of long, rather than short rates of interest; a finding which can be explained in terms of the greater statistical variability of short rates. In measuring the return on long-dated government securities, it is normal to assume that the expected capital gain on bonds over the holding period is zero. An exception to this approach is provided by the study of Grice and Bennett (1984) who include a measure of expected capital gains within their opportunity cost measure. Two alternative ways of generating the series are considered. The first method assumes perfect foresight, in that expected capital gains are proxied by the *ex post* actual values. The second procedure is based upon the 'rational expectations' approach of Nelson (1975) and McCallum (1976). This method involves the generation of a series for the expected relative return on gilts (including capital gains), using the predictions from the equation that is believed to determine the actual relative return. Included among the explanatory variables in this equation are several interest rate terms and various expenditure and wealth variables.[19] Grice and Bennett find that the opportunity cost measures generated from these two approaches are each statistically significant in a demand function for sterling $M3$.

Several studies have included more than one opportunity cost variable in the money demand function.[20] Such an approach is based upon Friedman's belief that money is a substitute for all assets, both real and financial, so that the rates of return on a whole range of assets are relevant. For example, studies by Hamburger (1977b) and Laidler (1980), using US data, have stressed the importance of the rate of return on equities (and thus on physical capital) as proxied by the dividend–price ratio ruling in the stock market. A similar effect is isolated for the UK by Hamburger (1977a) in a demand function for narrow money. Such findings suggest that claims against the earnings and real assets of firms are effective substitutes for money. With the increasing integration of domestic and foreign capital markets, there is also some evidence to suggest that account should be taken of the rate of return on international securities. The interest rate on such assets is also less subject to manipulation by the authorities than many of the domestic short rates, such as the Treasury bill yield, and may therefore be a better measure of the opportunity cost of holding money. Hamburger (1977a) finds that the three-month eurodollar deposit rate is a significant variable in the UK demand function for narrow money. In a study of the demand for sterling $M3$, Adam (1991) assumes that the return on foreign assets is determined by both the eurodollar deposit rate and the expected depreciation in the sterling exchange rate. An assumption of perfect foresight is made, in which *ex ante* exchange rate expectations are proxied by their actual *ex post* outcomes. Adam's hypothesis is consistent with the findings of Arango and Nadiri (1981) for real cash balances, while Howard and Johnson (1983) find a role for exchange rate expectations in a demand function for sterling-denominated sight deposits. In the latter study, the insignificance of the eurodollar interest rate appears to indicate that the relevant substitute for sterling sight deposits is foreign notes and coin, rather than eurodollar deposits.

Friedman (1956) argues that the rate of return on real assets is related to the expected rate of inflation, so that money holdings should fall when inflationary expectations rise. Cagan (1956) suggests that such an opportunity cost variable is particularly relevant to the demand for money during times of rapid and highly variable rates of inflation, since it is then that expectations are likely to change most rapidly. Traditionally, such influences have been particularly important in developing countries, while the past two decades have also witnessed several periods of very high inflation in the major industrialised economies, so that the use of the expected or actual rate of inflation as a potential determinant of the demand for money has increased. Early studies using US data, such as Goldfeld (1973), found a role for the expected inflation rate, measured either as a weighted average of past actual rates of inflation, in accordance with the adaptive expectations hypothesis, or else constructed from opinion survey data. For the UK, Artis and Lewis (1976) experiment with different expectations generating mechanisms and find that inflationary expectations are best modelled by the current rate of change of prices. Such a variable is found to have a significant influence upon holdings of $M1$ balances, but not upon the wider $M3$ aggregate. In other studies, Hendry and Mizon (1978), Hendry (1979, 1985), Taylor (1987) and Hendry and Ericsson (1991b) use general distributed lag models to analyse the demand for both narrow and broad money, in which the actual rate of change in the price level is included as an explanatory variable in the estimated equation. The results indicate that the variable has a negative effect upon the demand for money, as theory would predict. Strong evidence of inflation effects is also found by Budd and Holly (1986) in a demand function for sterling $M3$, which is estimated using annual data for the period 1878–1984. Similarly, Hall *et al.* (1990) find a powerful role for the rate of inflation in cointegrating regressions for both $M3$ and $M4$ for the data period 1968–87. The use of an inflation rate variable in empirical demand for money equations is therefore now well established and the significant role found for the variable in these studies would appear to indicate that inflation has an effect upon the demand for money, over and above any indirect influence it might exert via the nominal interest rate.[21]

Although much of the early theoretical work treated money as an asset bearing a zero rate of return, such an assumption is hardly empirically accurate and most types of money now provide a positive pecuniary return. Furthermore, empirical studies have increasingly found evidence to support the view that the own rate of return on money is a relevant factor to include in the demand function, as well as one or more opportunity cost measures. Initially, these attempts at modelling the return on money, such as the US studies by Barro and

Santomero (1972), Klein (1974a and 1974b) and Startz (1979), concentrated upon measures of the 'implicit service yield' on money. Such an approach is based upon Friedman's view that money is held because it provides a flow of services, just like any consumer durable or capital good. In a similar vein, Klein (1977) finds that a variable measuring the short-term unpredictability of the price level has a positive effect upon the US demand for money over the period 1879–1972. It is argued that uncertainty over the predictability of the value of money has the effect of reducing the services provided by a given quantity of real balances and so causes agents to compensate by increasing their money holdings.[22] Kent (1985) applies the principles of capital theory to the demand for money and develops a measure of the relative 'implicit rental price', or 'user cost' of money, for use as an explanatory variable in a demand equation for US narrow money. The composite variable is constructed from the own rate of return on money, the opportunity cost rate on a substitute asset, the tax rate and the price level.

For the UK, the construction of explicit own rate of return variables has been facilitated by the development of new financial instruments, such as certificates of deposit in the 1970s, and the more recent move towards the payment of interest on sight deposits. In consequence, variables representing the interest rate on money, or the differential between this return and an opportunity cost rate, are now frequently used in empirical studies. Hacche (1974) and Goodhart (1981) use a measure of the own rate of return, based upon the three-month certificate of deposit rate. The variable is shown to be important in explaining the rise in broad money holdings in the UK in the period immediately after 1971. Grice and Bennett (1984) and Adam (1991) construct composite measures of the own rate of return on sterling $M3$, based upon weighted averages of the interest rates paid on the different components of broad money. A similar composite rate variable is also used by Artis and Lewis (1976) to define a term in the relative return on money, in a demand function for the $M3$ aggregate. Taylor (1987) has stressed the importance of the own rate of return, in a demand function for sterling $M3$, using a measure based upon the seven-day deposit rate and the return on high-interest cheque accounts. Finally, Hendry and Ericsson (1991b) have shown that a satisfactory explanation of $M1$ holdings, post-1985, requires consideration to be given to the interest rate on sight deposits.

Several US studies have attempted to verify the existence of a liquidity trap, or lower floor to the rate of interest, which is a fundamental element of the speculative demand for money, and associated with the belief that the relationship between money demand and the interest rate can be expected to be unstable over time. Bronfenbrenner and Mayer (1960) and Laidler (1966b) attempt to test for a liquidity trap by investigating the relationship between interest rates and elasticity values; they find no evidence to suggest that elasticity values increase as interest rates fall, as would be expected if there was a liquidity trap. However, other US studies such as Eisner (1971) and Spitzer (1976) use a different approach and find evidence of a minimum value for the interest rate. The evidence on the existence of a liquidity trap is therefore mixed; on balance, Laidler (1985) feels we cannot support the hypothesis. Such a conclusion is supported by the work of Starleaf and Reimer (1967); they attempted, without success, to find a role for the concept of a 'normal' rate of interest, based upon a weighted average of present and past actual rates. The empirical evidence from these US studies would therefore appear to cast some doubt on the validity of Keynes' speculative demand model.

The Scale Variable

In terms of the scale or constraint variables used in demand for money studies, measured income concepts are easier to test than wealth variables, where the usual proxy is permanent income, a definition which treats the present value of future labour income as part of the current stock of wealth. The early empirical literature, of which Laidler (1966a) is a typical example, suggested that permanent income was more appropriate than current income, although later studies such as Meyer and Neri (1975), Lieberman (1980) and Gupta (1980) dispute this conclusion. As we noted earlier, permanent income is most frequently modelled by a geometric distributed lag of current and past actual values of income. This leads to a short-run money demand relation, of the form given in equation (5.14), which is very similar to that obtainable from a partial adjustment model, with actual current income as the scale variable. In such cases, support for the permanent income hypothesis could therefore be misplaced, with the role of the lagged dependent variable purely attributable to adjustment rather than expectational lags. The model of Feige (1967), outlined earlier, was specifically developed to help resolve the problem of choosing between the two alternative theories. Feige's original study used annual US data for the period 1915–63 and found that the estimates of the adjustment parameter were not significantly different from unity, implying full adjustment to desired balances within the year, whereas estimates of the parameter underlying the modelling of permanent income produced values of 0.37 in the narrow money equation and 0.30 in the broad money equation. Laidler and Parkin (1970) estimate Feige's model, using quarterly UK data for 1956–67. Their results are not so conclusive as those of Feige, although the permanent income hypothesis is favoured, with the finding that the adjustment of actual to desired balances is almost complete within a year.

Some more recent studies have attempted to construct alternative measures of wealth, incorporating only non-human elements. Grice and Bennett (1984) use a series for financial wealth in a demand function for sterling $M3$. The variable, which has a significant effect upon the demand for money, is constructed from five different assets held by the non-bank private sector; namely money, gilts, national savings, local authority and Treasury bills and overseas assets. Grice and Bennett distinguish between changes in financial wealth due to new savings and those arising from the revaluation of existing asset prices. Money holdings react more slowly to wealth changes arising from asset price revaluations, although in the long run this channel of influence is found to be stronger. They find that wealth plays at least as important a role as income, with a long-run elasticity of 1.4 found for wealth against 0.3 for income. Adam (1991) argues that there is evidence of a long-run cointegrating relationship between sterling $M3$ and gross financial wealth, where both variables are expressed in real terms. Hall *et al.* (1990) find a measure of personal sector gross wealth, incorporating both financial and real assets (where the latter mainly reflects the value of owner-occupied housing) has a role to play in equations for both the $M3$ and $M4$ aggregates. For the latter definition of money, the estimates imply a long-run income elasticity of 0.28 and a wealth elasticity of 0.72. In general, elasticity values with respect to the scale variable differ considerably between studies, and range from less than one-half to well above unity, with the most common value either just above or slightly below unity. Broader definitions of money have, if anything, tended to produce higher long-run elasticity values; a finding that is consistent with the link between narrow definitions of money and transactions cost-based theories of the demand for money which, in their basic form at least, predict economies of scale in money holding.

In recent years, research on scale variables, using mainly US data, has also focused upon the construction of more comprehensive measures of transactions. Goldfeld and Sichel (1990) argue that the much-used Gross National Product variable may be an inadequate measure of transactions for use in the demand for money function, because it excludes all sales of intermediate goods, transfers, purchases of existing goods and transactions in financial assets, all of which may affect money demand. Similarly, Radecki and Wenninger (1985) argue that Gross National Product is not a good proxy for the total volume of transactions, when net exports or inventories are strongly affecting its growth rate. Mankiw and Summers (1986) consider a range of scale variables and find that consumer expenditure is the most empirically successful in explaining both narrow and broad money holdings. Similarly, Dotsey (1988) supports the use of an expenditure variable in a demand function for currency. Studies by Hall *et al.* (1990) and Westaway and Walton (1991), using UK data on the narrow *M*0 aggregate, also favour the use of transactions measures based upon total consumer expenditure or non-durable consumption.

Other Results

Long-term institutional influences upon the velocity of circulation (the ratio of nominal income to the money stock) are considered by Graves (1980) and Bordo and Jonung (1981, 1987, 1990). Graves focuses upon the role of urbanisation and shifts in the age distribution of the population, while Bordo and Jonung are particularly concerned with the impact of monetisation, economic stability and improved access to banking facilities. They argue that two stages of financial development characterise the typical economy, each of which leads to a particular trend in the velocity of circulation. In the first stage, the process of monetisation takes place, barter declines and a banking system develops; these all result in a tendency for the velocity of circulation to fall. Later, as economic stability improves and the financial system becomes more sophisticated, close substitutes for money become available and ways are found to economise on money balances, so that there is an upward trend in velocity. Within these long-term trends, short-term cyclical fluctuations may, at any given time, temporarily distort the long-run pattern. Using annual data from the 1870s to the late 1980s, for five different countries (including the UK and US) Bordo and Jonung find that variables designed to proxy financial development and the monetisation of the economy are significant in explaining variations in velocity. These variables are the currency to money ratio, the share of the labour force working outside agriculture and the ratio of non-bank financial assets to total financial wealth. The inclusion of these variables is also found to lower the implied income elasticity of the demand for money.

Other variables that have been incorporated into empirical money demand functions include measures of the 'riskiness' of bonds, which is stressed in Tobin's mean–variance model, and proxies for the brokerage fees involved in transferring funds between bonds and money, which is relevant to the transactions cost models. Unfortunately, the difficulties inherent in the modelling of such variables have severely limited their general applicability and it is difficult to make a judgement on their empirical importance.[23] Artis and Lewis (1976) include a measure of the standard deviation of bond yields, in order to proxy the 'riskiness' of bonds, in UK demand functions for both $M1$ and $M3$. According to mean–variance theory, a rise in the volatility of the yield of bonds should increase the uncertainty associated with holding alternative capital-uncertain financial assets and so lead to an increase in the demand for money. The variable is found to be generally significant, with the expected positive sign, in both sets of equations. Boughton and Tavlas (1991) find that a similar variable is significant in equations for both narrow and broad money in the US, but is insignificant when tested on UK data. Other studies using US data, such as Slovin and Sushka (1983), Koskela and Viren (1987), Hendry and Ericsson (1991b) and Baba *et al.* (1992), specify equations for narrow money which also isolate a significant role for measures of variability, based upon the standard deviation or variance of interest rates. The real wage rate has been used in US studies of the demand for money, such as Dutton and Gramm (1973), Khan (1973), Karni (1974) and Dotsey (1988). For the UK, Dowd (1990a and 1990b) has included a real wage variable in demand functions for both currency and non-interest-bearing personal sector deposits. The rationale for the inclusion of such a variable is the belief that wages foregone represent the opportunity costs of time and so make a suitable proxy for the transactions costs or brokerage fees, which are inherent in transactions and precautionary theories of money demand. In all these studies, the wage variable is found to have a significant positive effect upon money holdings, as theory would predict.[24]

6 Stability and the Demand for Money Function

The incorporation of proxies for risk and brokerage costs, and other specific tests of the theories outlined in Chapters 2, 3 and 4, are comparatively rare in empirical demand for money studies. Instead, most empirical work has concentrated upon the need to isolate a stable money demand function at the aggregate level, using the key opportunity cost and scale variables discussed in Chapter 5. Most studies published in the 1960s and early 1970s, such as Meltzer (1963), Brunner and Meltzer (1963), Laidler (1966a) and Goldfeld (1973) for the US, and Kavanagh and Walters (1966), Laidler and Parkin (1970) and Goodhart and Crockett (1970) for the UK, were able to find stable and well-determined money demand functions. The precise form of the equations, and the type and period of data used, varied between studies; static long-run equations of the form given in (5.3) were common for annual data, while studies using quarterly data generally estimated short-run equations, such as (5.6) and (5.14), which allowed for adjustment and expectational lags. The results, for the US in particular, were broadly invariant to the precise data period involved and the particular definitions of money, interest rate and scale variable used. Consequently, even though little attempt was made to test for stability in any rigorous manner, nobody seriously questioned the view that stable money demand functions could be isolated. Laidler (1971) was able to claim that, 'The evidence for Britain certainly points to the existence of a stable demand for money function in that economy. For the United States the evidence is overwhelming, and for Britain it is at the very least highly suggestive'.[1]

In contrast, studies undertaken since the mid-1970s, using quarterly data for both the UK and US, have often had difficulty in modelling the money market and have consequently questioned the existence of a stable demand for money relation. Indeed, this problem is not solely confined to the UK and US. Studies by Boughton (1979) and Fair (1987) showed that instability also appeared to be present in the money demand equations of several other countries in this period. Hacche

75

(1974) and Artis and Lewis (1976) were the first UK studies to highlight the instability problem. They found that the conventional short-run partial adjustment equations, which had explained the data well in the 1960s, were unable to forecast the quantity of money at all accurately in the early 1970s, with the estimated equations systematically underpredicting the actual UK money stock. When this data was incorporated into the observation period for estimation purposes, the results indicated that much of the explanatory power of the equations was due to the lagged dependent variable, with the coefficient estimates indicating an extremely slow rate of adjustment from actual to desired money holdings and, in consequence, implausibly large long-run elasticity values. The breakdown in the relationship was particularly apparent in the equation for broad money. For the US, studies such as Goldfeld (1976) and Enzler *et al.* (1976) found similar problems, although here the conventional short-run equations tended to overpredict the actual US money stock in the early 1970s, giving rise to the concept of 'missing money'. Also, in contrast to the UK experience, it was the narrow money equation which was particularly problematical. Difficulties were also encountered in the 1980s, when there was a noticeable decline in the velocity of circulation of most forms of money in both the UK and US; in consequence, the standard money demand equations were often found to underpredict the actual money stock in both countries. Studies undertaken since the mid-1970s, in both the UK and US, have therefore been largely concerned with explaining these apparent shifts in the demand for money function; this has led investigators to look for 'new' relationships which can explain money holdings over a longer data period than that used in the early short-run studies. In some cases, this search has involved the consideration of institutional factors specific to the different economies. We shall therefore concentrate on analysing the recent UK studies first of all, before turning to US studies later in the chapter.

NARROW MONEY

In an attempt to obtain more satisfactory money demand functions, many UK studies have looked at alternative specifications of the traditionally-estimated short-run relationships. Different functional forms, more flexible lag structures and additional explanatory variables have all been considered, and have been particularly successful in improving the demand equations for narrow money. Mills (1978) experiments with different functional forms and finds that the demand for narrow money is adequately explained by the conventional independent variables, regardless of which functional form is employed. Coghlan (1978) uses a model, allowing for a freely-estimated lagged structure, to isolate a transactions demand function based upon quarterly UK data for $M1$ over the period 1964–76. The preferred specification for nominal money balances takes the form

$$m_t = 0.379y_t - 0.216y_{t-3} + 1.326p_{t-1} - 2.069p_{t-2} + 1.675p_{t-3}$$
$$\quad (3.80) \qquad (2.17) \qquad (6.05) \qquad (5.73) \qquad (4.57)$$

$$\quad - 0.816p_{t-4} - 0.048r_t + 0.838m_{t-1}$$
$$\quad (3.53) \qquad (5.16) \qquad (18.62) \qquad R^2 = 0.99$$

where all variables are written in logarithmic form and the figures in parentheses refer to t-statistics. The lag structure implied by the results is complex and obviously different for each explanatory variable; adjustment to real income and price level changes is complete in less than a year, while adjustment to changes in the rate of interest is slower. A long-run income elasticity of unity is implied by the results. Coghlan concludes that there is no evidence of a breakdown in the demand function for narrow money in the 1970s.[2]

Hendry (1979, 1985) also finds that the demand for $M1$ exhibits greater parameter stability when a more flexible lag response is allowed, in a model in which the long-run real demand for money depends upon real income, the rate of interest and the expected rate of inflation. In addition to price homogeneity, an income elasticity of unity is assumed in steady state, implying that agents wish to hold money in proportion to their nominal incomes in the long run. Reparameterisation allows the unrestricted lagged model to be interpreted as an error-correction equation, so that while the growth in real balances depends upon the growth in prices and income, there is also a correction for any divergence from the long-run equilibrium demand relation. In this way, the approach allows the investigator to model the short-run dynamics around the long-run equilibrium demand for money function. Hendry's (1985) preferred short-run equation, obtained from quarterly data for the period 1961–82, takes the form

$$\Delta \tilde{m}_t = \underset{(0.01)}{0.04} + \underset{(0.13)}{0.37\Delta y_{t-1}} - \underset{(0.07)}{0.58R_t} - \underset{(0.12)}{0.80\Delta p_t} - \underset{(0.01)}{0.10(\tilde{m} - y)_{t-2}}$$

$$\underset{(0.07)}{-0.28\Delta \tilde{m}_{t-1}} \qquad\qquad R^2 = 0.71$$

where all variables, except the rate of interest, are expressed in logarithms and the figures in parentheses are the standard errors of the estimates. The symbol Δ is used to denote the first difference of the variable, so that the dependent variable represents the quarterly growth in real money balances, while Δp_t can be interpreted as a proxy for the expected rate of inflation. Income enters with a lag, while only the current interest rate is significant. The term $(\tilde{m} - y)_{t-2}$ represents the error-correction mechanism; previous disequilibria, in the relationship between the levels of real money balances and real income, affect the rate of change in real demand through this variable, which represents the ratio of lagged real balances to lagged real income. The hypothesis of a unitary long-run income elasticity is accepted by the data, while the coefficient on the error-correction variable indicates a feedback of 10 per cent from previous disequilibria between money and income. This is a relatively slow adjustment, possibly reflecting minimal costs of being out of equilibrium. In contrast, the results imply large immediate responses to changes in inflation and the interest rate. Given the high values frequently attained by both nominal interest rates and the rate of inflation over the second part of the data period used in the study, such findings indicate the importance of these variables to any explanation of money holdings post-1970.

Hendry and Ericsson (1991b) find that the coefficient estimates of the earlier Hendry studies change very little when the data period is extended to 1985, but that the model massively underpredicts money holdings over the remainder of the 1980s. Holdings of $M1$, in real terms, increased considerably over this period, leading Hendry and Ericsson to hypothesise that the advent of high-interest cheque accounts in the 1980s had the effect of increasing the demand for narrow money, once individuals had learnt of the availability of such accounts. A net opportunity cost variable, defined as the difference between the three-month local authority deposit rate and a measure of the retail sight deposit rate, is included in the estimated equations in order to measure this effect. The preferred equation for the period 1964–89 takes the form

$$\Delta\tilde{m}_t = \underset{(0.004)}{0.02} - \underset{(0.05)}{0.63RC_t} - \underset{(0.14)}{0.69\Delta p_t} - \underset{(0.06)}{0.17\Delta(\tilde{m} - y)_{t-1}}$$

$$\underset{(0.01)}{-0.09(\tilde{m} - y)_{t-1}} \qquad\qquad R^2 = 0.76$$

where RC represents the net opportunity cost variable. The figures in parentheses are standard errors, indicating that the coefficient estimates are all highly significant. The authors feel this equation represents an improvement over the previous Hendry specifications.

Using annual UK data for the period 1950–84, Beenstock (1989) examines the determinants of the ratio of cash holdings to bank sight deposits. Not surprisingly, the ratio is found to decline when the interest rate on sight deposits rises. The results also imply that the ratio rises when the returns on long-dated gilts and other liquid assets increase, suggesting that these assets are closer substitutes for sight deposits than cash. Increases in economic activity, or in the velocity of circulation, appear to lower the demand for cash relative to the demand for sight deposits. No role is found for the level of wealth in the determination of the ratio. The ratio of sight deposits to time deposits is also examined, with the results indicating that increases in the sight deposit rate, relative to the time deposit rate, had the effect of increasing the value of the ratio. No role is found for the interest rates on other assets, suggesting that the demand for both categories of deposits responded in a similar way to changes in the rates of return on competing assets.

Financial Innovation

Since the 1970s, the demand for narrow money, and cash holdings in particular, has been affected by institutional changes, improvements in transactions technology and the expansion of alternative payments mechanisms. For example, the increasing range of bank and building society accounts, the development in the use of direct debiting and standing order mandates, and the expansion in the use of credit and debit cards, have all enabled individuals to economise on cash holdings. In addition, the introduction of cash-point facilities, while possibly encouraging a greater use of notes in transactions, could equally well also lead individuals to reduce the average inventory of notes and coin held, by making cash withdrawals more convenient and so lowering brokerage costs.[3] At the same time, the trend has been for an increasing proportion of wages and salaries to be paid by cheque or credit transfer directly into bank accounts, rather than as cash in wage packets.

Johnston (1984) examines the determinants of the different components of $M1$ holdings, differentiating between interest and non-interest-bearing forms of the narrow money aggregate and paying particular attention to the influence of financial innovation. Different measures of innovation are considered, including variables representing the number of bank current accounts *per capita*, the number of building society share accounts *per capita*, the total number of cash dispensers and the number of credit cards. Applying 'general to specific' modelling techniques to data for the period 1965–82, demand functions are estimated for both notes and coin in circulation and the very narrow $M0$ definition of the money stock. The preferred equations incorporate only one innovation term, in either the bank current account or building society share account variables. In each case, these measures are found to exert a significant negative influence upon cash and $M0$ holdings. Johnston argues that financial innovation raised the velocity of circulation of both cash and $M0$ by about 3 per cent a year over the latter part of the period, and the results also appear to indicate that the interest sensitivity of these very narrow measures of money increased over the data period, in line with the innovations in cash management techniques and the general rise in nominal interest rates. The modelling of non-interest-bearing sight deposits proved more difficult, although the interest sensitivity of such deposits was found to be greater than that of both notes and coin and $M0$ holdings. Not surprisingly, a significant positive relationship is isolated between the variable representing the number of current accounts *per capita* and total holdings of non-interest-bearing sight deposits, but the other financial innovation variables exert no significant influence upon the aggregate. Complementary work indicated that the same measures of financial innovation were also unable to explain changes in the holdings of interest-bearing sight deposits, which had grown to become the major component of total $M1$ balances by the mid-1980s.

Applying cointegration techniques to quarterly data on narrow money for the period 1967–86, Hall *et al.* (1990) find that a long-run cointegrating vector cannot be established for $M0$, unless a measure of financial innovation is included among the set of explanatory variables. However, the results obtained using direct measures of innovation, based upon the number of cash dispensers, credit cards and bank current accounts, were felt to be unsatisfactory. Instead, the authors favour the use of a cumulative interest rate variable, which is designed to represent the innovation process; higher interest rates increase the opportunity cost of holding cash and therefore encourage individuals to adopt cash-saving technology and payments methods. Furthermore, once the new efficient cash management practices are adopted, they are likely to continue even when interest rates fall, so producing a kind of 'ratchet' effect upon the demand for $M0$. The preferred cointegrating vector relates $M0$ holdings to consumer expenditure and the cumulative interest rate variable. The residuals from the long-run cointegrating regression are used to construct an error-correction term, for use in a short-run dynamic equation for the rate of change of $M0$ holdings. Past rates of change in consumer expenditure and the price level, together with the level of the interest rate, form the other explanatory variables in the short-run equation. The wider $M1$ aggregate is also considered; in this case, some allowance must also be made for the rising proportion of narrow money which is interest-bearing. In a separate cointegrating regression, the growth in the interest-bearing element of $M1$ is shown to depend upon the wealth to income ratio, the own rate of interest and a variable representing the sharp increase in the size and turnover of the financial sector. In a follow-up study, Brookes *et al.* (1991) re-estimate the Hall *et al.* equation for $M0$, using an extended data set up to 1989. The results obtained, from both the long-run cointegrating regression and the short-run dynamic equation, are very similar to the original estimates, providing some evidence for the hypothesis of stability.

Westaway and Walton (1991) also find that financial innovation variables must be considered before a long-run cointegrating vector can be established for $M0$. Direct measures of innovation are considered, based upon the number of cash dispensers and the proportion of manual workers in the total employed. Manual workers traditionally receive their wage income in cash, so that $M0$ holdings should fall as the proportion of such workers in the labour force declines. However, a cumulative interest rate variable is found to dominate these measures.[4] The preferred cointegrating vector relates real money holdings to real non-durable consumption, the cumulative interest rate variable, the rate of inflation and the level of the interest rate. A short-run equation is also estimated, in which the growth in real $M0$ holdings is related to the growth in real consumption, the rate of change in the price level and an error-correction term, as represented by the lagged value of the residuals from the cointegrating regression.

BROAD MONEY

The search for a stable demand function for broad money in the UK
has proved more difficult. Hacche (1974) argues that these problems
emanate from the introduction of the Competition and Credit Control
regime of monetary control in 1971. With its emphasis upon greater
competition in the banking system, and the abandonment of lending
controls and the clearing banks' interest rate cartel, the new regime had
far-reaching consequences in the money markets. The clearing banks
began to compete more actively for funds by raising interest rates on
deposit accounts, issuing certificates of deposit and generally partici-
pating to a greater degree in the 'parallel money' markets. These
developments increased the attractiveness of interest-earning money to
asset holders and, according to Hacche, led to an upward shift in the
demand function for $M3$. This was especially the case for that portion
of $M3$ balances held by the company sector. Here, the arbitrage
operations surrounding the phenomenon of 'round-tripping' led to an
increase in both bank borrowing and the demand for large wholesale
deposits, in the periods when market pressures forced deposit rates
above borrowing rates. In an attempt to allow for these effects, in
equations for both aggregate $M3$ balances and company sector money
holdings, Hacche included a measure of the own rate of return on
money, based upon the three-month certificate of deposit rate. Using
quarterly data for the period 1963–72, this modification resulted in
more plausible coefficient estimates and an improvement in the overall
fit and predictive performance of the equations. In an extension of
Hacche's work, Goodhart (1981) estimates equations for both aggregate $M3$ and company sector money holdings, which include terms in
the certificate of deposit rate and the differential between this rate and
the banks' lending rate. The latter variable is designed to capture, more
explicitly, any 'round-tripping' effect. Using data for the period 1963–
73, the coefficients on both variables are found to be statistically
significant and together their inclusion results in an improvement in the
overall fit of the equations.

Hacche's model is a 'first-differenced' version of equation (5.8), the
reduced form obtainable from a nominal partial adjustment model, in
which corrections are also made for residual autocorrelation. It
therefore imposes several untested restrictions on the dynamic form
of the demand for money function, and has consequently been
criticised by Courakis (1978) and Hendry and Mizon (1978). Using
data on personal sector $M3$ holdings for the period 1963–75, Courakis

finds no evidence to suggest that the restrictions imposed by Hacche, including that of a unitary long-run price elasticity, are valid. Overall, Courakis' results show alarming variations over the different specifications tested and he questions whether it is possible to obtain reliable estimates of the demand for money parameters. Hendry and Mizon specify a general distributed lag model, which is reparameterised to incorporate an error-correction mechanism. The preferred specification, which makes some improvement to the overall fit of the personal sector $M3$ equation, over the period 1963–75, takes the form

$$\Delta \tilde{m}_t = 1.61 + 0.21\Delta y_t + 0.81\Delta r_t - 0.40\Delta p_t + 0.26\Delta \tilde{m}_{t-1}$$
$$\quad (0.65) \quad (0.09) \quad\quad (0.31) \quad\quad (0.15) \quad\quad (0.12)$$

$$-0.23(\tilde{m} - y)_{t-1} - 0.61r_{t-4} + 0.14y_{t-4}$$
$$\quad (0.05) \quad\quad\quad\quad (0.21) \quad\quad (0.04) \quad\quad R^2 = 0.69$$

where all variables are expressed in logarithmic form and the figures in parentheses represent the standard errors of the estimates. It is argued the statistical significance of the 'levels' terms indicates that it is invalid to include only first-differenced variables in the specification. The error-correction term implies a feedback of 23 per cent from previous disequilibria between money and income. Hendry and Mizon show that their results imply a plausible long-run equilibrium solution for the demand for money, with income, interest and inflation elasticities of the expected sign and of realistic magnitudes. However, the hypothesis of a unitary long-run income elasticity is rejected by the data.[5] Lubrano *et al.* (1986) also consider only personal sector holdings of $M3$. Separate equations are estimated for the periods 1963–71 and 1971–80, with the explanatory variables based upon the traditional real income, interest rate and price level series. They find that the parameters of the short-run equation changed with the introduction of Competition and Credit Control, but that the parameters of the underlying long-run equation are less affected by the policy change.

Grice and Bennett (1984) also allow a flexible lag structure in a demand function for aggregate sterling $M3$, which involves both wealth and income variables, a Competition and Credit Control dummy and terms in the own rate of return on money and the differential between the return on gilts (including expected capital gains) and that on money. The model is estimated using data over the period 1963–78, but the preferred specifications are not totally satisfactory; the lag responses are long and terms in the dependent variable, lagged up to five periods, provide much of the explanatory power. Nevertheless, their results lead them to conclude that the Competition and Credit Control reforms resulted in a permanent upward movement in the demand for broad money. Their conclusion is questioned by Taylor (1987) who finds no evidence of a structural break, following the imposition of Competition and Credit Control. Estimating a general distributed lag demand function for sterling $M3$ over the period 1964–85, he obtains the relation

$$\Delta \tilde{m}_t = 0.030 - 0.005(RTB_{t-1} - RM_t) - 0.003\Delta^2 RLB_{t-2}$$
$$\quad\ (0.007)\quad (0.002) \qquad\qquad\qquad (0.001)$$

$$\quad\ - 0.415\Delta p_t - 0.019(\tilde{m} - y)_{t-4} + 0.287\Delta \tilde{m}_{t-2}$$
$$\qquad\ (0.183)\qquad (0.006) \qquad\qquad (0.102)$$

$$R^2 = 0.76$$

where the figures in parentheses represent standard errors, Δ^2 is the second-difference operator, RTB is the Treasury bill rate, RLB is the yield on long-term government bonds and RM is the own rate of return on money, which is based upon the seven-day deposit rate and (towards the end of the data period) the rate available on high-interest cheque accounts. All variables, except the rates of interest, are expressed in logarithmic form. The performance of the equation deteriorates when the own rate variable is excluded, and Taylor concludes that both the return on money and the rate of inflation are important determinants of the demand for money over the estimation period.

Using the same data sets, Cuthbertson and Taylor (1990b) apply cointegration techniques to isolate a long-run relationship between real sterling $M3$ balances, real income, the Treasury bill rate and the own return on money. The preferred relation, which can be interpreted to be the long-run demand for money function, takes the form

$$\tilde{m}_t = y_t - 0.14RTB_t + 0.034RM_t$$

Although income homogeneity is imposed upon the relation, tests indicate that this is a valid restriction. The residuals from the cointegrating relation provide a measure of the short-run deviations from long-run equilibrium demand and are used to construct an error-correction term for use in a short-run general distributed lag equation. In this way, the growth in real money balances is adjusted for the difference between desired and actual holdings in the previous period. 'Testing-down' procedures produced a preferred short-run equation of the form

$$\Delta \tilde{m}_t = 0.04 + 0.19\Delta\tilde{m}_{t-1} + 0.44\Delta\tilde{m}_{t-2}$$
$$\phantom{\Delta \tilde{m}_t =} (0.01) \quad (0.09) \qquad\quad (0.09)$$
$$- 0.026(\tilde{m} - y + 0.14RTB - 0.034RM)_{t-1}$$
$$(0.006)$$

where the figures in parentheses are standard errors. Cuthbertson and Taylor argue that the low estimated value of the error-correction coefficient implies a very slow adjustment speed.

Adam (1991) uses cointegration techniques, in conjunction with a general distributed lag error-correction approach, to model the demand for sterling $M3$ over the period 1975–86. The identification of a robust long-run cointegrating relationship is hampered by the use of monthly data over a relatively short data period. However, the results indicate that a long-run relationship can be established between real money holdings and real wealth, the inflation rate and the differential between the own rate of return on money and the yield on foreign assets. The preferred short-run error-correction equation includes lagged and differenced terms in real income, the rate of inflation, the own return on money and the foreign interest rate. In spite of the considerable degree of financial innovation and deregulation which occurred over the data period, Adam feels his results suggest that it is possible to isolate a relatively stable short-run demand function for sterling $M3$. Particular importance is attached to the two interest rate terms, which capture the effect on money demand of the growth in interest-bearing sight deposits and the increased access to currency substitution opportunities over the period.

A particularly important potential source of instability in the $M3$ demand function is provided by the growth of building society deposits. The activities of banks and building societies have become much less distinct over the past twenty years and they both now offer the public a very similar and highly substitutable range of accounts. Transfers of funds between the two sets of institutions occur continuously and are capable of introducing a substantial element of instability into the $M3$ function. In contrast, the wider $M4$ aggregate, which encompasses both bank and building society deposits, is unaffected by such transfers. Instability can also arise in the $M3$

aggregate, independently of that of $M4$, because of the building societies' practice of holding part of their asset portfolio on deposit at the banks. Changes in these balances affect the growth of $M3$ balances, but not the $M4$ aggregate. Such deposits increased markedly in the 1980s as building societies began to show a preference for holding their assets in this form, rather than in short-dated gilts or local authority debt.

Hall *et al.* (1990) obtain cointegrating vectors for both $M3$ and $M4$, using quarterly data for the period 1968–87. The ratio of $M4$ to nominal income is linked to the wealth to income ratio, the rate of inflation, a Competition and Credit Control dummy and a variable based upon past falls in the stock market index. Significant interest rate effects could not be identified in the long-run cointegrating regression. The authors feel that this failure may be due to the problems of measuring appropriate own and competing rates in a period of financial change. It is also possible that different rates may be appropriate for different sectors of the economy, in which case a more disaggregated approach might be able to identify significant interest rate effects. 'General to specific' modelling techniques are used to estimate the short-run equation, with the preferred relation linking the proportionate change in $M4$ holdings to the lagged change and an error-correction mechanism, based upon the one-period lagged values of the residuals from the cointegrating regression. A similar cointegrating vector and short-run dynamic equation is obtained for $M3$, although in this case an allowance is also made for innovative behaviour by the building societies. In a follow-up study, Brookes *et al.* (1991) update the $M4$ equation using new observations which extend the data set to 1989. The parameter estimates obtained, from both the long-run cointegrating regression and the short-run dynamic equation, are almost identical to those obtained in the initial Hall *et al.* study, thus giving some support to the hypothesis of stability.

Cuthbertson and Barlow (1990) consider personal sector holdings of a wider liquid assets aggregate, which comprises cash, bank and building society deposits, tax instruments and three-month local authority debt. This group of assets corresponds closely to those which comprise the $M5$ money supply aggregate. Using quarterly data for the period 1968–86, a cointegrating vector is isolated, linking real liquid asset holdings to the inflation-adjusted own rate of return, an opportunity cost rate, the bank lending rate, real disposable income and the ratio of non-liquid gross financial wealth to income. The own return is taken to be the rate on three-month local authority debt, while the opportunity cost variable is represented by the return on gilts, which includes a measure of capital gains. The work of Sprenkle and Miller (1980), which we considered in Chapter 3, is used to justify the role of the bank lending rate, with the results supporting the hypothesis that a rise in the cost of borrowing reduces liquid asset holdings, as agents repay outstanding debt. An increase in the inflation rate also reduces liquid asset holdings as agents move directly into goods or equities, the expected return on which is likely to be correlated with inflation. The variable in the ratio of non-liquid financial wealth to income appears with a positively-signed coefficient; as illiquid wealth increases in relation to income, the risk associated with the overall portfolio rises and individuals increase their holdings of the safe liquid assets aggregate. Overall, the results imply a sensible long-run solution, leading the authors to argue both for the desirability of a disaggregated sectoral approach and for the benefits of considering a range of yield variables. The residuals from the estimates of the long-run cointegrating relation are used to generate an error-correction term, which forms part of a short-run general distributed lag equation for the proportionate change in real liquid asset holdings. The form of the error-correction equation implies that agents adjust their current liquid asset holdings, in response to the lagged four-period disequilibrium between actual and desired holdings. Davidson and Ireland (1990) also analyse the demand for the liquid asset holdings of the personal sector. Cointegration techniques are applied to quarterly data for the period 1968–88; the preferred relation links real liquid asset holdings to real income and the real value of gross financial wealth, with no role for interest rates.

US STUDIES

Most empirical work on US data has used either the narrow $M1$ aggregate or a broader $M2$ measure which includes small time and savings deposits at commercial banks. As we noted earlier, doubts about the stability of the US demand for money function first arose in the mid-1970s, just as similar misgivings were being expressed for UK data. However, whereas in the UK it has been the broader money equations which have proved to be particularly difficult to model, in the US it is the narrow money demand function which is more problematical. Goldfeld (1976), Enzler *et al.* (1976) and Laidler

(1980) all observe that the conventional restricted distributed lag models are prone to overpredict the stock of narrow money in the early 1970s, giving rise to the concept of 'missing money'.

Judd and Scadding (1982) and Garcia and Pak (1979) feel that the most likely cause of this apparent instability in the demand for money function is institutional change, and in particular innovation in financial arrangements, which allowed the private sector to economise on its holdings of transactions balances. This change appears to have been induced by high interest and inflation rates, and the existence of legal impediments to the payment of a market rate of return on transactions balances. Banks were consequently encouraged to provide their customers with new accounts for their transactions balances, which evaded the regulations on interest payments. Because these accounts fell outside the traditional definition of narrow money, their introduction had the effect of introducing instability into the $M1$ function. Such effects were not confined to the personal sector; high interest rates also encouraged large companies to use other liquid assets as alternatives to cash balances. In addition, innovations in cash management techniques, facilitated by changes in technology and particularly the increasing use of computers, had the effect of reducing the variance of cash flows, and thereby allowed firms to reduce their precautionary balances, as predicted by the Whalen (1966) model, which we discussed in Chapter 3. In a study of the $M1$ demand function for the period 1959–83, Cover and Keeler (1988) find a role for an indirect measure of financial innovation, based upon the previous peak interest rate. They hypothesise that high interest rates in the past encourage innovations in the management of cash balances and cause money holdings to fall via a kind of 'ratchet' effect.

Some of these effects were reversed in the early 1980s, as both nominal interest rates and inflation fell. In this period, the velocity of circulation of $M1$ began to show a marked decline, with the conventional models now tending to underpredict the actual money stock. This fall in velocity has been partly attributed to a change in the operating procedures of the authorities in the money markets between 1979 and 1982. New policies, occasioned by an attempt to move towards some form of monetary base control, seem to have had the effect of increasing the volatility of both the money stock and interest rates. Friedman (1983, 1984) argues that increased variability in monetary growth created a greater degree of uncertainty about future economic conditions and led to an increase in the precautionary demand for money. This hypothesis has received empirical support from narrow money aggregates in the work of Hall and Noble (1987) and Fisher and Serletis (1989) who find a negative relationship between velocity growth and measures of monetary variability based upon the standard deviation of monetary growth.

Several studies have also found a significant role for measures of the volatility of interest rates. For example, Hendry and Ericsson (1991b) and Baba *et al.* (1992) consider a variable based upon the standard deviation of the bond yield and find that it has a significant positive effect upon the demand for narrow money. Using a general distributed lag error-correction approach, it is claimed that the incorporation of such a variable can help explain the 'missing money' period of the 1970s, as well as the decline in velocity in the early 1980s. These studies also link the large increase in the $M1$ aggregate in the 1980s to the introduction of interest-bearing cheque accounts, which followed interest rate deregulation in 1981. As was the case in the UK, the growth of such deposits, which combine elements of both savings and transactions balances, had a considerable effect upon the demand for $M1$ in the 1980s. Funds were switched out of existing retail savings deposits, which comprise part of the non-$M1$ component of $M2$, and into these new interest-bearing accounts.

Hamburger (1977b, 1983, 1987) focuses upon the importance of including a broad spectrum of asset yields in the money demand function. Such an approach conforms to Friedman's demand for money function, being based upon the monetarist view that money is a substitute for a wide range of assets, both financial and real, and not merely for short-term financial assets. According to the monetarist hypothesis, the high rates of inflation after 1973 increased the nominal return to goods and induced a shift out of money towards real expenditure. Hamburger specifies a function for $M1$, in which the real demand for money depends upon real income, the lagged money stock and three rates of return, representing the rate on time deposits, the long-term bond rate and the dividend–price ratio ruling in the stock market. Hamburger argues that the latter variable is a proxy for the rate of return on equities, and therefore the yield on physical capital, and can be used to help explain the apparent shifts in the demand for money function over the past two decades. The value of the ratio certainly changed considerably in the period 1972–74 when stock market prices fell dramatically and dividend levels were maintained. Similarly, Hamburger argues that the increase in money holdings that occurred in the early 1980s was associated with a marked fall in the dividend–price ratio.[6]

The role of the dividend–price ratio, in empirical work, is open to other interpretations. For example, Friedman (1978) argues the majority of the variation in the ratio in the 1970s was in the price term, so that instead of indicating the opportunity cost of holding money, the variable could be interpreted as measuring the effects upon wealth of variations in stock market prices. The role of the stock market in influencing money demand is analysed by Friedman (1988). Using quarterly US data on the broader $M2$ aggregate for the period 1961–86, the real quantity of money demanded, relative to income, is found to be negatively related to the contemporaneous real stock price, and positively related to the real stock price lagged three periods. It is suggested that the former represents a substitution effect; the higher is the real stock price, the more attractive are equities as a component of the portfolio. The positive response to the lagged stock price variable is attributed to a wealth effect; a rise in stock prices results in an increase in nominal wealth. The wealth effect appears stronger, although a similar series of regressions, using annual data over the period 1886–1985, suggest that, until recently at least, the substitution effect was dominant over any wealth effect.

Cointegration techniques are applied to the analysis of the US demand for money function by Miller (1990, 1991) and Hafer and Jansen (1991). All three studies find that a long-run cointegrating relationship exists between the broad $M2$ aggregate, real income, prices and an interest rate variable, but that the existence of an equilibrium relationship for narrow money is more doubtful. Miller's results are based upon quarterly data for the period 1959–87, while Hafer and Jansen also use quarterly data, but for a longer period encompassing the years 1915–88. Baba *et al.* (1992) are more optimistic about the ability of investigators to isolate a stable long-run cointegrating equation for narrow money, arguing that such a relationship can be obtained for $M1$, using quarterly data over the period 1960–88, if consideration is given to factors such as the rate of inflation, the long-term bond yield, the own return on money and the 'riskiness' attached to bond holding. Lucas (1988) updates the long-run relationship estimated by Meltzer (1963), using a narrow definition of money and extending the data period to 1985. Although evidence of stability remains and the estimated elasticity values are in line with those obtained by Meltzer, the results appear to be dependent upon the restrictions imposed upon the estimated equation.

A rather different view is expressed by Wenninger (1988) who uses quarterly data, for the period 1915–87, to question the view that stability has been the norm in the past, and that it is only in the last two decades that the demand for money relationship has broken down. No attempt is made to hypothesise upon the factors which may be responsible for the recent instability in the estimated demand for money equation. Instead, a standard money demand function, incorporating partial adjustment, is estimated over three different data periods, in order to examine the way in which the relationship may have changed over time. Wenninger finds that the sub-period for 1950–73 was an unusually stable time for narrow money demand; a result which confirms the findings of previous work. When earlier (1915–49) or later (1974–87) sub-periods are considered, there is evidence of instability. The size of the estimated parameters varies considerably between the different periods, with the long-run income and interest elasticities much lower in the middle period. A much greater degree of constancy is found in the equation for broad money. Wenninger concludes that the stable demand for $M1$ over the 1950–73 period was a rather unique experience, and more the exception than the norm when other periods are taken into consideration.

Measurement Problems

A series of other studies have looked at particular problems, which arise out of the measurement of the dependent and independent variables in the empirical money demand function. Barnett (1980, 1982) and Barnett *et al.* (1981, 1984) focus upon the way in which money is measured in empirical studies. They construct 'Divisia' aggregates for the key monetary series, which recognise that the various items constituting money, such as cash, sight deposits and time deposits, are not perfect substitutes for each other and should therefore not be given equal weight, as is the case in the published monetary statistics. Instead, the individual components, within each aggregate, are weighted according to their relative 'moneyness', or contribution to money services, to form a more consistent series for money. The concept of a 'user cost' is used to measure the marginal money services provided by each money component. In each case, the 'user cost' is proportional to the difference between a representative market rate of interest and the component's own yield. The larger this differential, the greater must be the liquidity services which the asset in question yields to its holder, and hence the more likely it can be classified as 'true' money for transactions purposes. The weighting given to each component, in the construction of the 'Divisia' aggregate, is determined by the ratio of its own 'user cost' to the total 'user cost' from all components.[7] Proponents of the 'Divisia' approach argue that the rate of growth of the published monetary aggregates overstates the rate of growth of 'true' money, since most of the increase in the money stock has been in interest-bearing deposits, which possess a lower degree of 'moneyness'.

The empirical implementation of the model requires that the conventional aggregates are replaced by their 'Divisia' counterparts, with the 'user cost' indices used in place of the traditional opportunity cost variables. Tests over a range of different aggregates indicate that the 'Divisia' approach makes little difference to the performance of the narrower US monetary aggregates. However, for the broader aggregates, which include money market instruments, where we might expect the conventional series to incorrectly measure 'moneyness', the 'Divisia' counterparts do produce a more stable demand function. The approach continues to receive consideration in the US demand for money literature, in empirical studies such as Serletis (1987a, 1987b, 1991), while a review of theoretical developments in the construction of 'Divisia' aggregates is to be found in Barnett (1990). Few UK studies of money demand have considered the 'Divisia' approach; a notable exception is Belongia and Chrystal (1991) who use cointegration techniques to isolate an apparently stable money demand function for a 'Divisia' measure of the broad $M4$ aggregate. The authors are less confident about the existence of a cointegrating relationship for a narrower 'Divisia' measure, based upon non-interest-bearing bank sight deposits, interest-bearing bank retail deposits and interest-bearing building society sight deposits.

Kohn and Manchester (1985) argue that the interest rate in the conventional money demand equation acts as a proxy for the expected change in interest rates, which is central to Keynes' speculative demand model. This misspecification means that the observed interest elasticity will be dependent upon the expectations generating process for interest rates. An alternative model, involving a term in the expected change in the interest rate, is formulated and tested upon data from ten countries, along with a conventional money demand equation. The standard model is shown to lead to a downward-biased estimate of the true interest elasticity. These results are consistent with the theoretical work of Goodfriend (1985), who suggests that the importance of the lagged dependent variable in the conventional money demand equation is the result, not of any adjustment process, but of a serious errors-in-variables problem in the terms used to represent transactions and interest rates. It is argued that the interest rate and income variables, used in empirical demand for money functions, may only be imperfectly correlated with the theoretically appropriate opportunity cost and transactions scale variables. For example, interest rates are measured either as period averages or as end-of-period rates, both of which are only approximate measures of effective market interest rates. Also, to the extent that an individual's money demand decision is based upon anticipated expenditure and opportunity cost, the practice of using actual *ex post* values of these variables in conventional money demand regressions will introduce measurement error, by including the forecasting error as well as the forecast values for the variables. Because of this errors-in-variables problem, it is postulated that the estimated income and interest elasticities will be biased towards zero and positive autocorrelation will appear in the residuals of the equation. The lagged dependent variable captures this effect and therefore appears as a significant variable in the estimated equation, with a positively-signed coefficient, even though money holdings adjust completely each period to the interest rate and transactions variables, and lagged money plays no role in the true demand equation. In this way, Goodfriend argues that the errors-in-variables model can be used to rationalise the value taken by the coefficient on the lagged dependent variable in the conventional money demand equation, the magnitude of which often implies an unrealistically slow speed of adjustment of actual balances towards their desired level. The model can also be used to explain the problem of instability in the empirical money demand function. In the measurement error interpretation, the coefficients in the standard money demand regression are functions both of the parameters in the true relation and the regressor generating process parameters. Accordingly, Goodfriend states that the apparent downward shift in the US demand for money function, in the early 1970s, could be attributed to a shift in the expectations generating process for income or interest rates, rather than to any fundamental change in the underlying demand function.[8]

In a similar vein to Goodfriend's analysis, Roley (1985) argues that the traditional use of temporally aggregated data, that is data which is averaged over periods, is larely responsible for the prominence of the partial adjustment model and in particular the large statistically significant coefficient on the lagged dependent variable. Using end-of-quarter data, which reduces the possibility of spurious correlation, the partial adjustment model is not found to be unambiguously better than the alternative involving complete adjustment of money demand within each quarter. Roley also feels that the neglect of simultaneity problems, in the regression equations, can lead to biases in the estimated coefficients that are potentially large.[9] Rose (1985) attributes the poor performance of previous demand for money equations to the widespread use of the traditional partial adjustment model, which ignores higher-order lags without justification. Using the general distributed lag approach, an error-correction equation for $M1$ balances is estimated using data for the period 1952–77. The preferred specification provides no evidence of instability during the 'missing money' period of the early 1970s, but when the data sample is extended to 1981, the various diagnostic tests indicate the presence of instability in the relationship and also provide some evidence of possible simultaneity problems. The timing of the breakdown in the equation appears to coincide with the decision of the authorities to use $M1$ more actively as a target for monetary policy.

Identification Issues

Gordon (1984) also argues that the conventional restricted-lag approach to the study of the short-run demand for money is plagued by severe problems of misspecification. In addition to the standard partial adjustment equation, a version of the permanent income model of money demand is developed to yield a specification which includes lagged income and interest rate terms. Other general distributed lag equations, involving lagged money terms and an error-correction mechanism are also estimated. The equations are tested on US data for $M1$ over the periods 1956–72 and 1956–83. Although the inclusion of lagged income and interest rate variables is shown to be desirable, no single specification is viewed to be markedly superior to any other. Instead, Gordon argues that his work offers an explanation of why all estimated equations are often unstable. His reasoning can be explained in terms of the identification problem of distinguishing between demand and supply equations. Gordon develops a money supply function for the case where the authorities operate a monetary rule. The form of the equation linking real balances to income and interest rates, with associated lagged money and price terms, is shown to be similar to that which would result from a model of money demand. Because of this similarity, the interpretation given to such equations is heavily dependent upon the policy regime in force over the estimation period. Over long data periods, which encompass different policy regimes, the estimated coefficients will represent a blend of money demand and money supply parameters, so that shifts in their values are to be expected and are as likely to represent changes in policy rules, as movements in the parameters of the underlying money demand function. Such arguments are, of course, very much in accord with the Lucas (1976) critique.

Gordon argues that the coefficients in the standard equation can be interpreted as parameters of money demand only if the authorities have followed a regime of interest rate stabilisation, in which the quantity of money responds to changes in the factors influencing demand. A move by the authorities from such a policy to a monetary targeting regime, will tend to cause systematic coefficient shifts in an equation explaining real balances. In particular, the sign response on the income coefficient may change from positive to negative, there may be a negative effect attached to the inflation rate variable and the sign of the coefficient on the interest rate may shift from negative to positive. These changes are possible because monetary restrictions are likely to be tightened in response to excess income growth or higher than desired inflation, while interest rates may be raised if monetary growth is excessive. The consistent tendency in the results for the coefficient on the income variable to decline in the 1956–83 period, as compared to 1956–72, gives support to this regime-shift interpretation of parameter instability. Similarly, the result that the coefficient on the inflation variable becomes more significantly negative, in several models over the longer data period, is also consistent with the view that the equation for real balances mixes together both demand and supply parameters. Of course, it could be argued that the rate of inflation, or more particularly the expected rate of inflation, also became a more important influence on money demand post-1970. Gordon states that, 'It is hard to avoid reaching the conclusion that these long-period equations represent a rather futile attempt to fit a single reduced form equation for real balances to a period when the underlying real balance equation was changing its stripes from something like a partial adjustment model for money demand to something like a money reaction function of the central bank'. The issues considered by Gordon have fundamental implications for the modelling of the money market and are analysed in detail in Chapter 7, when we introduce the concept of 'disequilibrium money'.

7 Disequilibrium Money and Buffer Stock Models

An alternative approach to the modelling of monetary aggregates is that based upon the notion of 'disequilibrium money'. Artis and Lewis (1974, 1976) were the first to formulate such a concept, in their attempt to explain the breakdown in the UK money demand function in the 1970s. In the traditional approach to estimating money demand equations, it is implicitly assumed that the actual money supply is always equal to the aggregate short-run demand, so that the money market is continually in equilibrium. Such an assumption is uncontroversial when the money stock is demand determined, as is generally assumed to have been the case in the UK in the 1950s and 1960s. However, the assumption appears to be a less applicable characterisation of the UK money market after 1970, particularly for broad money. Artis and Lewis argue that large independent changes in the UK money supply, in the early 1970s, led to a disequilibrium in the money market in which supply exceeded demand. This expansion in the money stock occurred for a number of reasons. An important factor was the Competition and Credit Control reforms, which created a new spirit of competition in the banking system and abolished the direct controls on bank advances. In addition, budget deficits incurred by the government in the early 1970s were largely financed by money creation.

Underlying such influences was a change in the basic policy stance of the authorities in the money and foreign exchange markets. Whereas in the 1960s, the UK authorities had been largely concerned with stabilising interest rates and maintaining the fixed value of the exchange rate, they now became willing to allow greater flexibility in both bond prices and exchange rates. The economic environment of the early 1970s therefore created a situation in which the broad money stock, at least, could no longer be automatically assumed to be demand determined by interest rates and nominal income; the supply of money was determined independently of demand and effectively exogenous for modelling purposes.[1] The UK authorities signalled their intention to exert an even greater degree of control over the money supply with the introduction of explicit monetary targets in 1976, and since then targets have continued to be applied each year to at least one monetary aggregate, albeit with varying degrees of intent and success.[2]

In practice, shocks to the quantity of money, emanating from the accommodation of external currency flows, changes in the PSBR and surges in bank lending to the private sector, meant that these targets were frequently exceeded, particularly for the broad monetary aggregates. Policy changes initiated by the government often contributed to the problems of monetary control. For example, the removal of exchange controls in October 1979 led to the freer movement of international capital funds, while the removal of the 'corset' controls on the growth of bank deposits in June 1980 led to a large expansion in the broad money supply in the following months.[3] Further deregulation of the financial system, later in the 1980s, produced similar effects as competitive forces were unleashed and personal sector borrowing from both banks and building societies increased. Nevertheless, although precise control of the money supply has proved to be difficult, such 'shock' effects serve only to cast further doubt upon the appropriateness of modelling the money market through a traditional demand function, in which the quantity of money is endogenous, and interest rates, prices and real income are the exogenous variables. It is only in an economic environment in which the supply of money responds passively to variations in the demand for it that this approach can lead to a correct specification of the behaviour of the money market. In other cases, the aggregate demand for money may have to be viewed as adjusting to a largely exogenous money supply, through variations in one or more of the arguments of the demand function; that is interest rates, real income or the price level.

PARTIAL ADJUSTMENT AND EXOGENOUS MONEY

We now consider the implications of an exogenous money stock for the conventional short-run partial adjustment equation.[4] For the purposes of this analysis, we will assume that prices and income are constant in the short run, with only the interest rate variable. Because the partial adjustment model implies continuous market clearing at the aggregate level, the impact effect of an exogenous increase in the money supply must be borne solely by the rate of interest. Given constant prices and income, the rate of interest has to change by a relatively large amount in the short run, in order to equate demand to the new supply. In the longer term, with prices and income both variable, the adjustment required of the interest rate is less. The assumption of an exogenous money supply, in conjunction with the short-run partial adjustment equation, would therefore appear to imply that the rate of interest has to initially 'overshoot' its long-run equilibrium value, in order to compensate for short-run price and income stickiness.[5]

More fundamental comments can be made about the validity of using partial adjustment models in conjunction with an exogenous money supply. The partial adjustment hypothesis is justified in terms of the costs incurred by individual agents, as they adjust their money holdings towards the desired level. At the aggregate level, the model implies that the supply of money must adjust passively to variations in the quantity demanded, in order to ensure market clearing. However, with an exogenous money supply, the concept of aggregate partial adjustment for the economy as a whole becomes nonsensical, even though individual agents can still be assumed to adjust their own money holdings, in response to changes in the interest rate, real income and price level.[6] Instead, it is argued, what we are really observing with such models is the transmission mechanism, by which an exogenous increase in the money supply influences the arguments of the aggregate demand for money function. The exogenous money supply creates an environment of disequilibrium in the money market, which in turn generates adjustment of varying degrees, and with different timing, in the interest rate, real income and prices. The assumption of an exogenous money supply therefore implies a pattern of money market dynamics, which is very different to that underlying the conventional partial adjustment hypothesis. We now consider some alternative models of money market adjustment, both single and multi-equation, which have been developed specifically for the analysis of this disequilibrium situation.

LAIDLER'S 'STICKY-PRICE' MODEL

Laidler (1982) demonstrates that the reduced form of the partial adjustment model is consistent with a model of price adjustment, in which long-run equilibrium prices are set at the level which ensures equality, in real terms, between the exogenously determined money supply and the aggregate demand for money. This can be shown using an equation for the equilibrium price level of the form

$$p_t^* = m_t^s - \gamma - \alpha r_t - \beta y_t - v_t \tag{7.1}$$

where m^s is the nominal money supply and the other terms represent the arguments of the long-run real demand for money function given by equation (5.3). In addition, if prices are 'sticky' and adjust gradually towards this equilibrium value, we can write

$$p_t - p_{t-1} = \theta(p_t^* - p_{t-1}) \tag{7.2}$$

where the adjustment parameter, θ, should take a value between zero and unity. Substituting (7.1) into (7.2) produces the short-run price equation

$$p_t = -\theta\gamma - \theta\alpha r_t - \theta\beta y_t + \theta m_t^s + (1 - \theta)p_{t-1} - \theta v_t \tag{7.3}$$

Adding m_t^s to both sides of equation (7.3), and rearranging the terms, produces the relation

$$(m^s - p)_t = \theta\gamma + \theta\alpha r_t + \theta\beta y_t + (1 - \theta)(m_t^s - p_{t-1}) + \theta v_t \tag{7.4}$$

or equivalently

$$(m^s - p)_t = \theta\gamma + \theta\alpha r_t + \theta\beta y_t + (1 - \theta)(m^s - p)_{t-1} \\ + (1 - \theta)\Delta m_t^s + \theta v_t \tag{7.5}$$

where Δm_t^s represents a term in the change in the money supply. Equation (7.5) can be compared with the reduced form of the real partial adjustment model of money demand, as given in equation (5.6). Given $\tilde{m} = m - p$ and equating m^s with m in equation (5.6), we obtain the specification

$$(m^s - p)_t = \theta\gamma + \theta\alpha r_t + \theta\beta y_t + (1 - \theta)(m^s - p)_{t-1} + \theta v_t \tag{7.6}$$

so that (7.5) and (7.6) are equivalent, but for the additional term in the change in the money supply in equation (7.5).[7]

Under this interpretation, the presence of a lagged dependent variable in an aggregate demand for money function can therefore be explained in terms of gradual price adjustment to a change in the exogenous money supply. The low values of the adjustment parameter, found by empirical studies, imply a slow pattern of price adjustment to nominal money supply changes, an interpretation which may be intuitively more acceptable than the slow adjustment of actual to desired balances which underlies the traditional partial adjustment view. In the light of this interpretation, it is also not surprising that the conventional short-run functions have proved unsatisfactory in recent years; when the money supply is volatile, it seems likely that the transmission mechanism, emanating from a monetary disequilibrium, will be incorrectly represented by a single constant parameter. In addition, the typical short-run equation ignores the influence of the term in the change in the money stock, which the 'sticky-price' model indicates should be included in the estimated equation. Following Lucas' (1976) arguments, it is also evident that policy regime changes, which cause the transmission mechanism to vary, can be expected to produce shifts in the structure of the so-called 'short-run' demand for money function.

Laidler's interpretation of the short-run demand for money equation has been rejected in an empirical study by MacKinnon and Milbourne (1988). Using US narrow money data, they test the proposition that the endogenous variable in the money market is really the price level. Money demand functions are reformulated as price equations and tested over different data sets, both pre- and post-1973. In each case, the estimated coefficients do not lend support to the view that the price level is determined in the money market. Using UK data on $M1$, Hendry (1985) and Hendry and Ericsson (1991b) reach a similar conclusion.

THE ARTIS–LEWIS MODEL

Artis and Lewis (1976) suggest an alternative model in which the rate of interest clears the money market. Such an approach necessitates the 'inversion' of the traditional money demand function, so as to obtain a relationship in which the rate of interest assumes the role of dependent variable, and income and money are exogenous. Artis and Lewis begin with a long-run money demand function for nominal balances of the form

$$m_t = \gamma + \alpha r_t + \beta(p + y)_t + v_t \tag{7.7}$$

where m is the logarithm of the money stock and $(p + y)$ is the logarithm of nominal income.[8] Rearranging equation (7.7), and assuming demand equals supply, it is possible to obtain the relation

$$r_t^* = -\frac{\gamma}{\alpha} - \frac{\beta}{\alpha}(p+y)_t + \frac{1}{\alpha}m_t^s - \frac{1}{\alpha}v_t \qquad (7.8)$$

where m^s is the exogenous supply of money and r_t^* is the long-run equilibrium rate of interest, which equates the demand for money with the money supply. However, Artis and Lewis assume that the money market does not necessarily clear instantaneously and specify a partial adjustment mechanism for the rate of interest of the form

$$r_t - r_{t-1} = \theta(r_t^* - r_{t-1}) \qquad (7.9)$$

where θ is the adjustment coefficient, which assumes a value between zero and unity. The gradual adjustment of the rate of interest, implicit in the mechanism outlined in (7.9), is very different to the 'overshooting' implied by the conventional short-run partial adjustment model, when there is an exogenous change in the money stock.[9] Furthermore, because the rate of interest moves only gradually towards its long-run equilibrium value, a disequilibrium will prevail between demand and supply in the short term, with agents temporarily forced 'off' their long-run demand function until full adjustment has taken place.[10] Substituting the long-run equilibrium rate given in equation (7.8), into the adjustment mechanism in (7.9), we obtain the short-run relation

$$r_t = b_0 + b_1(p+y)_t + b_2 m_t^s + (1-\theta)r_{t-1} + u_t \qquad (7.10)$$

where $b_0 = -\theta\gamma/\alpha$, $b_1 = -\theta\beta/\alpha$, $b_2 = \theta/\alpha$ and $u_t = -\theta v_t/\alpha$. Estimation of equation (7.10) therefore allows the identification of the parameters of the long-run demand for money function (γ, α, β).

Artis and Lewis also consider the possibility that market clearing is achieved through changes in the level of income, by specifying a demand equation in which the ratio of money balances to nominal income is the dependent variable. The long-run desired value of this ratio is assumed to depend upon the rate of interest and the level of real *per capita* income, and can be represented by the relation

$$\left[\frac{M}{PY}\right]_t^* = \gamma + \alpha R_t + \beta \bar{Y}_t + \varepsilon_t \qquad (7.11)$$

where $\bar{Y}$ is real *per capita* gross domestic product and ε is an arbitrary error term. Again, adjustment to this desired level is not assumed to be instantaneous and a partial adjustment mechanism is specified in order to model the gradual adjustment of the actual money to income ratio to the desired level. This mechanism can be written as

$$\left[\frac{M}{PY}\right]_t - \left[\frac{M}{PY}\right]_{t-1} = \theta\left\{\left[\frac{M}{PY}\right]_t^* - \left[\frac{M}{PY}\right]_{t-1}\right\} + \varphi S_t \qquad (7.12)$$

where θ is the adjustment coefficient and the variable S represents the set of factors which may generate changes in the actual money to income ratio, independently of the gradual adjustment process. Substitution of (7.11) into (7.12) produces a short-run relation of the form

$$\left[\frac{M}{PY}\right]_t = b_0 + b_1 R_t + b_2 \bar{Y}_t + \varphi S_t + (1 - \theta)\left[\frac{M}{PY}\right]_{t-1} + u_t \qquad (7.13)$$

where $b_0 = \theta\gamma$, $b_1 = \theta\alpha$, $b_2 = \theta\beta$ and $u_t = \theta\varepsilon_t$. In estimating equation (7.13), the S term is variously represented by changes in high powered money, the domestic borrowing requirement and the latter variable in combination with an index of bank lending controls. Such series represent supply constraints and are therefore an attempt to capture the influence, exerted upon the adjustment process, by the sudden increase in the UK money stock which took place in the early 1970s. They can be interpreted as a preliminary attempt to consider the role of money as a buffer stock, which we will consider in more detail later in this chapter.

Artis and Lewis test the specifications derived in equations (7.10) and (7.13), using quarterly UK data on both $M1$ and $M3$ for the period 1963–73.[11] The parameter estimates obtained from these relations exhibit a greater degree of stability than those resulting from the conventional partial adjustment model, although the $M3$ versions of equation (7.10) are much more encouraging than those obtained for $M1$. This finding may reflect the likelihood that the assumption of an exogenous money supply is more appropriate for broad money. One interesting point of comparison, between the results obtained from equations (7.10) and (7.13), is that the speed of adjustment implied by the money-income equation is slower than that implied by the interest rate equation. This is consistent with the view that the money market clears in the short run through adjustment in the interest rate, while income adjustment becomes more important in the longer run. Unlike

Hacche's scenario, which we discussed in Chapter 6, Artis and Lewis do not claim that the demand for money function has shifted. Their empirical results lead them to conclude that the demand for money function remained stable in the early 1970s, but that variations in supply conditions created a disequilibrium in the money market, which gave the misleading appearance of a breakdown in the relation. In effect, because the supply of money had expanded too rapidly for demand to adjust to it, observations on the quantity of money represented points lying 'off' a largely unchanged, and therefore stable demand function.

In an extension of their work, Artis and Lewis (1984) estimate a long-run demand function of the form

$$(m - p - y)_t = \gamma + \alpha r_t + v_t \qquad (7.14)$$

in which the dependent variable is the logarithm of the ratio of money to nominal income. Annual UK data over the period 1920–81 is used to test the relationship. In order to obtain such a lengthy run of data, the 'old' $M2$ definition of the money stock had to be used; this is a slightly less broad definition of money than $M3$. The results suggest that a long-run stable demand for money function can be isolated using equation (7.14), provided that the observations on the period 1973–76 are removed.[12] Artis and Lewis feel that such findings lend support to their disequilibrium hypothesis, indicating that the supply shocks of the early 1970s temporarily forced the private sector 'off' its demand curve, until prices, income and interest rates, and the money supply itself, adjusted sufficiently to restore the ratio of money to income to its long-run equilibrium path. Observations in later years more closely conformed to the basic relationship; the same degree of monetary disequilibrium was not present because the magnitude of the money supply shocks was less and the markets were no longer so easily 'surprised'. Nevertheless, the Artis and Lewis studies indicate the importance of allowing for monetary disequilibrium in any analysis of the money demand function. At particular times, supply and demand may be different, so that the market cannot be assumed to be continuously in equilibrium. This should be more of a problem for broad definitions of money; narrow money is more likely to be determined by demand factors because of its link with transactions requirements. This difference would help explain why, over the past twenty years, the traditional models have been more successful, in the UK at least, when applied to narrow definitions of money.

For the US, Laidler (1980) discusses the arguments for and against the assumption of an exogenous money supply, before going on to consider the instability issue in the context of the possible adjustment processes underlying the short-run demand for money function. Following Artis and Lewis, separate models involving interest rate and income adjustment are estimated, with the better statistical fits found for the broader $M2$ definition of money rather than the narrow $M1$ aggregate. Laidler concludes that the $M2$ function is relatively robust; no matter what form of short-run dynamic adjustment process is hypothesised, the size and statistical significance of the parameters of the function vary very little. The same is not true of the function for narrow money.

MULTI-EQUATION DISEQUILIBRIUM MODELS

The single-equation disequilibrium models described above all have the drawback that only one argument of the demand for money function can be chosen as the dependent variable. However, the transmission mechanism of monetary policy is complex and subject to long and variable time lags, and may be expected to involve adjustments in all of the arguments of the demand function, albeit at different rates. Therefore, any attempt to capture its operation in a single-equation framework, with either the price level, or the interest rate, or real income as the dependent variable, is likely to be unsatisfactory. Such considerations lie behind the development of models which allow for the simultaneous adjustment of several expenditure and portfolio variables. Multi-equation models have been applied, with some success, to the UK economy by Knight and Wymer (1978), Laidler and O'Shea (1980), Davidson (1987) and Davidson and Ireland (1990), and to the US economy by Laidler and Bentley (1983) and Miller (1990,1991).

In these 'more complete' models, disequilibrium effects, as measured by the difference between the money stock and the underlying long-run money demand, are allowed to influence a wide range of real and nominal variables, such as the exchange rate and the level of foreign exchange reserves, as well as income, prices and the interest rate. In this way, the models capture several channels of the transmission mechanism and show how excess money balances affect the economy as a whole, through an all-embracing real balance effect. Such a system is representable by the $(n + 1)$ relations

$$\Delta X_{it} = \sum_{k=1}^{m} c_{ik} Z_{kt} + d_i (M_t^s - M_t)$$

$$M_t = \gamma + \alpha R_t + \beta Y_t + \delta P_t$$

$$i = 1, \ldots, n$$

where Δ is the first-difference operator, X_i is the ith endogenous variable and Z_k is the kth predetermined variable, which represents the set of other influences on the dependent variable. The c_{ik} represent the coefficients on these variables, while d_i is the coefficient on the money market disequilibrium term. Substituting the money demand relation into the monetary disequilibrium term, produces an n equation system of the form

$$\Delta X_{it} = \sum_{k=1}^{m} c_{ik} Z_{kt} + d_i M_t^s - d_i \gamma - d_i \alpha R_t - d_i \beta Y_t - d_i \delta P_t$$

$$i = 1, \ldots, n$$

which can be tested empirically to determine the different responses to monetary disequilibrium.[13] The money supply can either be assumed to be exogenously determined, or else modelled in relation to the accounting identities surrounding the government budget constraint and the banks' balance sheet. The latter approach enables the investigator to relate changes in the broad money supply to the source of shocks, emanating from the PSBR, bank advances and external currency flows.

In the Knight and Wymer (1978) model, disequilibrium money is allowed to influence current consumption and the interest rate, and is also included in the equation for the private sector's liabilities to foreign residents, thereby affecting the capital account of the balance of payments. A broad definition of money is used, with the model tested on quarterly data for the period 1955–72. The findings suggest that disequilibrium in the money market did not have a significant effect upon consumption over the sample period, but significant disequilibrium effects were isolated in the other two equations. Laidler and O'Shea (1980) incorporate lagged monetary disequilibrium terms in equations for output and the level of reserves. The expenditure flows resulting from excess money balances can therefore involve foreign goods and assets, and may also divert domestic production from or into exports, as well as leading to changes in domestic output. Annual data over the period 1954–70 is used to estimate the model. The $M3$ definition of the money supply is used, with the results indicating that monetary disequilibrium is a significant influence upon the balance of payments, but not the level of output. In so far as the excess money balances influence expenditure, the goods involved are therefore either imported, diverted from exports or drawn from existing stocks, rather than being added to current output. Both the Knight–Wymer and Laidler–O'Shea studies use 'early' data periods when disequilibrium effects might be considered to be less important.

Davidson (1987) estimates a series of equations for both financial and real variables. 'General to specific' modelling techniques are used, with each equation given an error-correction interpretation through a lagged monetary disequilibrium term. The residuals from the long-run money demand equation are used to provide an estimate of this disequilibrium error. In this way, it is possible to test the hypothesis that previous-period monetary disequilibria cause current-period adjustments in a wide range of economic variables. Using broad sterling $M3$ and $M5$ definitions of money, and data for the period 1964–82, Davidson finds that the lagged monetary disequilibrium effect is most noticeable in the equation for bank loans to the non-bank private sector, where it appears with a negatively-signed coefficient. Other significant effects are found in the equations for the price level and the private sector's net capital liabilities to overseas residents. Monetary disequilibria appear to have no effect upon real income, the exchange rate and the current account surplus. These results seem to imply that a significant proportion of excess money holdings are extinguished via a reduction in outstanding bank borrowing, with no apparent effect upon real expenditures.

Davidson and Ireland (1990) include a disequilibrium liquidity variable in various equations representing categories of personal sector expenditure and credit utilisation. In this case, cointegration techniques are applied to quarterly data over the period 1968–88, in order to determine the parameters of the long-run demand function for the liquid asset holdings of the personal sector. The residuals from the cointegrating regression are then used to construct a measure of disequilibrium liquidity, with the lagged value of this series used to represent an error-correction mechanism, in a series of equations for total consumer expenditure, the share of expenditure taken by durable goods, private sector housebuilding, consumer credit and other personal sector credit. The disequilibrium liquidity variable has the expected positive effect upon the three categories of expenditure and a negative effect upon the credit aggregates, although its coefficient is insignificant in the total consumption and housebuilding equations.

For the US, Laidler and Bentley (1983) incorporate a monetary disequilibrium term in equations for output and the real rate of interest. Using annual data for the period 1954–78 and a broad definition of money, the effect is found to be particularly strong in the output equation. Miller (1990) uses both cointegration analysis and error-correction modelling to test the disequilibrium money hypothesis, in a series of equations for the interest rate, price level and both nominal and real income. In each case, the current rate of change in the chosen dependent variable is related to an error-correction term and past rates of change in the dependent variable. The error-correction term represents the previous-period or short-run disequilibrium error between the money stock and long-run equilibrium demand, with the residuals from a cointegrating regression for broad money providing an estimate of the disequilibrium error. The model is tested using quarterly US data for the period 1959–87. The coefficient on the error-correction term is significant in each case and appears with a negative sign in the interest rate equation and a positive sign in the real income, nominal income and price level equations. This result is consistent with *a priori* expectations; when the money supply exceeds the long-run money demand, we would expect real output and the price level to rise, and the interest rate to fall. However, apart from the price level equation, the overall explanatory power of the equations is poor. Nevertheless, Miller feels that the results are broadly supportive of the disequilibrium money hypothesis, and that the apparent instability in the US money demand function, which has been observed over the past two decades, is due to periods of temporary disequilibrium in the money market, occasioned by instability in money growth rates arising out of a more exogenous money stock.

Using the same US data set, Miller (1991) adopts a similar, if more general, approach to the estimation of the short-run equations. The first difference of each variable in the cointegrating equation is regressed on lagged values of the first differences of all of the variables, plus the error-correction term. This means an equation is specified for the rate of change of money holdings, as well as for the proportionate change in income, prices and the interest rate. The coefficient on the error-correction term in the money equation is negatively signed, which is consistent with the view that money stock growth rates are reduced in response to a positive disequilibrium gap, between supply and demand, in the money market. Across the range of equations, those error-correction coefficients, which are significantly different from zero, are all of the 'correct' sign. Causality tests are carried out in order to determine whether each variable should be considered to be exogenous or endogenous. No clear conclusions emerge, but there does appear to be a two-way relationship between many of the variables and particularly between the money stock and the interest rate.

MONEY AS A BUFFER STOCK

Implicit in the disequilibrium models discussed so far is the view that money fulfils the role of buffer stock or shock-absorber in the individual's portfolio. Increases in the money supply are initially absorbed into total money holdings, before being dissipated in the form of extra expenditure on goods and financial assets, in accordance with the transmission mechanism of money. The lags involved in this real balance effect may be long and variable. The principles behind the approach are considered by Laidler (1984, 1987), Knoester (1984) and Goodhart (1984). It is argued that money is the residual or buffer asset of the portfolio, because individuals are willing to allow their balances to fluctuate up and down in response to extraneous shocks. At the micro-level, the concept has been related to the target-threshold models of the transactions demand for money, which we discussed in Chapter 3. According to models of this type, such as Miller and Orr (1966), money holdings are not optimally managed at each and every moment of time, but instead are allowed to fluctuate randomly between certain permissible limits and are only adjusted to an intermediate or return point if one of these bounds is reached. Because only the return point and the outer bounds are influenced by economic variables, agents do not have a single-valued demand function for money and actual balances can fluctuate within the bounds, regardless of movements in income or interest rates.[14]

Money is assumed to fulfil a buffer role because the costs of adjusting money holdings are much less than the costs of changing the other, less liquid, assets of the portfolio. Adjustments are only made to the holdings of real and less liquid financial assets when changes in the economic environment are viewed to be permanent. If the changes are considered to be merely transitory, it is money holdings which bear the major part of any portfolio adjustment. Consequently, according to the buffer stock approach, an exogenous increase in the aggregate money supply must be anticipated and perceived to be permanent before it will cause individuals to make major adjustments to their overall portfolios. If the change is unexpected, or expected to be reversed in the future, individuals are not likely to want to incur the present costs of changing their expenditure on real and less liquid financial assets, only to have to reverse the process later. Instead, the extra balances will be absorbed into buffer stock money holdings. The same process can be considered in terms of the arguments of the demand for money function. If individuals find their income has suddenly risen, they will only make permanent adjustments to their overall portfolio if they feel the change will be maintained. If this is not the case, transitory money balances will be temporarily increased to absorb the surplus funds. In this sense, total money holdings, at any given time, can be assumed to comprise a permanent or planned element, which is dependent upon expectations held about the future levels of income and rates of return, and a transitory or unexpected component which is related to unanticipated shocks, such as those arising from unexpected receipts or disbursements. Satisfactory models of the demand for money must attempt to take account of both elements, so that if transitory money holdings represent a substantial and volatile part of total money balances, we might expect the conventional theories, which fail to allow for the possibility of such balances, to show evidence of parameter instability over time. Advocates of the buffer stock approach therefore feel that it can be used to explain the apparent instability in the post-1970 demand for money function. This has involved the development of a number of different models and surveys of these alternative approaches to the treatment of money as a buffer stock are made by Cuthbertson and Taylor (1987a) and Milbourne (1988).

THE CARR–DARBY MODEL

Carr and Darby (1981) utilise the notion of buffer stock money to analyse the short-run dynamics of the money market. Like the disequilibrium model of Artis and Lewis (1976), they consider the effect upon money holdings of independent changes in the money supply, but make a distinction between those changes which are expected and those that are unanticipated. Their hypothesis is that anticipated changes in the money supply are neutral, in that they are reflected in immediate changes in the price level, which leave real balances unaffected, while unanticipated shocks to the money supply lead to temporary changes in real money holdings, because prices adjust much more slowly to such effects.[15] Unexpected increases in the money supply are temporarily absorbed into total balances, with little or no change in interest rates, so that the 'overshooting' implied by the conventional short-run partial adjustment model need not occur. The hypothesis therefore leads to a relationship in which short-run money holdings, in real terms, are related to the unanticipated component of the money supply, as well as the usual arguments.

The formal specification of the Carr–Darby model is based upon a long-run desired demand for real balances of the form

$$\tilde{m}_t^* = \gamma + \alpha R_t + \beta y_t^p + v_t \tag{7.15}$$

where all variables, except the rate of interest, are expressed in logarithms and y^p is the logarithm of permanent real income. Unanticipated changes in the nominal money supply exert their influence through an extended real partial adjustment mechanism, which can be written as

$$\tilde{m}_t - \tilde{m}_{t-1} = \theta(\tilde{m}_t^* - \tilde{m}_{t-1}) + \S y_t^T + \varphi(m - m^e)_t \tag{7.16}$$

where y^T is the logarithm of transitory real income, defined as the difference between actual real income and permanent real income. The unanticipated component of the money supply is represented by $(m - m^e)$ where m^e is the logarithm of the anticipated money supply. The mechanism in (7.16) indicates that the gradual adjustment of money balances towards the desired level is also subject to the influence of 'shock' effects, arising from changes in transitory income and unexpected increases in the money supply. The adjustment coefficient, θ, takes a value between zero and unity, while the parameters $\S$ and φ measure the influence of transitory income and monetary shocks. The inclusion of the term in transitory income reflects the work of Darby (1972); it is there to cater for the possibility that money holdings may temporarily absorb unexpected variations in income. Substitution of equation (7.15) into (7.16) produces the short-run relation

$$\begin{aligned}
\tilde{m}_t = {} & b_0 + b_1 R_t + b_2 y_t^p + (1 - \theta)\tilde{m}_{t-1} + \S y_t^T \\
& + \varphi(m - m^e)_t + u_t
\end{aligned} \tag{7.17}$$

where $b_0 = \theta\gamma$, $b_1 = \theta\alpha$, $b_2 = \theta\beta$ and $u_t = \theta v_t$. The first four terms in equation (7.17) determine the planned element of short-run money holdings, while the transitory income and unanticipated money variables indicate the unplanned component. Under the shock-absorber hypothesis, the magnitude of the coefficient on the unanticipated money term should lie between zero and unity; the precise value depends upon the proportion of any shock which is held in money balances.[16]

The model is applied to monetary series from several countries, including UK data on $M1$ for the period 1957–76. The anticipated money supply is modelled in terms of past values of the actual money supply, using a univariate ARIMA process. The results vary between the different data sets, but the coefficients on the unanticipated money variables are all significant and take values between 0.63 and 1.18, so lending general support to the buffer stock model. The transitory income term does not perform so well and is generally insignificant.[17]

For the UK data, the preferred equation produces a statistically significant coefficient value of 0.69 for the unanticipated money term, while the coefficient of transitory income is positive and exceeds that of permanent income. Laidler (1980) estimated a similar model, using annual US data on $M1$ for the period 1953–76. The unanticipated money term is significant and the forecasting performance of the equation is found to be superior to that obtained from other more conventional models.

MacKinnon and Milbourne (1984) are sceptical of Carr and Darby's results, because the correlation between the unexpected money variable and the error term in equation (7.17) is likely to produce biased and inconsistent single equation estimates.[18] In an attempt to overcome this simultaneity problem, they suggest that the buffer stock hypothesis should be tested using a different formulation of the basic equation. A description of their approach requires a distinction to be drawn between the unanticipated money term and the other variables which influence money holdings, so that (7.17) becomes

$$\tilde{m}_t = bx_t + \varphi(m - m^e)_t + u_t \tag{7.18}$$

where b is a vector of coefficients and x is a vector representing the set of all other influences on real balances held.[19] The procedure adopted by MacKinnon and Milbourne involves the addition of a term in φp_t to each side of equation (7.18), and the rearrangement or reparameterisation of the resulting equation, to produce an alternative testable relation of the form

$$\tilde{m}_t = b^\dagger x_t + \varphi^\dagger (m^e - p)_t + u_t^\dagger \tag{7.19}$$

where $b^\dagger = b/(1 - \varphi)$, $\varphi^\dagger = -\varphi/(1 - \varphi)$ and $u_t^\dagger = u_t/(1 - \varphi)$. Equation (7.19) includes a term in the anticipated quantity of nominal money deflated by the current price level. Because the Carr–Darby hypothesis implies a value of φ between zero and unity, $\varphi^\dagger$ should take a non-zero negative value. MacKinnon and Milbourne also add a term in anticipated money to equation (7.18), resulting in the specification

$$\tilde{m}_t = bx_t + \varphi(m - m^e)_t + \lambda m_t^e + u_t \tag{7.20}$$

where λ is the coefficient which measures the influence of anticipated money. Adding a term in φp_t to each side of equation (7.20), and reparameterising, produces the testable relation

$$\tilde{m}_t = b^\dagger x_t + \varphi^\dagger(m^e - p)_t + \lambda^\dagger m_t^e + u_t^\dagger \tag{7.21}$$

where $\lambda^\dagger = \lambda/(1 - \varphi)$. Under the Carr–Darby hypothesis of neutrality, anticipated money does not influence real balances, so that $\lambda^\dagger$ should be zero. MacKinnon and Milbourne estimate their model for US data, using an autoregressive process to generate a series for anticipated narrow money. The parameter estimates imply a significant role for anticipated money and a significant, but negative, influence for unanticipated money, thus refuting the Carr–Darby hypothesis.[20]

Other studies have considered the relative merits of the basic Carr–Darby equation and the alternative MacKinnon–Milbourne formulation. Cuthbertson (1986a) uses both models to test the shock-absorber hypothesis, for quarterly UK data on $M1$ over the period 1964–81. General distributed lag versions of the two equations are also estimated and in each case an autoregressive model is used to generate the series for anticipated money. Evidence of misspecification is found in the conventional Carr–Darby-type partial adjustment equations, although the estimated coefficients support the buffer stock hypothesis. All the estimated MacKinnon–Milbourne-type equations imply rejection of the hypothesis.

In order to determine series for anticipated money, all of the above studies assume that agents use univariate fixed-coefficient ARIMA models, estimated over the whole sample period. The predicted values from the ARIMA models are used to generate an expectations series for use in the real money holdings equation, with the residuals taken to represent the unanticipated values. Cuthbertson and Taylor (1986) specify an alternative expectations generating mechanism, which is based upon a money growth equation, involving lagged values of the interest rate and money. This, more structural approach, is developed from the work of Mishkin (1982, 1983). Using UK data on $M1$ for the period 1964–81, Cuthbertson and Taylor test versions of equations (7.18) and (7.20), with the results lending support to the buffer stock hypothesis. As in previous studies, a two-stage approach is adopted. First of all, an expectations mechanism is used to generate predictions for the anticipated money supply and then this series is incorporated in the equation explaining money holdings, in order to test the Carr–Darby hypothesis. Cuthbertson and Taylor feel a more consistent approach is to estimate jointly the money balances equation and the expectations generating mechanism for the anticipated money supply. This alternative procedure, which utilises the methodology developed by Mishkin, allows the investigator to test, not only the significance of the anticipated and unanticipated money coefficients, but also the validity of the cross-equation 'rationality' restrictions, which are implicitly imposed in the two-stage model.[21] Using the money growth expectations mechanism, Cuthbertson and Taylor find that, although the joint estimation procedure produces a coefficient on unanticipated money which is strongly significant, the results imply a rejection of the cross-equation 'rationality' restrictions. Such a result undermines their previous findings and also casts some doubt on the earlier studies of the Carr–Darby model, which have not been tested for consistency in this way. Cuthbertson and Taylor (1988) apply the same procedures to US data on narrow money for the period 1960–83. Again, the two-step approach leads to coefficient values which support the shock-absorber hypothesis, while joint estimation of the system produces results which reject the 'rationality' restrictions required for model consistency. Therefore, although the shock-absorber view of money holdings may have some empirical validity, Cuthbertson and Taylor feel that their results indicate that this cannot be coupled with the notion that agents form expectations according to the rational expectations hypothesis.

Cuthbertson and Taylor (1987c) relax the assumption of full information and costless, instantaneous learning, which is implicit in the standard rational expectations approach, and formulate an alternative expectations generating mechanism, that allows agents to update the coefficients of the forecasting model as new data becomes available. This method, which mimics a learning process, involves the use of the Kalman filter.[22] The particular model used to generate expectations is arbitrary. Cuthbertson and Taylor suggest that agents are likely to use a fairly simple model, with expectations of the money supply based upon a linear time trend which allows for seasonal variation. Applying the Kalman filter, a series is generated for anticipated money from UK data on $M1$ over the period 1963–83, and then incorporated in general distributed lag error-correction versions of equations (7.18), (7.19) and (7.21), in order to test the shock-absorber hypothesis. The results suggest a significant role for unanticipated money, but also that anticipated money has no effect upon real money holdings, thus lending support to the Carr–Darby hypothesis.

A more fundamental issue concerns the interpretation given to the basic Carr–Darby shock-absorber equation. Implicit in the MacKinnon–Milbourne critique of the Carr–Darby equation is the view that the nominal money stock is an endogenous variable. Cuthbertson and Taylor (1986, 1988) argue that such an assumption implies that agents are irrational; they generate forecasts about the anticipated money supply using a particular expectations generating mechanism, and then choose a value for endogenous money holdings, and hence the actual money supply, using equations such as (7.21), which take these expectations into account.[23] Because of this inconsistency, Cuthbertson and Taylor feel that the shock-absorber model does not make sense unless money is taken to be exogenous, even though this is a somewhat extreme view in the context of narrow money. Of course, even with an exogenous nominal money supply, real money holdings, which also depend upon the price level, will still be endogenous at the aggregate level, so that it is legitimate to estimate equations such as (7.17). In a rejoinder to MacKinnon and Milbourne (1984), which clarifies the initial Carr–Darby paper in this respect, Carr *et al.* (1985) also assert that the nominal money stock should be treated as exogenous at the aggregate level, with the shock-absorber equation interpreted as a model of price adjustment.[24] This can be seen more clearly if we rearrange equation (7.18) to produce the price equation

$$p_t = m_t - bx_t - \varphi(m - m^e)_t - u_t \qquad (7.22)$$

or, alternatively, by adding m_t^e to each side of equation (7.22), we can show

$$p_t = m_t^e - bx_t + (1 - \varphi)(m - m^e)_t - u_t \qquad (7.23)$$

Equation (7.23) illustrates that changes in anticipated money are immediately and fully reflected in current prices, whereas changes in unanticipated money are only partially reflected in current prices for values of $(1 - \varphi)$ between zero and unity. This interpretation of the shock-absorber equation would appear to be based upon a view of money market adjustment similar to that expressed by Laidler (1982), which we considered earlier in this chapter. However, in that case, no distinction was made between anticipated and unanticipated changes, and all exogenous money creation led to the slow adjustment of prices.

Carr *et al.* do not estimate explicit price level equations such as (7.22) or (7.23). Instead, they estimate an equation of the form given in (7.20), in which a term in anticipated money is added to the basic Carr–Darby equation. The variable is found to have no effect upon real money holdings, a finding which is used to support their neutrality hypothesis that anticipated changes in the money stock are fully reflected in the price level. Using the same data set on US narrow money, a version of equation (7.22) is estimated by MacKinnon and Milbourne (1988). On the basis of the estimated coefficients, they find no empirical support for the view that the price level is determined in the way hypothesised by Carr *et al.*

OTHER BUFFER STOCK MODELS

Browne (1989) is sceptical of the value of distinguishing between anticipated and unanticipated money, arguing that the empirical evidence is contradictory and that the series are difficult to model at the empirical level. Browne formulates an alternative model of buffer stock money, in which no such distinction is made, and attention is focused upon the source of money supply shocks. The adjustment mechanism in equation (7.16) is replaced by the relation

$$\tilde{M}_t - \tilde{M}_{t-1} = \theta(\tilde{M}_t^* - \tilde{M}_{t-1}) + \sum_{i=0}^{n} \varphi_i S_{t-i} \tag{7.24}$$

where the term S is used to represent the set of factors determining current and past changes in the nominal money supply; these are assumed to be responsible for displacing agents from their short-run demand for money function. The long-run desired demand for real balances is specified as

$$\tilde{M}_t^* = \gamma + \alpha R_t^e + \beta Y_t^p + \delta \dot{P}_t^e + \varepsilon_t \tag{7.25}$$

where the superscript e denotes an expected value, $\dot{P}$ is the rate of inflation, Y^p is permanent real income and ε is an arbitrary error term. Substitution of (7.25) into (7.24) yields the short-run equation

$$\tilde{M}_t = b_0 + b_1 R_t^e + b_2 Y_t^p + b_3 \dot{P}_t^e + (1 - \theta)\tilde{M}_{t-1} + \sum_{i=0}^{n} \varphi_i S_{t-i} + u_t$$

where $b_0 = \theta\gamma$, $b_1 = \theta\alpha$, $b_2 = \theta\beta$, $b_3 = \theta\delta$ and $u_t = \theta\varepsilon_t$. The use of the lagged monetary change variables means that it is possible to model explicitly the lagged effects over time of exogenous money creation on balances held. The existence of a buffer stock mechanism requires at least the impact, and perhaps more recent, φ_i parameters to be positive, while the non-existence of a buffer stock element in the long run requires negative values for some previous φ_i, so as to ensure that the sum of the responses to any given shock equals zero. Although the model is not applied to UK data, it has been tested, with some success, using a broad money series for Ireland. Given the degree of financial integration between the Irish and UK economies, changes in the UK monetary base and PSBR are used as alternative proxies for excess money creation in the Irish economy. The results indicate a buffer stock reaction by Irish money holders in response to money creation in the UK. Prices adjust slowly to these exogenous money shocks, although in the long run real money balances are unaffected, with the price level adjusting proportionately after about three years. Such findings give general support to the buffer stock notion.

Other buffer stock models are based upon a more explicit theoretical framework, taking into account the costs of portfolio adjustment. Santomero and Seater (1981) develop a formal model, based upon a general theory of partial adjustment. Individuals are assumed to compare the costs of being out of long-run equilibrium with the search costs of finding alternative investment opportunities, when a shock leads to a change in money holdings. Long-run equilibrium balances are determined according to Whalen's (1966) model of the precautionary demand for money and depend upon the cost of illiquidity, relative interest rates and the variance of transactions. Because individuals do not have full information on the alternative assets available, adjustment to a shock occurs only slowly, with search intensity and the speed of adjustment varying according to the size of disequilibrium balances and the source of the initial disturbance.[25] The model is tested using US data on both the narrow $M1$ and the broader $M2$ aggregate over the period 1952–72. Permanent income is used as the scale variable and the monetary shock term is represented by a distributed lag on both transitory income and the change in the money supply, all expressed as a proportion of permanent income. The variable is found to have an immediate, but short-lived, impact upon real money holdings.

Forward-looking Models

Kanniainen and Tarkka (1986) develop a model in which money balances held by individuals are the outcome of optimising forward-looking behaviour. They consider the role of expected future shocks to the money supply as well as current monetary injections. The model implies that any current injection, whether anticipated or not, ought to have a positive impact upon real balances held, while any anticipated future injection ought to have a negative impact upon current money holdings, with the weights on expected future shocks declining geometrically as we move further into the future. Empirically the source of monetary shocks is related to Domestic Credit Expansion, the surplus on the current account of the balance of payments and the government's net borrowing from abroad. The model is tested on data from five countries, including the US, but excluding the UK. The authors claim that their results support the buffer stock hypothesis, by suggesting that monetary injections from the various sources, force agents, at least temporarily, 'off' their money demand curves.

Cuthbertson and Taylor (1987b, 1989) and Cuthbertson (1988a) develop a forward-looking buffer stock model, in which individuals consider the expected future values of the determinants of their demand for money, and on this basis plan their optimal holdings of money over time. The individual is assumed to have a long-run desired demand for nominal balances, which depends upon the interest rate, real income and the price level. We can represent this function, at time t, by the relation

$$m_t^* = \gamma + \alpha R_t + \beta y_t + \delta p_t$$

where all variables, except the rate of interest, are expressed in terms of their logarithmic values. Disequilibrium and adjustment costs are explicitly introduced into the analysis and the individual economic agent is assumed to choose his planned short-run money holdings, at time t, so as to minimise the multi-period quadratic cost function

$$MQC = E_t \sum_{j=0}^{T} D^j [\Psi(m_{t+j} - m_{t+j}^*)^2 + \omega(m_{t+j} - m_{t+j-1})^2] \qquad (7.26)$$

where E_t is the expectations operator for information up to time t, T represents the time horizon or number of future periods beyond t relevant to the planning decision, D is the discount factor, and Ψ and ω represent the respective weights attached to the disequilibrium and adjustment costs of money holdings.[26] The first term of the expression in (7.26) represents the current and expected future discounted costs of being out of equilibrium in each period, while the second term is used to approximate the current and expected future discounted costs of changing money holdings for each period. The planned short-run demand for money at time t, which we write as m_t^p, can be represented by the relation

$$m_t^p = (1 - \lambda)(1 - \lambda D) \sum_{j=0}^{T} (\lambda D)^j (\gamma + \alpha R_{t+j}^e + \beta y_{t+j}^e + \delta p_{t+j}^e)$$

$$+ \lambda m_{t-1} \qquad (7.27)$$

where λ is a coefficient which depends upon the disequilibrium and adjustment cost parameters (Ψ and ω) and the superscript e denotes the expected value of a variable. Planned holdings are therefore related to previous-period balances and the current- period expectations of the future evolution of the determinants of long-run money demand. Actual money holdings, at any time, comprise this planned element and an unplanned or buffer component, which depends upon the current-period unanticipated values of the arguments of the demand for money function. The actual short-run equation, which can be tested empirically, takes the form

$$m_t = b_0 + \sum_{j=0}^{T} b_{1j} R_{t+j}^e + \sum_{j=0}^{T} b_{2j} y_{t+j}^e + \sum_{j=0}^{T} b_{3j} p_{t+j}^e + \lambda m_{t-1}$$

$$+ \varphi_1 (R - R^e)_t + \varphi_2 (y - y^e)_t + \varphi_3 (p - p^e)_t + v_t$$

where the b coefficients are composites of the model parameters, the φ parameters represent the coefficients on the unanticipated values of the explanatory variables in the long-run money demand function and v is an arbitrary error term. Money holdings, in any time period, are therefore dependent upon forward-looking variables in the expected values of the arguments of the long-run demand function, a backward-looking variable in the lagged money stock and a series of terms representing unanticipated changes in the factors determining desired holdings. The model implies a restriction between the forward and backward-looking variables: the weights on the expected future variables should decline geometrically as the time horizon is extended and in addition be related to the coefficient on the lagged dependent variable.

The basis of the model is that an expected future rise in the price level or real income (or an expected fall in the interest rate) will lead to a small rise in current money balances, which continues into future periods until a new long-term equilibrium is reached. Adjustment is not instantaneous because costs of adjustment are non-zero. In contrast, an unanticipated rise in the price level or real income (or an unanticipated fall in the interest rate) leads to an immediate increase in unplanned money holdings. If the shock is reversed in subsequent periods, money holdings will return to their previous level. However, if the unanticipated changes are subsequently interpreted as permanent movements, they will result in a revision of the expected future levels of the interest rate, real income and prices, so that planned money holdings will change to a new level. The forward-looking model also reduces the likelihood of interest rate 'overshooting', which is required in the conventional short-run partial adjustment equation, in order to restore equilibrium following an exogenous money supply shock. If the increase in the money supply is accompanied by an unanticipated increase in prices or real income, this leads to a temporary rise in buffer holdings. Also, to the extent that the shock may cause revisions to be made to the expected future paths of the arguments of the money demand function, there will be a further immediate change in current money holdings. Consequently, any disequilibrium in the money market is alleviated, without the need for large changes in the current value of the interest rate or any of the other arguments of the function.

Empirical implementation of the model requires a theory of expectations formation. Using a fourth-order vector autoregressive process to generate expected future values for real income, the price level and the rate of interest, Cuthbertson and Taylor (1987b) apply the model to quarterly UK data on $M1$ for the period 1963–83.[27] The equation for short-run money holdings is estimated jointly with the expectations generating mechanism, and a test of the cross-equation 'rationality' restrictions suggests that these cannot be rejected. The results yield parameter estimates of the correct *a priori* sign and lend support to the view that forward-looking variables should be included in the short-run demand for money function. Although the results indicate a slow pattern of adjustment, in response to changes in the expected future values of real income, prices and the interest rate, the authors are unable to reject the hypothesis that the long-run real income and price elasticities are unity. Cuthbertson (1988a) uses both autoregressive and vector autoregressive forecasting schemes for the independent variables of the demand for money function, and time horizons of four and eight quarters. Cuthbertson and Taylor (1989) use the Kalman filter to incorporate a learning mechanism in an expectations generating function, which is based upon a time trend with seasonal variation. An arbitrary time horizon of eleven periods is chosen. Both of these latter studies use quarterly data on $M1$ for the period 1964–79. In each case, the results are similar to those obtained by the earlier study and again lend support to the buffer stock role of money, with the current-period impact on money holdings, of a 1 per cent increase in the expected future values of the arguments of money demand, found to be much smaller than that resulting from the corresponding unanticipated changes. For example, Cuthbertson's results indicate that an unanticipated change in real income has approximately twice the impact effect of an anticipated increase in income, although the effect of the latter is more powerful in the long run. Both studies also make a comparison between the forward-looking model and a backward-looking error-correction model, similar to that reported in Hendry (1985). Although the latter is found to fit the data more closely, this is to be expected because a general distributed lag approach allows the dynamics to be determined by the data, which is not the case in the forward-looking model, where restrictions are imposed between parameters.

On the basis of these studies, Cuthbertson and Taylor argue that the forward-looking model is superior to other formulations which do not consider the role of the expected future values of the arguments of the money demand function. At the empirical level, the explicit modelling of agents' expectations formation, in a separate equation, helps to circumvent the Lucas (1976) critique, by making it easier for the investigator to isolate the structural parameters of the underlying long-run demand equation. The empirical form of backward-looking distributed lag models does not allow such a separation, in that the estimated coefficients are a mixture of expectations, adjustment and structural parameters, with the expectations generating process, in particular, likely to alter under alternative policy regimes. According to the Lucas critique, equations estimated using this approach are therefore only really suitable for the analysis of data over a period in which policy has been relatively unchanged. They should not be applied to periods where policy changes, or other extraneous factors, have altered the data generating process of the expectations variables or indeed the costs of adjustment. In such circumstances, the parameters of the model are likely to display great variability, even if the long-run equilibrium relationship remains invariant to the change. Given the changing institutional environment and developments in the emphasis of monetary policy in the UK, such factors provide a powerful rationale for the apparent instability that has plagued many distributed lag demand for money equations in recent years.

Muscatelli (1988) is more cautious in his support for the forward-looking model. He amends the cost function, given in relation (7.26), so as to incorporate the disequilibrium and adjustment costs incurred with respect to the other assets of the portfolio. At the same time, adjustments in money holdings are made costless, which it is argued, is more in accord with the assumed role of money as a buffer stock. Expectations of future savings decisions are also assumed to enter the plan for current money holdings. Adoption of a modified cost function leads to a different dynamic structure and Muscatelli makes an empirical comparison of his model with the Cuthbertson and Taylor approach, using quarterly data for $M1$ over the period 1963–84. Muscatelli's results do not lend clear support to any particular model and he finds that there are problems with all the estimated equations, which can probably be attributed to dynamic misspecification. He concludes that the use of theory in buffer stock models to infer a precise dynamic structure for the demand for money is unsatisfactory, and that the data should be allowed to play a greater part in determining the final specification. In this sense, Muscatelli reasons that it may be more appropriate to concentrate future research on traditional backward-looking models, by adopting a 'general to specific' model selection procedure. Of course, because of the problem of 'observational equivalence', it can be difficult, in practice, to distinguish between backward and forward-looking models.[28] Using the same data set on $M1$, Muscatelli (1989) compares the results from a general distributed lag equation, which follows the approach of Hendry (1979, 1985), with those obtainable from a forward-looking buffer stock model. On the basis of the estimated parameters and other diagnostic tests, he argues that the 'general to specific' approach is to be preferred and that there must be doubts as to whether the demand for $M1$ can have a forward-looking interpretation. Hendry (1988) also makes an attempt to discriminate between the two approaches in the context of a study of the demand for $M1$. Using various diagnostic tests, he contrasts the equations in Hendry (1985) and Cuthbertson (1988a); he argues that his findings imply a rejection of the forward-looking expectations-based interpretation of the demand for money function, with the autoregressive equations used to generate forecasts for prices, income and interest rates found to be unstable over the sample period.[29] In contrast, Cuthbertson and Taylor (1990b) find in favour of a forward-looking model for sterling $M3$. Although the reduced form implied by the model is shown to be a constrained version of an error-correction formulation, tests indicate that it is not possible to reject the restrictions implied by the forward-looking 'rational expectations' model. A similar conclusion is reached by Domowitz and Hakkio (1990) in a cross-country comparison of money demand.

A comparison of different approaches to the empirical analysis of money demand is also made by Boughton and Tavlas (1990, 1991). Using data on both narrow and broad money from five different countries (including the UK and US) for the period 1963–88, the authors consider the partial adjustment, general distributed lag and Carr–Darby buffer stock models. Various formulations of the Carr–Darby model are tested, involving different expectations generating mechanisms and a consideration of the role of anticipated money. Although post-sample forecasting tests often favour the buffer stock approach, the goodness of fit statistics and intertemporal stability tests lend support to the general distributed lag models. The results indicate that the adjustment lags differ considerably between the different explanatory variables, a pattern of response which is not allowed in the conventional partial adjustment model. Similarly, although the different formulations of the Carr–Darby model all produce results which are broadly supportive of the buffer stock hypothesis, the authors argue that their diagnostic tests imply that the approach fails to capture important dynamic and systematic influences upon the short-run demand for money. Overall, the Boughton and Tavlas findings support the development of more general dynamic models, and therefore appear to favour the use of a 'general to specific' modelling strategy. A contrasting view is provided by Hall et al. (1990) who feel that the way forward is not to play with increasingly complex dynamics, but rather to use cointegration techniques to determine the correct form of the long-run money demand equation. Once such a relation is obtained, they argue that the resulting dynamics may often turn out to be relatively straightforward. The debate over the different methodological approaches to the modelling of money demand is obviously set to continue.

BUFFER STOCK MODELS: A REVIEW

The analysis in the preceding sections of this chapter illustrates that a variety of different models have been developed and tested empirically, in an attempt to explain and verify a buffer stock role for money. Unfortunately, the empirical findings are not conclusive in their support for the buffer stock hypothesis, and many of the models suffer from severe statistical shortcomings. The results obtained from the different Carr–Darby-type models are often contradictory, while it is difficult to obtain a tractable forward-looking model for empirical purposes. Swamy and Tavlas (1989) review the different approaches and conclude that the buffer stock hypothesis, although attractive, still awaits the development of an empirical model that can serve as a true test of its validity. Other reviewers, such as Milbourne (1987), have also been critical of the theoretical basis of the buffer stock model. The studies cited above have, in the main, tested their models using data on narrow money. This can be rationalised in terms of the association, at the micro-level, between the role of money as a buffer stock and the target-threshold models of the transactions demand for money. It might be expected that an individual agent's incoming receipts and outgoing payments will normally initially involve additions to, or deductions from, narrow money balances. However, Milbourne uses a simple target-threshold model to demonstrate that the behaviour of individual agents will not necessarily translate into a significant aggregate buffer stock effect. Following an unexpected monetary injection, some individuals will increase their buffer stock balances, but still remain within their threshold limits, while others will reach their upper threshold and proceed to reduce their money holdings to the intermediate target or return point. The aggregate effect upon total money holdings may therefore be small or non-existent.[30] Of course, this conclusion is heavily dependent upon the implicit assumption that the monitoring of money balances is continuous and costless. If monitoring is costly or takes place only occasionally, the aggregate effect is likely to be much greater.

Milbourne argues that wider definitions of money may be more appropriate to the role of money as a buffer stock. Supply-side shocks, such as those central to the Carr–Darby model, are more likely to be applicable to the broader monetary aggregates and, in the UK context, changes in the PSBR, external currency flows and bank lending to the private sector, all have the potential to cause sharp movements in the stock of broad money. Unfortunately, as we can see from our discussion of the empirical literature, there have been very few attempts to apply buffer stock models to broad monetary aggregates. For a more complete evaluation of the concept, there would therefore appear to be a need for a more comprehensive analysis of the applicability of the different buffer stock models to the wider UK monetary aggregates, which encompass bank time deposits or even building society deposits.[31] In other circumstances, short-term private sector liabilities, in the form of credit card debts or bank overdrafts, may act as the buffer stock of the portfolio. Large firms, who can borrow from the banking system at more favourable rates of interest than individuals and small firms, are particularly likely to use their outstanding borrowings as a financial buffer. In reality, it is therefore likely that more than one financial asset or liability assumes the role of a buffer stock: alternative buffers may be chosen by different agents at the same time, or indeed by the same agent at different times, as transactions costs and market conditions change, or the source of the shock varies. The factors influencing the choice of the financial buffer are considered in more detail by Bain and McGregor (1985). One way to resolve the issue would appear to be through the specification and estimation of a complete portfolio model of private sector behaviour, in which the selection of the buffer stock item becomes an empirical matter. Unfortunately, such models are difficult to test empirically, as we shall see in Chapter 10.

8 Bank Lending Equations

Variations in sterling $M3$ are often closely associated with changes in sterling bank lending to UK residents. Such lending increased considerably after the removal of direct controls in the Competition and Credit Control reforms of 1971. The company sector, in particular, reduced its traditional reliance on the capital markets in the 1970s and increasingly began to use bank lending as a source of external finance. It is therefore not surprising to find that the breakdown of the broad demand for money function in the 1970s was accompanied by similar problems in the modelling of bank lending equations. Whereas studies based upon data periods covering the 1950s and 1960s, such as Norton (1969) and Artis (1978), had indicated that reasonably stable bank lending equations could be isolated, Cuthbertson and Foster (1982) found that, when later data periods were considered, the isolation of such functions became more problematical. Their study looked at bank lending to industrial and commercial companies, and in particular how such lending was modelled in versions of three large macro models current in the early 1980s.

COMPANY SECTOR BORROWING

Bank lending to companies has traditionally been assumed to be dominated by demand factors, with the banks meeting all loan demand at the prevailing rate of interest. This view is central to the study of Cuthbertson (1985b), who specifies a lending equation in which the major determining variables are income, relative interest rates, the net borrowing requirement of companies, the rate of inflation and a Competition and Credit Control variable. A general distributed lag model is formulated and tested using quarterly data over the period 1965–80. The preferred specification can be interpreted as an error-correction equation of the form

$$\Delta^4(l-p)_t = -0.079 + 0.59\Delta^2(l-p)_{t-1} + 0.98\Delta(l-p)_{t-3}$$
$$\quad\quad (2.5) \quad\quad (10.7) \quad\quad\quad\quad (14.1)$$

$$+ 0.22\Delta^4 y_t - 0.16(l-p-y)_{t-4} - 0.55\Delta RBL_{t-2}$$
$$\quad (2.2) \quad\quad\quad (3.8) \quad\quad\quad\quad (2.5)$$

$$+ 0.65\Delta(RLA - RBL)_t + 1.5(RLA - RBL)_{t-2}$$
$$\quad (2.1) \quad\quad\quad\quad\quad (4.1)$$

$$+ 0.029 BRC_t + 0.23 REUBL_t - 1.29\Delta p_{t-1}$$
$$\quad (8.2) \quad\quad\quad (4.1) \quad\quad\quad (4.0)$$

$$- 0.76\Delta p_{t-2} + 0.038 CCC_t$$
$$\quad (2.4) \quad\quad\quad (10.3) \quad\quad\quad\quad\quad\quad\quad\quad (8.1)$$

where the figures in parentheses are t-statistics. The symbol Δ is used to denote the difference operator, so that Δ^4 represents the fourth difference of the variable and Δ^2 the second difference. The dependent variable, written in terms of logarithms, therefore represents the annual growth, in real terms, in sterling bank lending to industrial and commercial companies, while y is the logarithm of real gross domestic product, p is the logarithm of the price index, RBL is the bank lending rate, RLA is the representative short rate on liquid assets, BRC is the real net borrowing requirement of companies, $REUBL$ is a variable representing the differential between the three-month Eurodollar rate and the bank lending rate, and CCC is a dummy variable which is designed to capture the effects of Competition and Credit Control.

The relative interest rate terms indicate the differential between the cost of borrowing and the return on liquid assets, both at home and abroad. A reduction in liquid asset holdings can be viewed as an alternative to extra bank lending, although in some circumstances firms may increase their borrowing in order to hold more liquid assets. In particular, when the differential between the two rates moves in favour of liquid assets, the phenomenon of 'round-tripping' can occur by which companies increase their borrowing from banks, in order to place more funds on deposit in the wholesale money market. Such behaviour, which was particularly profitable in the early years of Competition and Credit Control, leads to an increase in both bank lending and the liquid asset holdings of firms.[1] Overseas interest rates are relevant because, with the increasing integration of domestic and foreign capital markets, large multinational companies are able to borrow and make deposits in a variety of different currencies and international centres. The income variable mirrors transactions needs, while the borrowing variable is used to measure unanticipated financing requirements. Its significance implies that bank lending acts as a buffer stock for companies. The price variables used to measure the inflation rate have a negative effect upon bank lending. Cuthbertson attributes this response to the greater uncertainty arising from inflation, which has the effect of reducing firms' investment expenditure and hence their demand for loans. Of course, the lagged price terms could be interpreted as representing the lagged adjustment of advances to changes in the price level. The long-run static equilibrium solution implied by equation (8.1) is plausible and indicates an income or transactions elasticity of unity.

Moore and Threadgold (1985) also consider the possibility that bank borrowing fulfils a buffer stock role for the company sector. Their hypothesis is that companies increase their short-term bank borrowing, in order to finance their extra working capital requirements, whenever there is a rise in production costs.[2] Changes in the wage bill, raw material costs, corporate tax payments and stockbuilding are used to represent these effects. Using quarterly data for the period 1965–78, all four variables are found to be significant determinants of the change in bank lending to industrial and commercial companies. The other explanatory variables are the real lending rate and a 'round-tripping' variable, defined as the excess of the three-month certificate of deposit rate over the bank lending rate. Although the real lending rate is significant, the magnitude of the effect is small and indicates that the demand for bank credit is highly interest inelastic. This result is attributed to the fact that the majority of company sector borrowing is primarily for short-term purposes. The finding does, however, imply that the ability of the authorities to control the volume of company borrowing indirectly, through variations in interest rates, is extremely limited. Dummy variables were also included in the estimated equations, in order to capture the effects of Competition and Credit Control, quantitative restrictions on bank lending and the 'corset' controls on the growth of bank deposits. None of the variables had a significant effect upon the dependent variable. The Competition and Credit Control variable may be duplicating the effect that is captured by the 'round-tripping' variable, while the non-significance of the control dummies is understandable, given that the restrictions were directed primarily at lending to the personal sector. The explanatory power of the equation is high and overall the results are consistent with the view that the quantity of bank lending to companies is largely demand determined. Unfortunately, when the data period is extended to 1981, there are marked changes in the parameter estimates and the explanatory power of the equation falls considerably. Nevertheless, the model is useful because it highlights the chain of causation through which money supply shocks, induced by changes in bank lending, can create a temporary disequilibrium in the money market.

PERSONAL SECTOR BORROWING

The market for personal sector bank advances is more likely to be characterised by a disequilibrium situation, in which demand and supply differ at the ruling interest rate. This situation can arise if the lending rate is set at a level different from the market clearing rate, so ensuring either an excess supply or an excess demand for loans. In the former case, the banks are left with surplus funds, while an excess demand for loans means that market clearing can only be achieved by credit rationing, through the operation of non-price factors such as collateral requirements or the length of the repayment period. Rationing may also be required if the authorities impose direct quantitative controls upon the amount of lending which the banks are able to provide. Restrictions on the free operation of the advances market were common in the pre-Competition and Credit Control era, when the lending rate was tied to the Bank Rate set by the authorities and lending was frequently subject to both quantitative and qualitative guidance. In the 1970s, the 'corset' controls had a similar effect, even though they were imposed upon the liabilities (deposits) of the banking system, rather than upon their asset portfolio.[3]

A model of the market for personal sector bank advances, which takes account of these factors, implies a supply equation for the stock of advances of the form

$$S = a_1 X_s + b_1 C \tag{8.2}$$

where X_s refers to the set of explanatory variables relevant to the supply function, C represents the non-price market clearing variables and a_1 and b_1 are the parameters of the relation. The stock demand equation can be written as

$$D = a_2 X_d - b_2 C \tag{8.3}$$

where X_d is the set of factors affecting demand and a_2 and b_2 are parameters. The quantity 'traded' in the market, A, is determined from an appropriately weighted sum of the supply and demand equations. We can write

$$A = w_1 S + w_2 D \tag{8.4}$$

with w_1 and w_2, the respective supply and demand weights, given by the formulae

$$w_1 = \frac{b_2}{b_1 + b_2} \quad \text{and} \quad w_2 = \frac{b_1}{b_1 + b_2} \tag{8.5}$$

where $w_1 + w_2 = 1$. By substituting relations (8.2), (8.3) and (8.5) into equation (8.4), we can remove the market clearing 'unobservables', leaving the 'reduced form' relation

$$A = \left[\frac{b_2 a_1}{b_1 + b_2}\right] X_s + \left[\frac{b_1 a_2}{b_1 + b_2}\right] X_d \tag{8.6}$$

Equation (8.6) implies that the stock of advances is determined by a mix of supply and demand influences. Such an approach is implicit in the advances equations estimated by Artis (1978), in which supply factors are represented by the short bond rate (which measures the opportunity cost of making advances), Special Deposit calls and lending control dummies, and demand influences are indicated by permanent and disposable income, a capacity utilisation variable and the Bank Rate.

This type of model is most applicable to a market which is out of, but close to, equilibrium. There are obviously limits to the speed of response and the range over which non-price factors can be varied, and it is unrealistic to expect such variables to clear markets which are substantially out of equilibrium. In these cases, the quantity 'traded' has to equate to the minimum of the supply and demand values, at the prevailing interest rate. Such an approach, which necessitates the estimation of separate supply and demand equations, is based upon the work of Fair and Jaffee (1972) and has been applied to a model of bank lending in Canada by Laffont and Garcia (1977).[4] Early versions of the Treasury model, which are based upon the work outlined in Spencer and Mowl (1978), attemped to allow for these different ways of analysing the market clearing problem, in their treatment of personal sector bank advances. The form of the model enables demand and supply to be equated by the adjustment of unobservable non-price factors if there is only a moderate amount of disequilibrium in the market, while the greater the excess demand or supply the more closely the quantity 'traded' approaches the minimum of the two values.[5]

Finally, we can note that the considerations outlined in this chapter for the bank advances market are also relevant to the modelling of building society mortgage advances, although here the situation is complicated by the change in regime that occurred in the early 1980s. Prior to this time, mortgage funds were continuously rationed, with supply factors dominant in the market. Since the early 1980s, demand forces have become more important in influencing mortgages given. This change coincided with a noticeable decline in the building societies' share of total mortgage lending, as the banks entered the market in a committed way for the first time.

9 The Demand for Long-term Government Securities

In comparison to the plethora of empirical studies on the demand for money function, there have been few attempts to model the non-bank private sector's demand for long-term government securities (gilts). The issue was analysed by Norton (1969) in a pioneering study, while more recent models of the demand for government bonds are developed in Spencer (1981) and Hoggarth and Ormerod (1985). One of the main issues, analysed by these later studies, is the role and importance of expected capital gains in determining the demand for gilts. In each case, an attempt is made to model the relative return on gilts in each period, defined as the long-term rate of interest plus the *ex post* capital gain over the period, less the rate of interest obtainable on alternative capital-safe short-term assets.[1] Various models are used for this purpose, ranging from simple autoregressive forecasting schemes to more sophisticated 'structural' models, which relate the relative return to explicit economic information.

Spencer's preferred specification, obtained from quarterly data for the period 1967–77, takes the form

$$(RL + CG - RS)_t = 1509 - 0.01BAL_{t-1} - 2.24\dot{P}_{t-1} - 1.58\dot{P}_{t-4}$$
$$\quad (2.5) \quad (1.8) \quad\quad (2.56) \quad\quad (1.71)$$

$$-0.87REU_{t-1} - 3.72REU_{t-3} + 5.4REU_{t-4}$$
$$\quad (1.2) \quad\quad (2.3) \quad\quad (3.1)$$

$$+10.5RL_{t-1} - 1.85RS_{t-1} + 4.6nw_t$$
$$\quad (3.4) \quad\quad (1.3) \quad\quad (0.02)$$

$$-121.1y_t - 43.4sg_t + 53z_{t-1}$$
$$\quad (2.3) \quad\quad (1.26) \quad (1.0)$$

$$R^2 = 0.624 \quad (9.1)$$

where the figures in parentheses denote t-statistics. The dependent variable, $RL + CG - RS$, measures the relative return on gilts, given that RL is the rate of interest on long-dated gilts, CG is the *ex post* capital gain on gilts and RS is the three-month local authority rate. Of the explanatory variables, BAL is a balance of payments term, $\dot{P}$ is a measure of price inflation, REU is the three-month Eurodollar rate, z is the logarithm of a variable showing the effect of savings and inflation on real wealth, and nw, y and sg respectively denote the logarithms of the real values of net wealth, income and the stock of gilts at the beginning of the quarter. The negative coefficient on the balance of payments term may show the effect of confidence in the UK economy, with a surplus leading to capital inflows into sterling and in particular the gilts market, so reducing the required rate of return. The positive coefficient on RL_{t-1} probably reflects the behaviour of the authorities in the market over this period. By raising long rates abruptly by a large amount, the authorities encouraged investors to believe that interest rates would fall in the future, so producing the expectation of a capital gain, and ensuring a ready market for gilt sales. This tactic is often referred to as the 'Grand Old Duke of York' strategy, and is based upon a regressive view of expectations formation.

Following the 'rational expectations' approach, predictions from equation (9.1) can be used to provide a series for the expected relative return on gilts, for use as an explanatory variable in a gilts demand equation. Transactions in gilts are used as the dependent variable, rather than the market value of existing stocks, in order to avoid problems with revaluation effects.[2] Spencer's preferred specifications, which incorporate scale variables in either wealth or income, indicate that the flow demand for gilts is negatively related to the market value of stock already held. Changes in wealth also have a role to play, but apart from the expected differential return between long- and short-term assets, no other rate of return variables were found to be significant.

Hoggarth and Ormerod also model the demand for long-term government securities using a two-step procedure, although the set of explanatory variables utilised in each stage is not the same as that chosen by Spencer. Using quarterly data for the period 1975–83, their preferred specification for the relative return on gilts takes the form

$$(RL + CG - RS)_t = -0.42 - 0.0012\Delta ER_{t-3} + 0.008\dot{P}_{t-3}$$
$$ (0.1) \quad (0.003) \qquad\quad (0.004)$$

$$-0.013\dot{P}_{t-4} - 0.0057\Delta\pounds M3_{t-2} + 36.6RL_{t-1}$$
$$(0.004) \qquad (0.0037) \qquad\quad (6.7)$$

$$-0.018PSBR_{t-3} - 0.026PSBR_{t-4} + 0.72sgs_{t-1}$$
$$(0.007) \qquad\quad (0.008) \qquad\quad (0.18)$$

$$R^2 = 0.655 \qquad (9.2)$$

where the figures in parentheses are standard errors, ΔER is the change in the sterling exchange rate, $\Delta\pounds M3$ is the change in the sterling $M3$ money supply, $PSBR$ is the public sector borrowing requirement and sgs is the logarithm of the stock of long-term public sector debt held by the private sector (deflated by output). The positive and statistically significant coefficient on RL_{t-1} confirms the findings of Spencer, while the negative coefficients on the $PSBR$ terms are consistent with the view that higher interest rates, and hence lower gilt prices, and capital losses, are associated with increases in the $PSBR$. The statistical significance of the money supply variable is not very strong, but its negatively-signed coefficient suggests that the greater is monetary growth, the higher are interest rates expected to be to bring the growth rate back within target, and hence the greater the likelihood of capital losses on gilt holdings. Hoggarth and Ormerod feel that the positive coefficient on the stock of gilts outstanding probably reflects supply-side factors: the higher is the stock of gilts outstanding, the less the immediate need of the authorities to issue debt to finance the public sector deficit, and hence the more relaxed their attitude to interest rates.

Hoggarth and Ormerod estimated several equations for gilt sales to the non-bank private sector, using a variety of estimation methods. As well as the expected relative return on gilts, other determining variables considered were interest rates, wealth, income and the expected capital gain on equities which was generated separately. However, the expectations series obtained from equation (9.2), incorporating explicit economic information, was not statistically significant in most of the gilts equations estimated, and was found to be outperformed by a much simpler expected returns variable, related solely to the expected capital gain on gilts and which ignored the differential between long and short rates. Expectations in this case were generated from the equation

$$PCON_t = 35.50 - 1.19RL_{t-1}$$
$$(2.8) \quad (0.16) \qquad R^2 = 0.603 \qquad (9.3)$$

where *PCON*, the end-period price of consols, was regressed against the lagged value of the rate of interest on consols. The figures in parentheses represent standard errors. The mechanism outlined in (9.3) is based upon a simple extrapolative scheme of previous interest rates and contradicts the role of the lagged value of the long rate of interest in equation (9.2). The form of equation (9.3) suggests that the higher are long rates at the end of the previous period, the lower are consol prices at the end of the current period, and hence by implication the higher are long rates of interest.

A typical specification for the value of gilt sales produced the equation

$$GS_t = -0.017 - 0.00088FT_t^e + 0.0047PCON_t^e + 0.0011\Delta NW_t$$
$$(0.03) \quad (0.00029) \qquad (0.0019) \qquad (0.0005)$$

$$-0.0018\Delta^2 SGS_{t-1} + 0.002NW_{t-1}$$
$$(0.0006) \qquad (0.0007) \qquad R^2 = 0.372 \qquad (9.4)$$

where the figures in parentheses represent standard errors. The dependent variable, *GS*, represents sales of gilts (deflated by total expenditure), while FT^e is the expected value of the Financial Times All-Share Index, $PCON^e$ is a series for the expected price of consols which is generated from equation (9.3), *NW* is the net financial wealth of the non-bank private sector and $\Delta^2 SGS$ is the second difference of the outstanding stock of long-term public sector debt held by the private sector (deflated by total expenditure). The expected value of the All-Share Index is used to provide an indication of the expected capital gain on equities. The series is generated from an equation which relates the actual value of the Index to a variety of economic variables, including the sterling exchange rate, the interest rate on local authority deposits, real personal disposable income, private sector financial wealth and the gross trading profits of the company sector. Equation

(9.4) implies that gilt sales are positively related to the level of, and change in, net wealth and the expected capital gain on gilts, and are adversely affected by increases in gilt holdings in the past and improvements in the expectation of capital gains on equities.

10 Multi-asset Portfolio Models

In principle, it would seem to be preferable to examine asset demands (and supplies) within the context of a complete multi-asset portfolio model, rather than in single individual equations. The advantage of such an approach is that the allocation of the financial wealth of a sector among a variety of assets (and liabilities) is analysed as an interdependent decision: the demand equations explicitly take into account the fact that a decision to hold funds in a particular form is simultaneously a decision not to hold these funds in an alternative form. Furthermore, by examining the simultaneous response of sets of asset demands to changes in different explanatory variables, it is possible to impose, and to test, additional constraints upon the values that the coefficients in the system should take. For example, if the rate of interest on national savings is raised, it is possible not only to analyse the interest sensitivity of the demand for that asset, but also to see the extent to which the increase in demand is at the expense of the demand for money or other liquid assets. Such information, on the substitutability of different assets, is clearly of use to policy-makers.

We devote this chapter to a discussion of the multi-asset approach, beginning with a statement of the empirical form of the general portfolio model, as formulated by Brainard and Tobin (1968). We then consider the results of empirical studies based upon the multi-asset approach, concentrating in the main on UK studies. The work of the Treasury in developing a financial model of the UK economy is discussed in some detail. Contrary to expectations, we find that the insights provided by multi-asset studies have generally been minimal and that the empirical results obtained are often disappointing.

THE BRAINARD–TOBIN SYSTEM

The empirical form of the multi-asset portfolio choice model was first considered by Brainard and Tobin (1968) and this section draws heavily on the basic ideas which they developed. The main character-istics of the Brainard-Tobin system can be outlined as follows:

136

(1) The demand for each asset is a function of its own holding-period rate of return, the return obtainable on all other choice assets and the total wealth of the portfolio holder. There are many possible ways in which to formulate such a system of demand equations. The simple linear form, written in terms of the levels of the variables, can be represented by the relation

$$X_i = \sum_{j=1}^{n} f_{ij} R_j + c_i W \qquad (10.1)$$
$$i = 1, \ldots, n$$

where X_i is the quantity demanded of the ith choice asset in an n asset system, W is the total wealth of the portfolio holder and R_j is the (expected or actual) rate of return on the jth choice asset, which may include an element of capital gains. The f_{ij} and c_i are parameters of the model.

(2) Brainard and Tobin laid great emphasis upon the importance of not omitting any assets from the model, and on the need to meet a budget constraint. Accordingly, the typical portfolio model imposes the condition that the sum of asset holdings has to equal total wealth, so that we can write

$$\sum_{i=1}^{n} X_i = W \qquad (10.2)$$

We ensure that the budget constraint always holds, whatever the values of R and W, by imposing cross-equation or adding-up restrictions on the parameters of the model. These can be written as

$$\sum_{\substack{i=1 \\ \text{for all } j}}^{n} f_{ij} = 0 \qquad \sum_{i=1}^{n} c_i = 1 \qquad (10.3)$$

The first condition asserts that the total effect of a change in the rate of return on a particular asset, summed over the whole portfolio, must be zero. The second requirement means that all of the available wealth must be allocated among the competing assets.

(3) Portfolio forms are in essence demand systems and, given this, we should be able to impose sign restrictions on the rate of return

coefficients, which are analogous to some of the conditions imposed upon the price terms in classical demand theory. In particular, it seems intuitively reasonable to expect the own rate of return coefficients, the f_{ii}, to be positive. Under normal circumstances, an increase in the own return on any asset should increase the demand for that asset. Analogously, if we assume most assets, but not necessarily all, are substitutes for each other, then the cross rate coefficients, the f_{ij}, where $j \neq i$, should be predominantly negative.[1] Finally, it may be reasonable to assume symmetrical cross rate coefficients, so that the effect upon asset i, of a change in the rate of return on asset j, is equal in magnitude and sign to the effect upon asset j, of the same change in the return on asset i; that is, $f_{ij} = f_{ji}$.[2] The symmetry condition, combined with the adding-up restriction on the rate of return coefficients in (10.3), implies that the sum of the return coefficients in any equation is zero, so that we can write

$$\sum_{j=1}^{n} f_{ij} = 0 \qquad \text{for all } i$$

This condition is referred to as homogeneity of degree zero in rates of return. In economic terms, it implies that an equal change in all rates of return leaves the demand for each asset unchanged, so that only changes in relative returns exert any influence upon portfolio holdings.

(4)   The fourth point concerns the dynamic extension of the basic model. Brainard and Tobin stressed that it was unlikely that any portfolio holder would always be in equilibrium with respect to his desired portfolio. Long planning periods, habit persistence and high transaction and information costs would necessarily imply a disequilibrium portfolio, and hence the need for some kind of adjustment mechanism.

The Generalised Adjustment Mechanism

The simple partial adjustment mechanism, which we discussed in the context of the demand for money in Chapter 5, can be written as

$$\Delta X_{it} = X_{it} - X_{it-1} = \theta(X_{it}^* - X_{it-1}) \qquad (10.4)$$
$$i = 1, \ldots, n$$

where θ is the adjustment coefficient and X_{it}^* is the long-run desired holding of the ith asset at time t. The mechanism in (10.4) states that the change in the actual holdings of each asset, between the current and previous period, is a constant fraction, θ, of the difference between desired current holdings and previous actual holdings. Assuming that desired holdings are determined by the relation given in (10.1), we can substitute for X_{it}^* in (10.4), and by rearrangement obtain the specification

$$X_{it} = \theta \sum_{j=1}^{n} f_{ij} R_{jt} + \theta c_i W_t + (1 - \theta) X_{it-1} \qquad (10.5)$$
$$i = 1, \ldots, n$$

in which the demand for each asset also depends upon previous holdings of the asset. However, in a portfolio model, the sum of both the desired and the actual values of the different assets must satisfy the budget constraint at all times. This, in turn, implies that the sum of the deviations of actual from desired asset stocks must be zero and therefore a disequilibrium in the holdings of one asset must imply that the stock of at least one other asset is also in disequilibrium. Consequently, if the lagged value of asset holding affects the current demand for the asset, as described in equation (10.5), it must also affect the demand for at least one other asset in the opposite direction, so that the budget constraint can be maintained.[3]

Such considerations led Brainard and Tobin to develop the interdependent or generalised adjustment mechanism, in which the change in the holdings of each asset is influenced by all other desired portfolio adjustments. The system can be written as

$$X_{it} - X_{it-1} = \sum_{k=1}^{n} \theta_{ik}(X_{kt}^* - X_{kt-1}) \qquad (10.6)$$
$$i = 1, \ldots, n$$

where X_{kt}^* is the desired holding of the kth asset at time t and θ_{ik} is the adjustment coefficient for the kth asset in the ith asset demand equation. In system (10.6), the change in the holding of each asset, between the current and previous period, is assumed to depend upon not only the own gap between actual and desired holdings, but also the deviations of all the other assets in the portfolio from their desired levels. The overall speed and path of adjustment depends upon the sign and magnitude of both the own (θ_{ii}) and the cross (θ_{ik} for $k \neq i$) adjustment coefficients, where each θ_{ik} illustrates the effect upon holdings of the ith asset of a disequilibrium in the holdings of the

kth asset. The approach therefore permits a much more flexible and varied dynamic response than that allowed under simple partial adjustment. Thus, for example, the speed with which a discrepancy between desired and actual holdings of bonds is eliminated now depends upon whether the bond disequilibrium is the counterpart of a discrepancy between desired and actual money balances or desired and actual equity holdings.[4]

The budget constraint imposes restrictions on the adjustment system such that

$$\sum_{i=1}^{n} \theta_{ik} = 1 \qquad \text{for all } k \tag{10.7}$$

This requirement means that any disequilibrium, between desired current holdings and previous-period actual holdings of a particular asset, must be exactly accommodated, between the two periods, either by changes in the holdings of the asset itself, or by changes in one or more of the other assets of the portfolio, or by some combination of the two responses. Intuitively, we would expect the values of the majority of own and cross adjustment coefficients to lie between zero and unity. For example, there should normally be some positive movement, to correct any existing disequilibrium gap, between the long-run desired values and the actual holdings of each asset. A value of the own adjustment coefficient greater than unity would imply over-adjustment to such a disequilibrium. Similar reasoning applies to the cross adjustment coefficients. In a complex asset choice system, it does not seem unreasonable to expect a positive disequilibrium gap, in one asset, to have a positive impact upon many, if not all, of the other assets in the portfolio.[5]

The theory of the process of adjustment is typically poorly specified and the adjustment coefficients are generally treated as constant parameters of the system, so that the speed of adjustment does not depend upon relative interest rates, the availability of liquid funds, or any other exogenous variable. Sharpe (1973) and Christofides (1976) have shown that the generalised adjustment scheme, specified in relation (10.6), can be derived from the hypothesis that economic agents choose their asset holdings, so as to minimise the quadratic cost function

$$AQC = \sum_{i=1}^{n} \Psi_i (X_{it} - X_{it}^*)^2 + \sum_{i=1}^{n} \omega_i (X_{it} - X_{it-1})^2 \tag{10.8}$$

subject to the constraint that the sum of actual asset holdings equals the sum of desired asset holdings. The first term in relation (10.8) represents the costs of being out of equilibrium for each of the assets, with Ψ_i equal to the cost per unit of disequilibrium. The second term represents the costs of adjustment for each asset, with ω_i equal to the cost per unit of adjustment in each case. The values taken by the parameters Ψ_i and ω_i determine the magnitudes of the adjustment coefficients.[6]

The Short-run Equation

Assuming that long-run desired asset holdings are determined by equation (10.1), and substituting for this relation in the adjustment mechanism in (10.6), we can derive flow demand equations for the change in asset holdings, between the current and previous period. These will take the form

$$\Delta X_{it} = \sum_{j=1}^{n} \sum_{k=1}^{n} \theta_{ik} f_{kj} R_{jt} + \sum_{k=1}^{n} \theta_{ik} c_k W_t - \sum_{k=1}^{n} \theta_{ik} X_{kt-1}$$

$$i = 1, \dots, n$$

Rearranging these flow equations, it is possible to derive short-run demand specifications for the stock of each asset at time t. These can be written as

$$X_{it} = \sum_{j=1}^{n} \eta_{ij} R_{jt} + \phi_i W_t + (1 - \theta_{ii}) X_{it-1} - \sum_{\substack{k=1 \\ k \neq i}}^{n} \theta_{ik} X_{kt-1} \qquad (10.9)$$

$$i = 1, \dots, n$$

with the demand for each asset dependent upon the set of rates of return, wealth and the lagged value of the stock of all assets in the portfolio. The η_{ij} and ϕ_i represent short-run, or impact, coefficients and are defined as follows

$$\eta_{ij} = \sum_{k=1}^{n} \theta_{ik} f_{kj} \qquad \phi_i = \sum_{k=1}^{n} \theta_{ik} c_k$$

They give the effect upon the dependent variable of a unit change in an explanatory variable, in the period in which the change occurs.

The system of equations in (10.9) can be rewritten in matrix notation as

$$X_t = \eta R_t + \phi W_t + (I - \theta)X_{t-1} \tag{10.10}$$

where $\eta = \theta F$, $\phi = \theta C$ and I is the identity matrix. From the estimates of the system given in (10.10), we can obtain values for the matrices η, ϕ and θ. The long-run coefficients, given by the matrices F and C, can then be determined by applying the formulae

$$F = \theta^{-1}\eta \qquad C = \theta^{-1}\phi$$

where θ^{-1} is the inverse of the matrix of adjustment coefficients. The long-run coefficients show the total increase in the stock of the choice variable, caused by a unit change in the explanatory variable, after all adjustment has taken place. In the simple partial adjustment model, we expect the magnitude of the short-run coefficient, on any independent variable, to be less than that of the long-run coefficient. In the generalised scheme, there is no guarantee that this will be the case, because the pattern of adjustment is dependent upon the sign and magnitude of both the own and the cross adjustment coefficients. The short-run and long-run values may even display different signs. Furthermore, even if the long-run rate of return coefficients display symmetry, the property may not carry over to the short-run coefficients, because the matrix of adjustment parameters cannot be assumed to be symmetric. However, we can impose cross-equation restrictions on the short-run coefficients, which are analogous to the conditions imposed upon the long-run coefficients, as outlined in (10.3).[7] We can therefore write

$$\sum_{i=1}^{n} \eta_{ij} = 0 \qquad \sum_{i=1}^{n} \phi_i = 1$$
$$\text{for all } j$$

A Portfolio Shares Model

The linear equation system described in equation (10.1) has the advantage of simplicity. However, the comparative static properties of such a system may be considered to be unrealistic: the response to a change in wealth does not depend upon the relative rates of return on the different assets, while the effect of a change in each of the return variables is independent of the overall level of wealth. An alternative approach, which removes these shortcomings, is to specify the asset demand equations in terms of portfolio shares, with the dependent variable deflated by wealth. Such a system of equations can be written as

$$\frac{X_i}{W} = c_i + \sum_{j=1}^{n} f_{ij} R_j \qquad i = 1, \ldots, n$$

The form of the equation implies that the demand for each asset is homogeneous of degree one in wealth. The system can be re-expressed as

$$X_i = \left(c_i + \sum_{j=1}^{n} f_{ij} R_j\right) W \qquad i = 1, \ldots, n$$

Such a reformulation involves several composite variables in rates of return and wealth. The comparative static properties of this model are more realistic than those implied by the simple linear model, with the response to a change in rates of return now dependent upon the total wealth of the portfolio holder and the effect of a change in wealth now influenced by the relative returns on the different assets. The cross-equation restrictions implied by this model are the same as those outlined in (10.3) for the simple linear model.

A PORTFOLIO MODEL FOR BANKS

The general portfolio model is particularly applicable to the empirical analysis of personal sector asset allocation decisions. When analysing the portfolio behaviour of banking institutions, some modifications have to be made to the basic model. These arise because of the special nature of the items in a bank's balance sheet, the form of which can be represented by the identity

Assets $\equiv$ Liabilities $+$ Net Worth

Net worth, or wealth, is very small for banks and principally comprises capital and reserves. For the most part, banks allocate borrowed money, so that it is more important to consider their total liabilities, which principally comprise deposits, rather than their net worth. Also, the general portfolio model assumes that agents act as price-takers in all markets, with interest rates exogenously determined. This need not always be true for a bank; in some markets, banks may act as rate-setters, with the quantity of such assets in their portfolios dependent upon the amount of the asset supplied by other market participants at the selected rate.[8] In addition, constraints may be placed upon the way in which the banks allocate their deposit holdings between different assets. The authorities normally impose reserve asset requirements on the banks, as well as implementing other policy measures at various times in order to influence the composition of the portfolio.[9] A consequence of such restrictions is that the items in a bank's balance sheet have to be dichotomised into a choice or decision set, held freely by the bank, and an exogenous set in which holdings are determined by extraneous factors. The allocation problem can become even more complex if we allow the banks to engage in liability, as well as asset management, so that elements of their liability holdings become part of the choice set.[10] In order to simplify the model of bank portfolio allocation, we shall ignore this possibility. Instead, we assume that the portfolio choice problem facing the banks is one of allocating a given total of net worth and liabilities among certain choice assets, subject to the restrictions imposed by the exogenous asset set. Accordingly, we replace the system, given in equation (10.1), by a specification of the form

$$X_i = \sum_{j=1}^{n} f_{ij} R_j - \sum_{q=1}^{m} b_{iq} X_q + \sum_{g=1}^{p} a_{ig} L_g + d_i NW \qquad (10.11)$$

$$i = 1, \ldots, n$$

where X_i is the quantity demanded of the ith choice asset, R_j is the rate of return on the jth choice asset, X_q is the quantity of the qth exogenously determined asset, L_g is the quantity of the gth liability in the portfolio and NW is the value of net worth. The f_{ij}, b_{iq}, a_{ig} and d_i are parameters of the model.

The balance sheet constraint takes the form

$$\sum_{i=1}^{n} X_i + \sum_{q=1}^{m} X_q \equiv \sum_{g=1}^{p} L_g + NW$$

Its imposition means that the parameters of the model are subject to a series of cross-equation restrictions. In this case, these restrictions will take the form

$$\sum_{i=1}^{n} f_{ij} = 0 \qquad \sum_{i=1}^{n} b_{iq} = 1 \qquad \sum_{i=1}^{n} a_{ig} = 1 \qquad \sum_{i=1}^{n} d_{i} = 1$$

$$\text{for all } j \qquad\qquad \text{for all } q \qquad\qquad \text{for all } g$$

Combining the exogenous asset, net worth and liability terms into one general exogenous variable, we can rewrite equation (10.11) as

$$X_i = \sum_{j=1}^{n} f_{ij} R_j + \sum_{s=1}^{m+p+1} c_{is} Z_s \qquad\qquad (10.12)$$
$$i = 1, \ldots, n$$

where Z_s refers to the sth exogenous balance sheet item and the c_{is} represent the parameters of the composite term. Assuming that the form, given in equation (10.12), can be used to represent the long-run demand equation for the desired level of each choice asset, we can substitute the relation into the generalised adjustment scheme, given in (10.6), and by manipulation obtain a system of short-run demand equations for the stock of each asset at time t. These can be written as

$$X_{it} = \sum_{j=1}^{n} \sum_{k=1}^{n} \theta_{ik} f_{kj} R_{jt} + \sum_{s=1}^{m+p+1} \sum_{k=1}^{n} \theta_{ik} c_{ks} Z_{st} + (1 - \theta_{ii}) X_{it-1}$$

$$- \sum_{\substack{k=1 \\ k \neq i}}^{n} \theta_{ik} X_{kt-1} \qquad\qquad (10.13)$$

$$i = 1, \ldots, n$$

The properties of the model are comparable with those of the general portfolio model discussed earlier.

AN INTEGRATED MODEL OF SAVINGS AND PORTFOLIO ALLOCATION

The Brainard–Tobin framework is concerned with the portfolio allocation of a given level of wealth, which is determined by previous-period asset holdings and current-period saving and capital gain accruals. By assuming that these different elements of wealth are predetermined, Brainard and Tobin separate the consumption–savings decision from the portfolio allocation problem, so that decisions about the accumulation of wealth are distinct from decisions about its allocation. Purvis (1978) argues that such a separation is over-restrictive and questions its validity when there are adjustment costs to changing the level of individual asset holdings. Instead, Purvis proposes an integrated model of savings and portfolio allocation, embodying the key features of the Brainard–Tobin approach, but in which wealth is no longer assumed to be predetermined. The simple wealth restriction is replaced by a wider budget constraint, in which asset holdings in the previous period, plus income, Y, received during the period, equal current-period asset holdings plus consumption, E, during the period. We can therefore replace the budget constraint, embodied in (10.2), with the relationship

$$\sum_{i=1}^{n} X_{it} + E_t = \sum_{i=1}^{n} X_{it-1} + Y_t$$

Purvis' model leads to a $(n+1)$ equation short-run system, involving consumption and asset flow demand relationships, which can be written in the form

$$E_t = \sum_{j=1}^{n} g_j R_{jt} + h_0 Y_t + \sum_{k=1}^{n} \tau_k X_{kt-1}$$

$$\Delta X_{it} = \sum_{j=1}^{n} \eta_{ij} R_{jt} + \phi_i Y_t - \sum_{k=1}^{n} \theta_{ik} X_{kt-1} \qquad i = 1, \ldots, n$$

The balance sheet requirement imposes restrictions upon the parameters of the system with

$$g_j + \sum_{i=1}^{n} \eta_{ij} = 0 \qquad h_0 + \sum_{i=1}^{n} \phi_i = 1 \qquad \tau_k - \sum_{i=1}^{n} \theta_{ik} = 0$$
$$\text{for all } j \qquad\qquad\qquad\qquad\qquad\qquad\qquad \text{for all } k$$

In the integrated model, consumption is therefore affected by the process of adjustment of actual towards desired asset holdings. The same variables, namely rates of return, income and asset holdings in the previous period, influence both consumption and asset flow demands. Smith (1978) questions the desirability of such a restriction and Owen (1981) extends the model to account for the possibility that there may exist variables which are relevant to the consumption–savings decision, but influence the portfolio allocation decision only to the extent that they affect the overall level of wealth to be allocated.

THE ESTIMATION OF PORTFOLIO MODELS

A system of empirical demand equations, derivable from a portfolio model of a particular sector, will take the form

$$X_i = \sum_{q=1}^{s} \Omega_{iq} H_q + \varepsilon_i \qquad i = 1, \ldots, n$$

where X_i refers to the ith choice variable of the system and H_q represents the qth predetermined variable, encompassing the set of rates of return, scale variables and lagged asset holding terms, which are viewed to be relevant to the decision process. The Ω_{iq} refer to the parameters of the system and ε_i represents the disturbance term, which takes account of all other unaccountable factors that may influence the demand for each asset. If all n equations of the system contain the same set of independent variables, single-equation estimation techniques, applied separately to each equation, will automatically ensure that the cross-equation parameter restrictions implied by the budget constraint are satisfied.[11] Furthermore, it is normally only necessary to estimate $(n-1)$ equations in the system. The form of the nth equation can be determined as a residual from the appropriate adding-up restrictions, so ensuring that the budget constraint is satisfied.[12] However, if particular variables are excluded from some of the equations, restricted estimation methods, involving the whole system, are required in order to ensure that the cross-equation restrictions are met. Such methods must normally also be used if symmetry and homogeneity restrictions are to be imposed upon the rate of return variables in the system of equations.

In addition to a consideration of the overall explanatory power of each of the equations, tests of the empirical validity of portfolio models tend to focus upon the sign and significance of the own and cross rate of return coefficients, and the magnitude of the own and cross adjustment coefficients. Unfortunately, as we shall see in the rest of this chapter, it is not easy to obtain meaningful results from fully-specified portfolio models. This is partly because of the large number of parameters which have to be estimated in such multi-asset models. The collinearity of many of the data series used, particularly for interest rates, means that the estimated coefficients are often imprecise. Furthermore, many models display extremely slow or unstable dynamic adjustment patterns.

FINANCIAL SECTOR MODELS

A knowledge of the behaviour of financial intermediaries, such as banks and building societies, is important because of their role in the determination of the money supply and the general transmission mechanism of monetary policy through the economy. Because of this need to understand the factors influencing the asset choice decisions of such institutions, a number of studies have analysed their behaviour using the portfolio approach. Much of this work emanates from the mean–variance model developed by Parkin (1970) in his study of the portfolio behaviour of the UK discount houses. Parkin attempts to explain, at the aggregate level, these institutions' holdings of call money, Treasury bills, commercial bills and other short-term assets. The demand functions for each asset are related to a constraint variable and the set of expected interest rates on the choice assets. Various ways of generating these expectations are considered, with the preferred specification involving the use of actual rates. Using quarterly data over the period 1955–67, a number of interest rate coefficients are found to be statistically significant, with the estimated values appearing to indicate that some of the assets in the portfolio are complements. Symmetry is imposed upon the cross interest rate coefficients in some versions of the model, although unconstrained estimation of the system suggests that this is not always a valid restriction.[13] Parkin tries to incorporate a generalised or interdependent adjustment mechanism into his model, but finds that this results in less satisfactory equations. Although the explanatory power of the estimated relations improves, they become dominated by the lagged dependent variable, with a consequent loss of precision in all the other coefficients. This outcome is attributed to the considerable degree of collinearity which exists between both the different interest rate series and the various lagged balance sheet terms. Courakis (1975) re-estimates Parkin's equations and tests for both symmetry and homogeneity of degree zero in the interest rate coefficients. These restrictions cannot be validated, and in comparison to Parkin's findings, a greater number of interest rate coefficients are found to be statistically insignificant.

Using a similar framework, the portfolio behaviour of the London Clearing Banks is analysed by Parkin *et al.* (1970) and Courakis (1974), using quarterly data over the period 1953–67. Call loans, Treasury bills, commercial bills and government bonds are selected to be the choice assets, with demand functions for these assets specified in terms of expected rates of return and the expected levels of the other items in the balance sheet, which are assumed to be exogenous to the decision process of the banks. Deposits and advances are the main items of the balance sheet treated in this way.[14] In the estimated equations, actual values are used to model expectations for both rates of return and balance sheet items. The return on bond holding is measured by the rate of interest on short-dated gilts and no attempt is made to incorporate an explicit measure of capital gains over the holding period. Parkin *et al.* are encouraged by the overall explanatory power of their specifications, with many of the interest rate coefficients found to be statistically significant. Courakis is again more sceptical of the validity of the portfolio approach. Using a variety of different specifications, which extend the basic Parkin *et al.* model, he concludes that none of the formulations can provide a satisfactory statistical explanation of bank behaviour over the data period. Many interest rate coefficient estimates are insignificantly different from zero, and the sign and magnitude of the various responses appears to be very sensitive to the particular specification estimated. The results differ markedly from those obtained by Parkin *et al.* and the general lack of robustness, in the estimated equations, makes it difficult to place much confidence in the pronouncements made by Parkin *et al.* on the substitutability and complementarity of different assets. Of course, the form of the mean–variance model implies that the estimated interest rate coefficients are functions of the variances and covariances of asset returns. If these are variable over the estimation period, instability will be introduced into the parameters of the estimated relationships.

Both Parkin *et al.* and Courakis exclude advances from the choice set of bank assets. In support of this treatment, they stress the alleged importance of demand factors to the determination of advances, and the ceilings imposed upon bank lending by the authorities for much of their data period. Nevertheless, such an approach can be criticised because it precludes, within a portfolio framework, any direct test of the determinants of advances. White (1975) formulates a model which distinguishes between loans that were typically not subject to credit restrictions in the 1960s and those which had controls imposed upon them at various times by the authorities. Included in the first category are loans to the public sector and those used to finance exports under official schemes. Since these were thought to be categories of advances which had been largely given on demand and where the banks had, as a result, exercised little or no effective control, they were treated by White as being exogenous to the decision process. Subtracting these exogenous advances from total advances leaves a category he defines as other advances, where controls were often imposed, but where, he argues, exogeneity is not necessarily a valid assumption. This is because the level of advances frequently diverged substantially from the level implied by the controls. Furthermore, he feels, to argue that these advances were wholly demand determined is unrealistic, as it implies that the banks put loans before everything else, regardless of the opportunity cost. In some specifications, White therefore treats these other advances as part of the choice set and finds that the results obtained, from quarterly data for deposit banks over the period 1963–70, lend support to this approach.

In another departure from Parkin *et al.* and Courakis, White also incorporates the Brainard-Tobin generalised adjustment scheme into some versions of his model. Again, the results display a lack of robustness and on the basis of the estimated coefficients it is difficult to judge between the static and dynamic versions of the model. The rate of return coefficients in many specifications are often insignificantly different from zero and no support is found for the hypothesis of symmetric interest rate effects. In the dynamic versions of the model, the largest own adjustment coefficients are found in the equations for call loans and other advances. White argues that this is not unreasonable because call loans are the most liquid of non-cash assets, while the banks generally prefer to make advances. Unfortunately, the sign and magnitude of many of the cross adjustment parameters is unrealistic. Implausibly large negative signs are displayed by some terms, implying that increases in the holdings of one asset are exaggerated as a result of a shortage (below the desired level) of some other asset.

Bewley (1981) attempts to resolve some of the problems involved in the classification of advances, by developing a model which allows the status of advances to vary according to the regime in force; advances are assumed to be determined exogenously when lending controls exist and are treated as part of the choice set when these controls are inoperative. The model incorporates the generalised adjustment system and is estimated using monthly data over the period 1963–71. The majority of interest rate coefficient estimates are again statistically insignificant and Bewley highlights the problem of the negative own rate sign response in the bond equation. This apparently perverse result is also present in some of White's results and is consistent with the view that the banks have extrapolative expectations in the short run and sell bonds, as the rate of interest rises, in order to avoid further capital losses.

Berndt *et al.* (1980) re-estimate the model used by Parkin *et al.* and reject their assumed hypothesis of a non-autocorrelated error term. Using an estimation technique which explicitly takes account of autocorrelation in the residuals, they find that the estimated coefficients differ considerably from those obtained by Parkin *et al.* Although the presence of autocorrelation probably reflects the omission of a dynamic adjustment process from the model, their findings illustrate, even more conclusively, that the results obtained from portfolio studies are strongly affected by the form of the specification and the estimation procedures adopted. All the above studies test models of portfolio behaviour using aggregate data on groups of banks. Courakis (1980) criticises this practice, arguing that the models should be tested on data for individual banks. A mean–variance model is formulated and tested using data on individual clearing banks over the period 1959–67. The results are not uniform between the different banks, indicating that individual institutions may respond in different ways to changes in rates of return and exogenous balance sheet items.

Spencer (1984) estimates a model of bank behaviour, under the Competition and Credit Control conventions, for the period 1972–80. The choice set assets are assumed to be cash balances, reserve assets, local authority deposits, gilts, foreign currency assets net of liabilities and the money market position, as represented by net claims in the inter-bank market less certificate of deposit issues. In contrast to the models estimated using pre-1971 data, both asset and liability management is therefore allowed. The exogenous items of the balance sheet are taken to be advances, retail sterling deposits and other liabilities including net worth. It is assumed that cash and reserve assets are held for precautionary purposes to meet outflows of funds and consequently these items are modelled in a different way to the other choice items, where risk–return factors are paramount. The overall explanatory power of the equations is high, with the own rate response coefficients all significant and positively signed. The symmetry restriction is imposed upon the cross rate responses, the coefficients of which are negatively signed and nearly always significantly different from zero. The results indicate that the immediate impact of changes in both retail deposits and advances is felt mainly in the holdings of cash and reserve assets, and in the money market position, whereas the long-run effect is concentrated upon holdings of local authority deposits and gilts.

Models of the portfolio behaviour of life assurance companies have been developed by Ryan (1973) and Honohan (1980). Such institutions hold large portfolios, comprising equities, gilts, company securites and property. Ryan specifies a simple partial adjustment model, in which net asset acquisitions are related to the change in wealth and expected yields, with the latter proxied by autoregressive schemes and actual returns. The results are not particularly conclusive and illustrate the multicollinearity problems which are present in such models. Honohan applies a mean–variance model to the investment portfolios of life assurance companies in the UK. Prior information is used to generate series for the variances and covariances of the different asset yields, which are then used to obtain 'mixed' estimates of the parameters of the demand equation. The theory leads to a non-linear system of equations, but the results are disappointing and do not lend support to the mean–variance model. Honohan also amends the basic model to allow for the possibility that life assurance companies have some monopoly power in the market, with the return on each asset related to the demands of the institutions in the market.

The behaviour of building societies has been investigated in a number of studies, including Ghosh and Parkin (1972), O'Herlihy and Spencer (1972), Foster (1975) and Anderson and Hendry (1984). Foster is solely concerned with the demand for building society share and deposit accounts. Using data for the period 1961–73, the percentage change in building society deposits is shown to be positively related to the own interest rate, the expected rate of inflation and the level of personal disposable income, and negatively related to the interest rate on bank deposits. Ghosh and Parkin specify a mean–variance portfolio model of building society behaviour, in which the choice items are Treasury bills, local authority bills, long-term government securities, local authority securities, mortgages, and shares and deposits. The deposit and mortgage rates are assumed to be exogenous to the decision process of individual societies. The explanatory power of most equations is good and there are several significant interest rate coefficients of the 'correct' *a priori* sign. The own rate response coefficients in the mortgage and share and deposit equations are particularly well-determined.

O'Herlihy and Spencer do not specify a full portfolio model, but consider the four main financial flows affecting building societies: deposit inflows, deposit withdrawals, mortgage advances and mortgage repayments. In addition, equations are specified for the mortgate rate and the rate of interest offered on shares and deposits. The equations are estimated using quarterly data over the period 1955–70. The flows of gross receipts and withdrawals, into and out of building societies, are found to be income elastic and sensitive to changes in the standard rate of income tax, the share and deposit interest rate and the rate of return on competing assets. The lags in adjustment are quite long, with flows of new deposits taking over a year to adjust fully to a change in one of the determining factors. The flow of new mortgages, in real terms, is found to be income elastic, although consumers appear to react quite slowly to changes in real income. The mortgage interest rate is insignificant, but mortgage rationing, as represented by a dummy variable, is found to be an important factor in determining the amount of funds advanced over the estimation period. A large element of mortgage repayments is due to the early termination of mortgages. Changes in the mortgage rate occur when the share and deposit rate is varied, with the ultimate response greater than the change in the latter rate. Changes in the share and deposit rate take place when the societies' liquidity or reserve ratios warrant such a change, although the adjustment is extremely slow.

The Anderson and Hendry model is also not in the pure portfolio tradition. Building societies are assumed to have the objective of meeting mortgage demand at a reasonable cost, taking into account the conflicting interests of borrowers and lenders. A cost function is specified, incorporating both disequilibrium and adjustment costs: the former consists of the costs of not meeting mortgage demand and of deviating from the long-run planned portfolio, while the latter consists of the costs of changing both mortgage lending and interest rates. Planned values for mortgage levels, the mortgage rate and the deposit rate are chosen so as to minimise the cost function, assuming that some information is known about the likely level of mortgage demand and the supply of deposits. Mortgage rationing exists if there is a deficiency of mortgage advances, relative to the perception that building societies have of the demand for mortgages. General distributed lag formulations are used by Anderson and Hendry to develop a series of equations for building society mortgages and deposits, and their associated interest rates. The key determining variables in the equation for mortgages are real disposable income, the post-tax mortgage rate, the rate of inflation and house price inflation. An error-correction term implies a long-run proportionate relationship between mortgage lending and building society shares and deposits. The supply of deposits equation indicates the importance of interest rate differentials to the societies' inflows. The deposit rate responds positively to movements in competing interest rates and the excess demand for mortgages, and is negatively related to the societies' liquidity position, while the mortgage rate is modelled as a variable mark-up over the deposit rate. The extent of the mark-up depends upon factors such as the tax rate, the societies' reserve ratio and other rates of interest.

PERSONAL SECTOR MODELS

There are fewer portfolio models specifically concerned with the personal sector. One of the earliest studies was that of Barrett *et al.* (1975), who analyse the demand for safe capital-certain non-marketable financial assets by the personal sector. The model is based upon the work of Gray and Parkin (1973), which we discussed in Chapter 3, and focuses on the stochastic nature of cash requirements, rather than the stochastic nature of asset yields, as the source of asset diversification. The choice set comprises a number of assets, including cash plus bank current accounts, bank time deposits, building society shares and deposits, Premium Savings Bonds, National Savings Certificates and National Savings Bank Ordinary Accounts. Demand functions for each asset are specified in terms of rates of interest, wealth and a variable representing the sum of consumer expenditure and tax payments, which is used as a proxy for the likely size of cash requirements. A dynamic version of the model, incorporating lagged dependent variables, is also estimated. The results of this precautionary approach are compared with the estimates obtained from a standard mean–variance model, with the former found to offer an improved explanation of all but one asset holding. However, many of the coefficient estimates display 'perverse' signs, again reflecting the problems inherent in the portfolio approach.

   Weale (1986) uses a portfolio model to analyse the demand for short-term capital-certain financial assets by the personal sector. A dynamic system of equations is specified in terms of portfolio shares and estimated for six different money and near-money assets: notes and coin, bank sight deposits, bank time deposits, savings bank deposits, building society deposits and local authority deposits. Using quarterly data for the period 1967–81, the explanatory power of the system is good, although several restrictions are imposed upon the estimated coefficients. Weale argues that his results do not suggest any sharp distinction, in terms of their degree of substitutability, between the various categories of asset.

Barr and Cuthbertson (1990, 1991) also use a portfolio approach to analyse the liquid asset holdings of the personal sector. The asset categories considered are notes and coin, bank sight deposits, bank time deposits, building society deposits and national savings investment accounts. Attempts were made to include other categories of national savings, such as savings certificates, and assets such as local authority temporary debt, but these proved difficult to model and were excluded from the final analysis. Cointegration methods are used to analyse the long-run portfolio share equations for each asset, using quarterly data for the period 1977–86. The estimated equations relate portfolio shares to the real return on each asset (the nominal return minus expected inflation), real wealth, a time trend and the expected level of transactions, as proxied by consumer expenditure. Symmetry and homogeneity restrictions are imposed upon the long-run rate of return coefficients; the estimates suggest that time deposits, building society deposits and national savings investment accounts are substitutes, with the own rate responses of the correct sign and larger than the cross rate effects in each case. An increase in the inflation rate reduces holdings of both notes and coin and sight deposits. A role is found for both wealth and expenditure; notes and coin and sight deposits appear to be inferior goods with respect to wealth and normal goods with respect to expenditure, while the reverse is true for the other three assets. The time trend variable captures a move into sight deposits and away from time deposits, presumably reflecting the increase in interest-bearing sight deposits that occurred over the data period. The lagged values of the residuals from the long-run regressions form error-correction terms for use in the short-run equations for each asset. These equations also involve differenced terms in the different explanatory variables.

Owen (1985, 1986) develops a model of UK personal sector behaviour, which attempts to integrate the portfolio allocation decision with the consumption–savings decision. The extension of the basic model in this way was considered earlier in this chapter and has also been applied to a model of household behaviour for the US economy by Backus and Purvis (1980). Owen uses an integrated approach to model equations for consumer expenditure on non-durables and the changes in the holdings of liquid assets, illiquid financial assets, life assurance and pension funds, consumer durables, the stock of dwellings, short-term loans and loans for house purchase. The dependent variable, in each case, is specified in real terms and explained in terms of own and cross rates of return, relative price indices, income, unemployment, capital gains and inflation variables and lagged stock terms. Quarterly data for the period 1963–78 is used to estimate the model and the results confirm the problems found in the standard portfolio models, with many of the parameter estimates not very precisely determined and the adjustment coefficients indicating very slow responses to own asset discrepancies.

Matthews and Minford (1980) also develop an integrated portfolio model, in which financial asset and real expenditure decisions are analysed together. A sequential decision-tree is assumed, involving a three-stage allocation process. The first stage analyses the choice between real and financial assets, while the second stage considers the division of total financial assets into liquid and non-liquid components. The demand for individual assets is considered in the third stage of the decision process. The model is estimated, using annual data for the UK, over the period 1946–74 and the results lend support to the approach adopted. A similar sequential model is used by Matthews (1984) to analyse private sector expenditure and asset accumulation in the inter-war period.

MULTI-SECTOR MODELS

There have been few empirical attempts to apply fully-specified portfolio models to the UK monetary sector in its entirety. An early multi-sector model was developed by Clayton *et al.* (1974). They consider nine distinct sectors (public, discount houses, deposit banks, other banks, building societies, other financial institutions, companies, personal, overseas) and sixteen different categories of assets and liabilities. The objective of each agent or institution is implicitly assumed to be the maximisation of expected net revenue and within this framework long-run demand functions are specified for the choice assets of each sector in terms of net worth, expected rates of return (including capital gains) and, where applicable, expected exogenous asset and liability values. In practice, expected values for both rates of return and balance sheet holdings are proxied by actual values. The dynamics of the allocation process is neglected, with no adjustment mechanism specified for any of the estimated relations. Unfortunately, the empirical results are largely disappointing. Most sectors have few well-specified equations; many estimated coefficients are insignificant, while a large number of own interest rate responses are negative.

Melitz and Sterdyniak (1979) develop a model of the UK monetary sector, in which behavioural equations are specified for the demand for broad money and the private sector's demands for government securities and bank loans. The equations are estimated using quarterly data for the period 1962–74, with the explanatory variables in each case drawn from real income, interest rates, the anticipated rate of inflation and dummy variables representing lending restrictions and the Competition and Credit Control reforms. The demand for government securities proved particularly difficult to model, with the positively-signed coefficient on the bond rate the only significant rate of return variable in the equation. The demand for money is negatively related to the overseas interest rate and the anticipated rate of inflation, while bank borrowing responds positively to anticipated inflation and is negatively related to the lending rate. The lending controls variable has a negative effect upon both bank borrowing and money holdings, whereas the Competition and Credit Control dummy has a positive effect in both equations.

A more recent study by Green (1984) follows the approach of a US study by Backus *et al.* (1980). A model of the monetary sector is specified, involving five sectors (banks, discount houses, non-bank private, overseas and government) and twelve different assets. The model is based upon a flow of funds matrix, in which each row (*i*) is an asset market and each column (*j*) is a sector. Each cell (*i, j*) in the matrix therefore indicates net purchases or sales of asset *i*, by sector *j*, over the decision period. Net liabilities enter as negative assets. The row sums of the matrix are zero, since net purchases of an asset must equal net sales, while each column (*j*) sums to the *j*th sector's surplus, or its net acquisition of financial assets. Each cell therefore represents a flow variable to be explained by a short-run asset demand or supply function.[15] The formal model develops these short-run functions from a Brainard–Tobin generalised adjustment scheme and a long-run stock demand function, in which desired demand depends upon interest rates, the appropriate constraint variable and other exogenous variables. In addition, an allowance is made for the possibility that agents may be forced 'off' their short-run demand curves, if interest rates are not able to move freely to clear all markets. In this way, disequilibrium in one market can lead to rationing and spillover effects in other markets. Equilibrium values for the various market interest rates can be determined from the short-run market clearing conditions for each asset. Green solves the model, assuming that the Treasury bill rate, the certificate of deposit rate, the loan rate and the equity yield are market determined, with the government bond yield, the call money rate and the exchange rate exogenously determined. The model is used to estimate demand and supply equations for the different sectors, using monthly data for the period 1972–7. The results are encouraging, given the problems posed by the need to estimate a large number of coefficients and the collinearity of the interest rate data. Although no statistically significant interest rate effects are isolated in the banking sector, a substantial proportion of the long-run interest rate responses, in the asset demand equations of the other sectors, are correctly signed and significantly different from zero. Similarly, apart from the case of the discount market equations, the terms in the adjustment coefficient matrices are generally sensibly signed.

Large Macro Models

The portfolio approach is also central to many of the large UK macro models. Keating (1985) describes a version of the monetary sector of the London Business School model, which encompasses nine distinct sub-sectors (persons, industrial and commercial companies, pension funds and insurance companies, building societies, banks, unit and investment trusts, other financial institutions, public, overseas) and thirteen different categories of assets and liabilities. No formal optimising model is developed for the banks and building societies. The banks are assumed to receive non-interest-bearing sight deposits and to set the interest rates paid on other deposits and charged on loans at given mark-ups above or below the market clearing bill rate. The building societies are treated in a similar way. The portfolio choice behaviour of the personal, company and pension fund-insurance sectors, is based, in each case, upon an amended mean–variance model, in which utility is also related to the quantity of each asset held.[16] In addition, adjustment costs are incorporated directly into the objective function, a practice which is a departure from the traditional Brainard–Tobin approach. The objective function is maximised subject to the relevant budget constraint, which in each case equals the sector's current-period income net of expenditure, plus previous-period asset and liability holdings, revalued to take account of current market prices. These prices are determined endogenously within the model. The optimisation process produces a relation in which the demand for each asset is dependent upon the relevant constraint variable, relative rates of return and the asset holdings of the previous period. The asset yields comprise three separate elements; the nominal interest rate, the expected capital gain or loss and a constant term representing the other non-pecuniary factors which provide utility from asset holding. The model is extended to allow for the possibility of rationing in particular markets, with consideration also given to the resulting spillover effects elsewhere in the system. In the personal sector, the assets subject to rationing are assumed to be loans for house purchase, other categories of bank loans, hire purchase loans and foreign currency assets (because of exchange controls prior to 1979). The results are unconvincing and there is evidence of misspecification in some asset demand functions, with many of the estimated equations dominated by the lagged dependent variable. In other equations, the coefficients are constrained to take particular values and are not freely estimated.[17]

The portfolio approach to analysing the demand for financial assets is particularly well-established in the Treasury model and has been the basis of several versions of the monetary sector since the late 1970s. The principal features of the monetary model were first described by Spencer and Mowl (1978) and the 1980 vintage of the model is described in Thompson (1984).[18] In this version, the banking and non-bank private sectors are both analysed in detail. The latter is defined to comprise persons, companies and non-bank financial intermediaries such as the building societies. The private sector's net financial wealth, in each period, is calculated by adding the current-period financial surplus to the existing stock of wealth, revalued to take account of the capital gains or losses resulting from movements in interest rates. Net wealth is allocated between government bonds, national savings and liquid assets, while decisions are also taken about the level of bank borrowing and other liability holdings.

Bank borrowing is disaggregated into that by persons, companies and non-bank financial intermediaries. A disequilibrium model is used to explain bank advances to persons; the outstanding quantity of advances is a weighted average of both demand and supply effects, where the weights themselves are variable and depend upon the degree of market disequilibrium. The demand for advances is negatively related to the loan rate, but responds positively to movements in real personal disposable income, the short rate as represented by the local authority rate, the expected rate of inflation and the level of borrowing in the previous period. The supply of advances is related solely to borrowing in the previous period, although dummy variables representing credit controls and the Competition and Credit Control banking reforms are included in the supply function in the original Spencer and Mowl study. Company borrowing and loans to other financial institutions are each modelled by a 'reduced form' in which demand factors are predominant. Included among the determining variables in the company lending equation is the arbitrage return from 'round-tripping', which is measured as the (positive) differential between the short rate and the bank lending rate.

An attempt is also made to model the private sector's demand for long-term government securities. The flow demand for gilts is negatively related to the market value of stock already held, but increases in line with improvements in both the expected relative return on bonds and the level of, and change in, gross financial private sector wealth (net wealth plus bank borrowing and other liabilities). The expected relative return on bonds is measured by the differential between the long rate (plus expected capital gains) and the short rate. Expected capital gains respond positively to changes in the current long rate and are negatively related to the current short rate, the expected change in prices and the ratio of the PSBR to the net worth of the public sector. The coefficients of the relation are imposed and the inclusion of lagged independent variables in the specification, with coefficients of the opposite sign to the current-period effects, ensures that permanent changes in these variables do not induce lasting expectations of capital gains or losses. The modelling of expected capital gains, in this way, appears to mirror the Keynesian belief that individuals have regressive interest rate expectations: the higher the level of interest rates and the greater the *ex ante* differential between the long rate and the short rate, the greater is the expectation of capital gains.

Of the other private sector portfolio decisions, flows into national savings are related to the personal sector's financial surplus, while holdings of liquid assets are determined as a residual from the sectoral budget identity. A further decision process is hypothesised in order to allocate the liquid assets aggregate among its constituent items. Five categories of asset are distinguished: non-bank holdings of Treasury and local authority bills, notes and coin, sight deposits, time deposits and 'parallel money' (local authority deposits and certificates of deposit). Of these items, time deposits are treated as the residual asset. Each of the other aggregates is related to demand factors, such as total expenditure and relative interest rates, as well as total liquid assets. This disaggregation enables the narrow money aggregate, $M1$, to be determined as the sum of the notes and coin and sight deposit holdings of the private sector. No explicit demand function is modelled for sterling $M3$ and the practice of specifying relations for all of the major asset choice decisions within the sector, except broad money, is a reflection of the problems which empirical investigators have encountered in their search for a stable function for this aggregate. Finally, within the non-bank private sector, separate equations are specified for building society shares and deposits, the stock of mortgages outstanding, repayments of principal to the societies and the ratio of their mortgage advances to average earnings.

The modelling of bank behaviour has similarities with the approach of Spencer (1984) which we discussed earlier in this chapter. The banks are assumed to set interest rates oligopolistically in the retail market, accepting the deposits that are offered to them at these rates. In addition, as already stated, bank lending to the private sector is modelled as a compromise between demand and supply variables. Given this information, and after allowing for Special Deposit calls, reserve asset requirements and non-deposit liabilities, the other items in the portfolio are allocated in such a way as to reconcile the deposit and loan aggregates, and satisfy the balance sheet requirement. The banks are assumed to have several possible options: they can bid for certificates of deposit, alter net foreign currency liabilities, or else change their holdings of notes and coin, excess reserves, local authority debt and gilts. The banks are therefore able to engage in both asset and liability-side portfolio management, and the ultimate choice among these options is based to a large extent upon relative costs and returns, as measured by the respective interest rates. Although certificates of deposit are treated as the residual item of the balance sheet, the banks have complete control over their issue and can accordingly exert an independent supply-side influence upon sterling $M3$. The supply of local authority deposits, which is the other component of 'parallel money', is largely determined by the financing requirements of local authorities. Hence, the total supply of 'parallel money' market assets can be equated with the private sector's demand function, to yield an equilibrium stock and interest rate for certificates of deposit. Sterling $M3$ can then be determined by adding private sector time deposit and certificate of deposit holdings to the demand-determined $M1$ aggregate.

The broad money aggregate is therefore implicit in the overall model and is determined as the residual which ensures consistency among the other allocation decisions of the non-bank private and banking sectors. In this way, both demand and supply factors exert an influence upon the quantity of money, and the money stock cannot be assumed to be solely demand determined by the non-bank private sector. Nevertheless, demand factors do have some influence upon the broad money stock because of the way in which the other portfolio decisions of the private sector are analysed. Factors such as wealth, income and relative interest rates, which affect these other allocation decisions, will exert an indirect influence upon money holdings.

Many revisions have been made since this initial analysis of the monetary sector of the Treasury model. The 1989 version of the model, described in Mellis *et al.* (1989), adopts a more simplified structure, although the dynamic specification of individual equations is typically more intricate and often based upon the general distributed lag approach. In addition, cointegration techniques are used to examine the long-run properties of some equations. Most equations are estimated using quarterly data over the past twenty years. A central role in the modelling of the monetary sector is played by the liquid asset holdings of the personal sector, which are now defined to comprise national savings, bank deposits and building society shares and deposits.[19] A sequential decision-tree is assumed, with the total liquid assets portfolio modelled by one equation and a separate set of equations then used to allocate these holdings across the three constituent assets.[20]

The main determinants of total real liquid asset holdings are real personal sector gross financial wealth, real personal disposable income which measures transactions requirements, the rate of return on liquid assets, the post-tax three-month inter-bank rate and the post-tax return on government securities. The rate of return on liquid assets is constructed as a weighted average of the returns on each of the constituent components, while the other two return variables are used to measure the opportunity cost yield on competing short and long-term assets. The return on government bonds is defined to include a measure of the expected capital gain on gilts, which is taken to be exogenously determined in this version, in order to alleviate the problems inherent in the modelling of the variable. The preferred equation includes an error-correction term in the ratio of lagged real liquid asset holdings to lagged real gross financial wealth, and a series of differenced and lagged terms in accordance with the 'general to specific' modelling approach. The coefficients imply that changes in wealth due to asset revaluations have a much smaller effect upon holdings of liquid assets than changes due to new saving. The coefficient estimates on the rate of return variables all display the 'correct' sign and the restriction of homogeneity of degree zero is accepted by the data, implying that equal changes in all rates of return have no effect upon the demand for liquid assets.

The individual components of personal sector liquid assets are modelled using a fully-specified portfolio model; equations are estimated for the change in the proportion of liquid assets held in bank deposits and in building society share and deposit accounts, with national savings fulfilling the role of residual. In the long run, these portfolio shares are assumed to depend upon the relative rates of return on the different assets. No role is found for income in this allocation decision. Lagged portfolio shares and a term in the inverse of the change in the size of the portfolio are included in the estimated equations in order to make the model dynamic. The results imply a very slow speed of adjustment to the long-run solution. Both bank and building society deposits act as buffer stocks when total liquid asset holdings rise, resulting in a fall in the national savings share in the short run. All six of the estimated interest rate coefficients are of the 'correct' sign, displaying positive own rate, and negative cross rate, responses. In five of these cases, the interest rate coefficients are also statistically significant. The restriction of homogeneity of degree zero is imposed upon the interest rate coefficients in both equations, although it is not accepted by the data in the bank deposits equation. Symmetrical interest rate responses are not imposed and are not supported by the data.

No formal model of bank or building society behaviour is developed, but a series of equations is specified for the different types of lending undertaken by these institutions. Four categories of bank lending are distinguished: loans to the personal sector for house purchase, other loans to the personal sector, lending to industrial and commercial companies and loans to other financial institutions. The share of lending for house purchase in total bank lending is positively related to both the total amount of lending and the relative profitability of mortgage lending, as represented by the differential between the mortgage rate and the inter-bank rate. In addition, a dummy variable is included in order to capture the banks' expansion in this market in the early 1980s. The form of the specification appears to indicate that this category of lending is predominantly determined by supply factors. The equation for other personal sector bank lending has proved more problematical, with the preferred specification involving a mix of both demand and supply variables. Cointegration techniques are used to analyse the long-run form of the equation; as well as price homogeneity, a long-run income elasticity of unity is imposed upon the relation. Other significant variables are real personal net financial wealth, real interest rates and various terms representing mortgage rationing, hire purchase availability, the 'corset' controls on the growth of interest-bearing deposits, Special Deposit calls and the Competition and Credit Control reforms. The residuals from the long-run cointegrating regression form an error-correction term for use in the short-run equation, with the dynamics of the relation also captured by various differenced terms in both the dependent variable and real income.

Bank lending to industrial and commercial companies is modelled by an equation in which the growth in lending, in real terms, is related to the growth in an expenditure variable, a 'corset' variable and an error-correction term, based upon the inter-bank rate and the ratio of bank lending to companies to the total stock borrowing requirement of the company sector. The form of this term, which implies a long-run proportionate relationship between such lending and the borrowing requirement, is derived from the application of cointegration techniques to the data set. Increases in the interest rate have a negative effect upon lending and the overall form of the equation implies that this category of lending is demand determined. Bank advances to other financial institutions are modelled by an equation in which present-period lending is related to lending in the previous period, an expenditure variable, the inter-bank rate lagged two periods and 'corset' and Competition and Credit Control dummy variables. An equation is also specified for building society mortgages outstanding. This is based upon an error-correction model, in which a long-run proportionate relationship is assumed between the stock of mortgages and the share and deposit liabilities of the building societies. Within this relationship, the growth in mortgages outstanding is also determined by the growth in the previous period in both mortgages and shares and deposits, the current and lagged mortgage rate, the value of council house sales and the growth over the previous two periods in both real personal disposable income and new house prices. Although the equation can be viewed as a 'reduced form' relationship, encompassing both demand and supply influences upon mortgage levels, the only demand influence which has an effect in the long run is the mortgage rate.

An equation is modelled for the quantity of notes and coin in circulation, reflecting the fact that the demand for currency has proved to be an easier aggregate to model than those forms of money which incorporate bank deposits. The relation estimated is a transactions-based specification, in which cash balances, in real terms, are determined by holdings in the previous period, real consumer non-durable expenditure, the lagged inflation rate, the number of cash dispensers, the proportion of manual workers in the total employed and an opportunity cost variable. The latter is represented by the current and lagged post-tax interest rate on seven-day bank deposits. Cash holdings are economised when increases occur in the rate of inflation or interest rates. Financial innovation, represented by the number of cash dispensers, also reduces balances, while a fall in the proportion of manual workers in the total workforce has a similar effect, because more people in this group are likely to receive their incomes in cash on a weekly basis. A unitary long-run elasticity is assumed with respect to the real expenditure variable and a long-run interest elasticity of minus one is also imposed upon the equation.[21] Summation of notes and coin in circulation with the exogenously determined bankers' balances at the Bank of England, enables the narrow $M0$ monetary aggregate to be determined.

Versions of the Treasury monetary model, current in the mid-1980s, specified explicit equations for both $M1$ and sterling $M3$, but in the 1989 version no consideration is given to either of these aggregates. Instead, the model acknowledges the increasing similarity between the activities of banks and building societies, by focusing upon the wider $M4$ aggregate, which also includes private sector deposits with the building societies. Underlying this change is a belief that the velocity of $M4$ may have exhibited greater stability than that of $M3$ in recent years. However, no single equation is modelled for $M4$; instead the monetary aggregate is determined, on a sectoral basis, from the summation of notes and coin in circulation, personal sector bank deposits, building society shares and deposits and company sector holdings of $M4$. The holdings of the latter, in real terms, are assumed to depend upon the real value of gross company sector wealth, a bank lending variable, the rate of inflation and the domestic inter-bank rate relative to the 'world' interest rate. It is argued, this sectoral approach to the modelling of broad money is desirable because of the widely differing growth rates of the individual components of $M4$.

There is no explicit demand equation for long-term government securities in the model. This probably reflects the difficulties inherent in the modelling of such a relationship, which we alluded to in our discussion of the 1980 version of the Treasury model, and which have also been highlighted by the other studies of bond holdings considered in Chapter 9. Instead, gilt purchases by the private sector (now defined to exclude building societies) are determined as a residual from the government budget constraint and the related accounting identities which link gilt sales to the PSBR, the change in $M4$, the change in national savings and the change in bank and building society lending. Gilt purchases by the personal sector are taken to comprise one-quarter of total sales to the non-bank private sector. As yet, no satisfactory model of equity holdings has been developed and purchases of equities by the personal sector are assumed to be exogenously determined.

11 Summary and Conclusions

The many changes that occurred in the format of the monetary sector of the Treasury model in the 1980s are indicative of the difficulties which are inherent in the modelling of asset demand equations. The multi-asset portfolio approach, although theoretically appealing, has not as yet proved to be empirically tractable for most sectors. The limitations of the available aggregate time-series data, and the complications involved in the simultaneous estimation of large systems of equations, have prevented any large-scale development of empirical work on financial systems along these lines. Much of the difficulty in estimating financial models can be traced to the high degree of multicollinearity among the variables. Although it is not hard to find asset demand equations which fit the data well, the coefficients on individual variables cannot be reliably estimated. In the Treasury model, the problems are to some extent alleviated by the imposition of specific separability restrictions on the asset aggregation scheme adopted, and the consequent development of a sequential decision-tree framework within which to analyse the allocation process. Such an approach increases the number of asset allocation decisions which have to be considered, but reduces the number of variables that are relevant to each stage of the decision process. However, it is doubtful whether the multi-equation portfolio approach has yielded empirical results that have really been significantly different from, or superior to, those obtained by single-equation studies. One solution to this problem may lie in the use of 'mixed' estimation techniques, which use prior information about the model coefficients to augment the sample data. This prior information can be obtained from a variety of sources: theoretical calculations, cross-section studies, previous time-series studies on different data, or even practical experience. Such an approach was adopted by Backus *et al.* (1980) in a study of the US financial system, using the method pioneered by Smith and Brainard (1976), while Honohan (1980) has used similar techniques to analyse UK life assurance companies.

In relation to the modelling of particular asset demand functions, more specific problems are posed by the need to generate a series for

167

expected capital gains in the demand equation for government bonds, by the treatment of disequilibrium and credit rationing in the loans market and, more fundamentally, by the attempts to isolate stable demand functions for the different monetary aggregates. Since the mid-1970s, empirical studies of the demand for money function have been plagued by instability and predictive failure. These findings are in marked contrast to those obtained by earlier studies, using 1950s and 1960s data, where a stable demand function was the norm. A variety of different explanations have been suggested for this apparent break-down in the relationship, involving both the consideration of new explanatory variables and the respecification of the dynamic form of the short-run equation. Particular suggestions hinge around the roles of inflation, the own return on money, interest rate volatility, financial innovation, competition and deregulation in the banking system, policy regime changes, measurement problems, disequilibrium money and the notion of money as a buffer stock.

The 1970s and 1980s witnessed a series of economic, financial and institutional developments which had substantial implications for the demand for money. Key economic variables, such as the level of nominal interest rates and the rate of inflation, fluctuated considerably and at times reached historically-high levels. The number of bank current accounts increased substantially and interest-bearing sight deposits became the major element of narrow money balances. Cash management behaviour was influenced by these and other forms of financial innovation, and the improvements in transactions technology, which led to the increased use of credit and debit cards and cash-dispensing machines. The activities of banks and building societies became more integrated, with the latter developing their own cheque book facilities, cheque guarantee cards and cash-point facilities linked to deposit accounts. This development rendered increasingly mean-ingless those money supply statistics, such as $M1$ and $M3$, which exclude deposits with the building societies. Over the years, the range of accounts offered by the banks and building societies has become very similar and highly substitutable, yet the traditional money supply aggregates are affected if individual depositors transfer funds between the two sets of institutions. In the late 1980s, such considerations led to a switch of emphasis to the very narrow $M0$ measure of money, which excludes all deposits and the all-encompassing $M4$ aggregate, which includes deposits with both banks and building societies.

Regulatory and policy regime changes affecting the money market have been frequent, beginning in 1971 with the introduction of the

Competition and Credit Control regime of monetary control. The 1970s also saw the imposition of the 'corset' controls on the growth of bank deposits; these controls distorted the money supply figures and there was a considerable reintermediation of funds back into mainstream bank accounts when they were finally removed in 1980. The change from fixed to flexible exchange rates in 1972 and the abolition of exchange controls in 1979 also had implications for the money supply. Underlying these developments, throughout the 1970s, was the gradual move towards a policy of money supply control. The authorities first began to show an interest in controlling the quantity of money in the mid-1970s; a policy that was partly justified by the apparent success which empiricists had enjoyed in isolating a stable demand for money function for the prior period. In 1976, this policy was made more formal, when explicit monetary targets were adopted for the first time. Targeting the rate of growth of the money supply continued to be the focus of monetary policy until the mid-1980s.

Somewhat ironically, it has been argued that the breakdown of the empirical demand for money function in the 1970s broadly coincided with the move towards a policy of money supply control. This fact is acknowledged in Goodhart (1981) and has formed the basis of 'Goodhart's Law', which states that any observed statistical regularity is likely to prove unreliable if it is used for policy control purposes. The evidence from both the UK and US would seem to support this hypothesis. In the late 1970s and early 1980s, the main targeted aggregate in the UK was sterling $M3$ and, as we saw in Chapter 6, it is the broad definitions of money which have proved to be particularly difficult to model. Similarly, in the US over the same period, the main targeted aggregate was $M1$, which is precisely the definition of money which has produced the most evidence of instability in that economy.

Most empirical work on the demand for money function has focused upon the dynamics underlying the short-run equation, using either the traditional restricted distributed lag models or the 'general to specific' modelling approach. Although much of this work is unsatisfactory and often implies unrealistic long-run parameters, the failure of short-run equations does not necessarily preclude a stable underlying long-run money demand function. Unfortunately, little direct analysis has been applied to the long-run relation, although the development of the cointegration approach to the modelling of time-series data has meant that there has been a revival of interest in the long-run money demand function in recent years. Cointegration may prove to be a valuable technique for the analysis of the demand for money function, because it potentially provides a means of identifying and estimating the long-run function, without dealing with the more problematic issue of short-run adjustment. Proponents of the approach also attribute the failure of many earlier studies to the non-cointegration of the vector of variables used in these studies. However, much of this work is in its infancy and although there is broad agreement upon the range of variables which should be included in such a function, it is difficult to give an up-to-date assessment of the properties and stability of the long-run relation. In a changing financial environment, it is likely that both the parameters and the arguments of the long-run function will change over time.

Analysis of the short-run function suggests that the correct dynamic specification is not independent of the direction of causation between the quantity of money and the arguments of the long-run function, namely interest rates, prices and income. Consequently, tests of short-run money demand functions need to be seen as tests of a joint hypothesis, encompassing the form and arguments of the long-run demand function, and the dynamic process by which equilibrium is restored in the money market. These relations may involve not only an adjustment hypothesis, but also possibly some attempt to model the formation of expectations. In these models, the quantity of money must be assumed to be either endogenous or exogenous. Both positions represent extreme assumptions and in reality money aggregates are likely to be determined by the interaction of both demand and supply influences, regardless of the policy regime in force. At one extreme, the conventional partial adjustment approach models the gradual adjustment of aggregate demand in response to changes in the arguments of the long-run function, with supply responding to demand, so that there is continuous market clearing. However, under the assumption of an exogenous money supply, the aggregate demand for money has to be seen as adjusting to the existing stock, through variations in one or more of the arguments of the demand function. In effect, what is being modelled here is the transmission mechanism of money, and evidence suggests that it may not be possible to capture such a complex process in a single-equation framework. Implicit in this view of money market adjustment is the belief that money fulfils the role of buffer stock in the individual's portfolio, with holdings responding to unanticipated or disequilibrium-inducing supply shocks to the quantity of money. A variety of buffer stock models have been developed in recent years and money's role as such an asset has also been modelled in relation to the source of such shocks, and in the context of forward-looking models which consider expectations with respect to the components of money demand.

Although these developments have contributed to our understanding of the different demand and supply influences which determine the quantity of money, they also serve to highlight the problems involved in the empirical analysis of monetary aggregates. None of the approaches we have discussed is totally satisfactory and it is apparent that there is no such thing as a definitive model of money demand, with widespread empirical validity. Furthermore, the majority of UK empirical work, in recent years, has been confined to narrow money aggregates, and as yet has left largely unresolved the problem of the specification and estimation of a satisfactory equation for UK broad money. Of course, broad monetary aggregates, such as $M3$ or $M4$, encompass a wide range of types of asset and it is difficult to believe that the factors influencing the quantity of notes and coin in circulation are exactly identical to those determining certificates of deposit or even interest-bearing cheque accounts. Therefore, instead of attempting to model broad money in its entirety, it may be desirable to estimate separate equations for each of its constituent assets. Similar reasoning suggests it may be fruitful to disaggregate total money balances according to the holder, so that separate equations are specified for personal and company sector holdings. Both the motives for money holding, and the composition of the monetary aggregates held, differ between firms and households; for example, households hold most building society deposits, but only a small proportion of certificates of deposit. Firms and households may also react differently to changes in the explanatory variables of the demand function; in particular, since active cash management is potentially much more important for firms, they might be expected to react more strongly to changes in both interest rates and inflation. A disaggregated approach was adopted in the Bank of England studies by Price (1972), Hacche (1974) and Goodhart (1981), and has also been used in recent versions of the Treasury model. Bank advances have traditionally been analysed on a sectoral basis and it is possible that future attempts to explain money holdings could benefit from such an approach. A more disaggregated treatment would certainly allow the investigator to analyse the changing trends, over time, in the relative contribution to monetary growth made both by each sector and by each type of monetary asset. Because they take no account of such changes, money demand studies using aggregate data are much more likely to display evidence of instability. Similar arguments suggest that more work on the 'Divisia' approach to the modelling of monetary aggregates might also prove worthwhile.

We conclude with a brief consideration of the policy implications of recent work on the demand for money. As we have already noted, monetary targeting was adopted in the 1970s, largely because the empirical evidence of the 1960s indicated that there was a close and predictable relationship between the aggregate quantity of money, however defined, and the major determinants of demand, namely income, prices and the rate of interest. Unfortunately, the empirical evidence of recent years suggests that this relationship is not nearly so simple or well-defined, and that the transmission mechanism of monetary policy involves long and variable lags between money, interest rates, the price level and aggregate expenditure. In consequence, the authorities are unable to predict the rate of monetary growth which will be consistent with the preferred path of output and prices. The apparent breakdown in the relationship also makes it difficult for the authorities to use interest rates to control the quantity of money. Indeed, if the demand for money is very sensitive to changes in the own rate of interest, we may observe an apparently perverse positive relationship between movements in the general level of interest rates and changes in the money stock. In such circumstances, movements in monetary aggregates become unreliable indicators of the stance of monetary policy.

Such problems are highlighted by Muscatelli (1990), who considers the difficulties involved in the implementation of a monetary targeting regime, in the context of a small macro model, in which the demand for money depends upon forward-looking behaviour and a buffer stock role is assumed for money. Following an unanticipated expenditure shock, various patterns of dynamic adjustment are shown to be possible in the money market, with the precise adjustment path dependent upon the values taken by the parameters of the model. Relevant factors here include the strength of the authorities' response to deviations of the money stock from its target value and the relative weights which agents attach to the costs of adjustment compared to the costs of being in disequilibrium with respect to their money holdings. Muscatelli argues that 'almost anything can happen in a money market where money plays a buffer role'. In such an environment, it is very difficult, if not impossible, to stabilise nominal incomes in the short run through monetary control and even the logic of applying a long-term targeting policy to the majority of monetary aggregates must be questioned. Consequently, an active targeting policy has not formed the centrepiece of UK monetary policy since the mid-1980s, and by the early 1990s targets were only being set for the very narrow $M0$ aggregate which, in modelling terms, has exhibited a greater degree of stability than the other definitions of money. The policy actions of the authorities have meant that the $M0$ aggregate has always been largely demand determined in the UK, so that movements in it can be assumed to serve as a useful indicator of changes in the level of economic activity. The aggregate is also a measure of the wide monetary base and, because of this, committed monetarists have often argued that strict control of its growth should form the basis of monetary policy. However, monetary base control has never been employed in the UK and it is quite likely that the equation for $M0$ would break down if such a policy was adopted.

In spite of the volume of empirical work on the demand for money, and the developments in econometric modelling techniques which have taken place in recent years, it is obvious that our knowledge of the major relations of the monetary system is still largely inadequate for policy purposes. At any given time, the stock of money in the economy is the outcome of a series of complex demand and supply interactions, which are necessarily difficult to model in any satisfactory manner. Nevertheless, the needs of monetary policy must justify a continued effort to improve our understanding of the different factors affecting the quantity of money, and in this work further analysis of the money demand function will play a central role.

Notes and References

1 An Introduction to Portfolio Analysis

1. In most textbooks, however, Tobin's model of the demand for money is treated as an extension of Keynes' speculative model; see, for example, Laidler (1985, pp. 69–77). Traditionally, of course, precautionary models of the demand for money are based upon uncertainty in the level of transactions, while in mean–variance models, it is the uncertainty in future bond prices which is important.

2 The Mean–Variance Approach

1. The effect of changes in the rate of interest on the overall level of wealth (through the effect on the value of existing bond holdings) is ignored in this analysis. This is because Tobin's model assumes that the division of the portfolio between cash and bonds is independent of the level of wealth, so that changes in wealth do not have any effect upon the relative shares of cash and bonds.
2. Sprenkle (1974) and Chang et al. (1983) have developed three-asset models, involving not only money and bonds, but also a relatively risk-free short-term asset. These show that narrow money will be dominated in the portfolio by the short-term asset, if the return on money is less than the return on such an asset and the variance of the return on the short-dated asset is small. The implication of such models is that the demand for narrow money, at least, may only be explainable in terms of transactions costs. Further discussion of these issues is to be found in Sprenkle (1984) and Chang et al. (1984).
3. At the minimum-risk point in the case of independent returns, it can be shown (Tobin, 1965, p. 25) that the proportion of the portfolio invested in the first asset is given by the relation $X_1 = \sigma_2^2/(\sigma_1^2 + \sigma_2^2)$, while the demand for the second asset is represented by $X_2 = \sigma_1^2/(\sigma_1^2 + \sigma_2^2)$.
4. When returns are perfectly negatively correlated, it can be shown (Tobin, 1965, p. 25) that the proportion of the portfolio invested in asset one at the minimum-risk point is given by $X_1 = \sigma_2/(\sigma_1 + \sigma_2)$ and that in asset two by $X_2 = \sigma_1/(\sigma_1 + \sigma_2)$.
5. Hicks (1967, pp. 117–25) makes an attempt to analyse situations in which the investor takes account of skewness.
6. Markowitz (1959) devotes Chapter 9 to a consideration of the semi-variance. A review of risk surrogates, including the semi-variance and the mean absolute deviation of returns, is to be found in Allen (1983, p. 46).
7. For a short account of the empirical evidence on the validity of the normality assumption for security returns, see Allen (1983, pp. 79–80).
8. This follows from the Central Limit Theorem.

9. For a proof of the equivalence between the maximisation of the expected value of the utility function in (2.7) and the use of the maximand in (2.8), see Freund (1956, p. 255).

10. One of the few attempts to measure explicitly the variances and covariances of asset returns is made by Honohan (1980) in a mean–variance model of UK life assurance companies.

11. For example, moving from a policy of interest rate stabilisation, to one of controlling the money supply by Open Market Operations, is likely to alter both the variance of returns on long-term government securities and the covariance of returns between such government debt and other private sector assets.

12. Above the level where $\pi = k/2c$, the utility function implies a negative marginal utility of returns which does not make economic sense.

3 Transactions and Precautionary Demand Models

1. The alternative interest-earning asset could equally well, and perhaps more realistically, be considered to be time deposits held in banks or building societies.

2. Tobin (1956) concentrates on this case, proving that these encashments will be equally spaced in time and equal in size. Tobin's approach is slightly different; instead of minimising transactions and interest costs, he assumes that the individual maximises interest earnings net of transactions costs. This enables the individual to consider whether interest earnings are high enough to justify any investment at all. It will not be profitable to buy bonds, when income is received in cash, if the cost of buying and selling them is more than the interest they would earn. In this case, all income will be retained in cash.

3. An early model analysing the effect of credit on the transactions demand for cash was developed by Rama Sastry (1970), although some of his results have been challenged by Wrightsman and Terniko (1971) and Litzenberger (1971), and are acknowledged in Rama Sastry (1971). Lewis (1974) makes further amendments to the model, arguing that the introduction of credit into the Baumol framework makes the interest elasticity of the demand for cash less negative and possibly even positive. More recently, Bar-Ilan (1990) analyses the demand for money in a Baumol framework, in which access to overdrafts is allowed at a penalty rate.

4. Santomero also distinguishes between cash and demand deposit holdings, deriving separate demand functions for each of these categories of money. Further analysis of this issue is to be found in Santomero (1979) and Dotsey (1988).

5. In a more general version of the model, Grossman and Policano (1975) argue that the positive relationship between inflationary expectations and commodity inventories does not necessarily hold.

6. A short-run income elasticity of unity, implying a constant velocity of circulation in the short run, is a prediction of the traditional classical models of the Quantity Theory of Money, as embodied in Fisher's (1911) equation of exchange.

7. For a synthesis of this critique, see Cuthbertson (1985a, pp. 25–8).
8. In the context of the model, this is obviously an unrealistic assumption, although recently banks have begun to offer their customers 'sweep accounts', by which funds are automatically transferred between interest and non-interest-bearing accounts, whenever certain thresholds are reached.
9. More generally, Miller and Orr (1968) show that the various elasticity predictions are crucially dependent upon the nature of the transfer costs assumed in the model.
10. Akerlof and Milbourne argue that their models offer an explanation for the empirically observed low short-run income elasticity of the demand for money. Empirical studies, such as Goldfeld (1973), typically find short-run income elasticities that are very small (of the order of 0.2 in quarterly data) but long-run elasticities near unity. These results are consistent with the view that the velocity of circulation of money varies almost proportionately with income over the course of the business cycle, but nears constancy in the longer run. In this sense, the authors reverse the simple Quantity Theory view about the velocity of circulation, embodied in the work of Fisher (1911), which argues that velocity is constant in the short run due to institutional requirements and variable only in the long run.
11. For an attempt to develop a model of the demand for money which integrates both approaches, see Frenkel and Jovanovic (1980).
12. This assumption is obviously unrealistic, but Whalen (1966, pp. 323–4) also develops his model for the case where the costs of illiquidity involve a proportional element, related to the size of the cash deficiency, as well as a fixed element.
13. This result is based upon a theorem of Tchebycheff. For a fuller explanation, see Whalen (1966, pp. 317–18).
14. For an alternative model involving overdrafts and the demand for interest-bearing money, see Bar-Ilan (1990).
15. The opportunity cost of overdrafts is $(r_c - r_b)$ and not r_c, since an amount equivalent to the overdraft will have been invested in the short-term liquid assets at a rate of return equal to r_b.
16. Sprenkle and Miller include broad money balances within their definition of short-term liquid assets, so that the demand for such balances will rise as r_b rises relative to r_c, and increased use is made of overdraft facilities. Such behaviour underlies the phenomenon of 'round-tripping', by which companies borrow funds from financial institutions, merely to re-deposit the money back within the banking system. This type of arbitrage activity was made profitable, in certain periods in the early 1970s, by the prevailing interest rate structure. It led to increases in the broad money supply in these periods.

4 Mixed Models and the General Utility Approach

1. See, for example, Pigou (1917).

5   The Empirical Demand for Money Function

1. An exception to this standard approach to the empirical analysis of the money demand function is provided by Beckman and Foreman (1988), who develop an experimental test of the Baumol–Tobin transactions demand model.

2. For a discussion of the identification and simultaneity issues in the context of the demand for money, see Cooley and LeRoy (1981).

3. The value taken by the adjustment coefficient is related to the size of the disequilibrium and adjustment costs, with $\theta = \Psi/(\Psi + \omega)$. If disequilibrium costs are zero, $\theta = 0$, so that $\tilde{m}_t = \tilde{m}_{t-1}$ and money holdings do not change from period to period. Alternatively, if adjustment costs are zero, $\theta = 1$, so that $\tilde{m}_t = \tilde{m}_t^*$ and actual money balances always equal desired holdings.

4. The system is exactly identified in that there are the precise number of estimated coefficients $(b_0, b_1, b_2, 1 - \theta)$ to determine the structural parameters $(\gamma, \alpha, \beta, \theta)$.

5. See Gordon (1984) for further discussion of this point.

6. Keating (1985) develops a model in which adjustment costs are incorporated directly into the objective function.

7. A problem arises in the empirical testing of this model because equation (5.14) is 'overidentified'; four structural parameters $(\gamma, \alpha, \beta, \lambda)$ have to be obtained from five estimated coefficients $(b_0, b_1, b_2, b_3, 1 - \lambda)$. We have more than one relation to determine one of the structural parameters; in this case, the estimate of λ obtained from the coefficient on the lagged dependent variable is unlikely to coincide with that obtained from the ratio of the coefficients on the two interest rate terms. To be consistent with the structural model, restrictions must be imposed upon the values of the estimated coefficients in the equation.

8. For a full derivation of this reduced form, see Thomas (1985, p. 300).

9. Again a problem arises with the empirical implementation of the model because there are six estimated coefficients $[b_0, b_1, b_2, b_3, 2 - \theta - \lambda, -(1 - \theta)(1 - \lambda)]$, but only five structural parameters $(\gamma, \alpha, \beta, \theta, \lambda)$. The equation is 'overidentified' and in order to determine the structural parameters, restrictions must be imposed upon the estimated coefficients.

10. General distributed lag models are not usually based upon any explicit optimisation framework, although Anderson and Hendry (1984) specify a cost-minimisation model of building society behaviour, in order to justify the use of such equations. Also, a simple model, involving 'differenced' and 'levels' terms, can be derived from the quadratic cost of adjustment framework, by adding a term which assumes that costs are lower, if the actual change in money holdings is in the same direction as the desired change. Such a formulation allows the change in all of the variables, determining desired money balances, to be included in the estimated equation as well as their levels. A simple equation of this form is derived in Cuthbertson (1985a, p. 67).

11. The change in the logarithmic value of a variable approximates the proportionate change in the variable. This is because

$$\Delta\tilde{m}_t = \tilde{m}_t - \tilde{m}_{t-1} = \log\tilde{M}_t - log\tilde{M}_{t-1} = \log\left[\frac{\tilde{M}_t}{\tilde{M}_{t-1}}\right] \approx \frac{\tilde{M}_t - \tilde{M}_{t-1}}{\tilde{M}_{t-1}}$$

Similarly, $\Delta y_t \approx \dfrac{Y_t - Y_{t-1}}{Y_{t-1}}$

12. It is possible to verify the validity of such a restriction, by adding additional 'levels' terms in lagged income to equation (5.20) and testing for their significance. If the restriction is valid, the coefficients on the additional terms will be insignificantly different from zero.

13. A stationary series is one with no trend in mean and a constant, finite variance. Consider two time series, X_t and Z_t, which are non-stationary in their levels, but stationary in their first differences. The series are cointegrated when a factor λ exists such that $W_t = Z_t - \lambda X_t$ is stationary. In the two-variable case, the cointegrating factor must be unique. More generally, we can state that the variables in an equation are cointegrated if the individual series are each integrated to order one (meaning that the observed time-series possess trends that can be removed by differencing the data once) and the residuals obtained from the estimation of the equation are integrated to order zero (that is stationary).

14. No additional 'levels' terms, in the variables which appear in the cointegrating relation, must appear in the short-run equation, otherwise the initial estimate of the cointegrating vector cannot be accepted as the long-run equilibrium demand function.

15. When more than two variables are involved, it is possible in principle to have more than one cointegrating vector. On the basis of the estimated coefficients, the investigator must then decide which vector appears to be the most plausible representation of the long-run relationship between the variables. For a particular approach to the problem of multiple cointegrating vectors, see Johansen (1988) and Johansen and Juselius (1990).

16. Sterling $M3$ differs from $M3$ by the exclusion of foreign currency deposits held with the UK banks by UK residents.

17. Retail deposits comprise small deposits, usually administered by banks through a branch network. Wholesale deposits are large deposits placed in the money markets.

18. The assumption of price homogeneity can be easily tested by adding a term in the current price level to a real demand for money function, such as that represented by equation (5.6). If the coefficient on the price term is significantly different from zero, the null hypothesis of homogeneity can be rejected.

19. This procedure is considered in more detail in Chapter 9.

20. The inclusion of extra interest rate variables does, of course, increase the likelihood of multicollinearity problems in the estimated relationship.

21. A cautionary note can be introduced here, for although these empirical findings would seem to indicate a role for the actual or expected rate of inflation in the demand for money function, the significance of lagged price variables could reflect slow adjustment of money balances to price

level changes (with homogeneity in the long run) rather than any inflationary effect. More particularly, Milbourne (1983b) notes that evidence of the significance of an inflation variable, in a real partial adjustment model, could equally well reflect support for a nominal partial adjustment model, in which long-run real money demand is independent of the rate of inflation. This can be seen if we reparameterise equation (5.8), the short-run relation produced by the nominal partial adjustment model, to produce the equation

$$\tilde{m}_t = b_0 + b_1 r_t + b_2 y_t - (1 - \theta)\Delta p_t + (1 - \theta)\tilde{m}_{t-1} + u_t$$

The set of explanatory variables included in this equation is the same as that which would be obtained if an inflation variable was added to equation (5.6), the short-run relation produced by the real partial adjustment model. However, the formulation described above implies that the coefficients on the lagged money term and the inflation rate variable are equal in magnitude and opposite in sign. A test of this restriction can therefore be used to differentiate between the two alternative hypotheses. Boughton and Tavlas (1991) attempt an alternative solution to the problem by using the lagged value of the inflation rate, as a proxy for inflationary expectations, in a real partial adjustment model; the variable is shown to have a significant effect upon broad money holdings in the UK, but not upon the narrow money aggregate. Significant effects are also isolated for the US in equations for both narrow and broad money. Further comments on the incorporation of inflation variables in partial adjustment models are made by Cuthbertson (1986b), Hafer and Thornton (1986), Milbourne (1986) and Goldfeld and Sichel (1987). As an alternative test, Friedman and Schwartz (1982) and Friedman (1988) have also suggested using the rate of change of nominal income, rather than the rate of change of prices, as a measure of the yield on real assets.

22. Klein's price uncertainty variable is based upon a measure of the variability of the rate of price change and involves a consideration of the standard deviation of the annual rate of inflation. His conclusions are questioned by Laidler (1980, pp. 230–2) who finds that the price uncertainty variable becomes negatively signed, when the equation is estimated using US data on $M1$ for the period 1953–76. Using similar data for the period 1960–73, Smirlock (1982) also finds a negative relationship between inflation uncertainty and the demand for real balances. The lack of an empirical consensus on this issue is also indicated by the work of Slovin and Sushka (1983) who find no role for a variable measuring the volatility of the rate of inflation. These contradictory findings are more understandable when it is realised that there are several competing justifications for the inclusion of an inflation uncertainty variable in the empirical demand for money function. As well as Klein's rationale, it can be argued that increased uncertainty about the inflation rate is likely to lead to an increase in the precautionary demand for money. On the other hand, the usefulness of money as a store of value and unit of account may be adversely affected by uncertainty over the

price level, and any increase in such uncertainty might create an incentive for agents to rearrange their portfolios towards assets which are better inflation hedges. This issue is considered further in Boonekamp (1978) and Koskela and Viren (1987).

23. These difficulties have also meant that other potentially important explanatory factors, such as the variability of net receipts or payments, which is stressed in the transactions model of Miller and Orr (1966) and the precautionary model of Whalen (1966), have not, as yet, been tested empirically in any satisfactory way.

24. The wage rate variable may, of course, exert a significant positive effect upon the demand for money for reasons other than the value of time hypothesis. For example, higher wage rates are likely to increase the level of income and through this channel exert an upward influence upon money holdings.

6 Stability and the Demand for Money Function

1. Using more sophisticated econometric techniques, involving cointegration analysis and an error-correction representation of the demand for money equation, Hendry and Ericsson (1991a) obtain results which indicate that a stable relationship can be isolated from annual UK data on broad money for the period 1878–1970. They also find that the demand for money relationship breaks down between 1970 and 1975. Their study is a critique of the work of Friedman and Schwartz (1982) who were also able to isolate a stable demand for money function for this long data period.

2. Artis and Lewis (1981, pp. 17–21) extend Coghlan's data period and find that, although the estimated equation yields long-run coefficients similar to those obtained by Coghlan, the short-run properties of the equation are unstable and the equation fails to predict subsequent movements in $M1$ holdings.

3. In a study of the Israeli experience, Paroush and Ruthenberg (1986) find that cash-dispensing technology increases deposits at the expense of currency holdings.

4. Westaway and Walton argue that the cumulative interest rate variable may represent a supply response on the part of the banks; higher interest rates offer the potential of increased bank profits and so encourage the banks to advertise their services in order to persuade more individuals to open bank accounts, and so reduce their average cash holdings.

5. The significance of the lagged real income term in the preferred equation means that the assumption of a long-run income elasticity of unity, implicit in the error-correction term, does not extend to the whole equation.

6. Hafer and Hein (1979) criticise Hamburger's model for constraining the income elasticity of the demand for money to unity, and claim that his results are heavily dependent upon this assumption. Laidler (1980) also finds that the deterioration of the $M1$ function after 1972 is considerably reduced when the dividend–price ratio is included in the equation. The variable appears to be a less important determinant of the broader $M2$ aggregate.

7. Spindt (1985) adopts a similar approach, in which the different components of money are aggregated according to their characteristics as a transactions medium, with the weights dependent upon the net turnover rate or velocity of each asset.

8. Using a forward-looking model (see Chapter 7) Cuthbertson and Taylor (1990a) reach a similar conclusion, arguing that the 'missing money' episode in the 1970s can be explained in terms of a shift in the expectations generating equations, with the underlying long-run money demand function remaining stable.

9. For a critique of Roley's results, see Goldfeld and Sichel (1990, pp. 330–1).

7 Disequilibrium Money and Buffer Stock Models

1. This is obviously an extreme assumption, but for the purposes of model formulation, the nominal money stock is assumed to be exogenous to money holders, if changes in the quantity of money are dominated by factors not related to the demand for money. Money is endogenous to holders, or demand determined, when agents are able to control their own nominal money holdings in the aggregate. It is important to note that the economic meaning of exogeneity, in the context of a structural model, is different from the statistical notion of exogeneity, which requires independence of the variable from the error term in the regression equation.

2. Initially, sterling $M3$ was the main targeted aggregate, but doubts about its appropriateness as a measure of the stance of monetary policy led the authorities to set additional targets for other monetary aggregates in the early 1980s. An increasing interest was also developing in the exchange rate as a tool of policy, and by the mid-1980s the level of the exchange rate had become, unofficially at least, as great a priority for the authorities. This concern with the exchange rate gradually became more obvious over the rest of the decade and was finally cemented with the entry into the European Exchange Rate Mechanism in October 1990. Although an active policy of targeting monetary growth effectively ceased to be the centrepiece of policy in the mid-1980s, targets continued to be set for the narrow $M0$ aggregate into the 1990s and were reintroduced for broad money ($M4$) in 1992. For a comprehensive review of the development of policy over the period, see Goodhart (1989a).

3. The Supplementary Special Deposits scheme, or 'corset', was first introduced in December 1973 and subsequently imposed at different times throughout the 1970s. Under the scheme, penalties were imposed upon individual institutions whose interest-bearing eligible liabilities (mainly sterling deposits) grew faster than a prescribed rate. These controls had the effect of distorting the money supply figures, since funds were often deposited outside the commercial banking system in order to evade the restriction. When the 'corset' was finally removed, the process was reversed and there was a considerable reintermediation of funds back into mainstream bank accounts, thus boosting the money supply.

4. The issues involved here have been made in a number of previous studies, dating back to Tucker (1966, 1971), Walters (1965, 1967) and Starleaf (1970). See also Coats (1982).

5. This implication of the short-run partial adjustment equation, when we assume an exogenous money stock, can be seen more clearly if we begin with equation (5.9), which represents a version of the short-run relation produced by the nominal partial adjustment model. Equating money supply to money demand, we can write equation (5.9) as

$$m_t^s = \theta\gamma + \theta\alpha r_t + \theta\beta y_t + \theta p_t + (1 - \theta)m_{t-1}^s + \theta v_t$$

where m^s is the exogenous money supply. Further rearrangement of this relation produces an expression for the rate of interest of the form

$$r_t = -\frac{\gamma}{\alpha} - \frac{\beta}{\alpha}y_t - \frac{1}{\alpha}p_t + \frac{1}{\theta\alpha}m_t^s - \left[\frac{1 - \theta}{\theta\alpha}\right]m_{t-1}^s - \frac{1}{\alpha}v_t$$

Assuming income and the price level remain constant, the short-run effect upon the interest rate of a change in the money supply is equal to $1/\theta\alpha$, while the long-run response (obtained by setting $m_t^s = m_{t-1}^s$) is $1/\alpha$. Given that the adjustment parameter, θ, takes a value between zero and unity, the short-run response must be greater than the long-run response. The reduced form of the partial adjustment model therefore implies 'overshooting' in the interest rate when it is applied to the case of an exogenous money supply.

6. Laidler (1982) has also offered a critique of the applicability of the partial adjustment model to aggregate data when the money stock is endogenous. He argues that a model, based upon the costs of adjusting money holdings at the individual level, should not be applied to a situation in which the supply of money has to adjust to aggregate demand.

7. In a similar way, it can be shown that the reduced form obtained from the nominal partial adjustment model of money demand, which is specified in equation (5.8), is equivalent to equation (7.4) if an additional term, given by $(1 - \theta)(\Delta m_t^s + \Delta p_t)$ is added to equation (5.8).

8. Given that nominal income is real income multiplied by the price level, we can write the logarithm of nominal income as $\log(PY) = \log P + \log Y = p + y$.

9. In this sense, the Artis–Lewis model is more realistic, because in practice, there is little evidence to indicate that interest rate 'overshooting' is a feature of financial markets.

10. White (1981) is sceptical of the notion of disequilibrium money embodied in this model. In an economy with a well-developed financial system, he argues that the rate of interest will always move quickly to eliminate any discrepancy between the supply of, and demand for money, so that disequilibrium money holdings should not exist.

11. The latter part of this data period, when the money stock was more likely to be exogenously determined, was obviously more suitable for the estimation of equations (7.10) and (7.13). However, Artis and Lewis felt that there was also sufficient doubt about the total endogeneity of the money stock in the 1960s to justify using the whole of the available data

set to estimate the equations. For example, even when the authorities are attempting to control interest rates, as was the case in the 1960s, shocks to the PSBR and bank advances can result in increases in the quantity of money which are independent of demand. Such points are made by Brunner and Meltzer (1976).

12. Patterson (1987) is critical of the absence of dynamics in the Artis–Lewis model. Using a general distributed lag version of the Artis–Lewis formulation, and the same data set, he finds a role for both lagged exogenous variables and lagged values of the dependent variable. Patterson is also sceptical of the Artis–Lewis claim that a stable demand for money relationship can be isolated using this data set.

13. As the disequilibrium term appears in each equation, the model yields cross-equation restrictions on the parameters of the long-run money demand function. The entire model has to be estimated before values for these parameters can be obtained. This also means that the estimated money demand coefficients are conditional upon the correct specification of the whole model.

14. Of course, changes in the level of income and interest rates will alter the threshold and return point values within which buffer holdings can fluctuate, and so affect the average money balance.

15. Such a hypothesis is in the 'new classical' tradition of monetary economics, as formulated in studies such as Barro (1978).

16. For a more general formulation of the Carr–Darby model, which allows past values of unanticipated money to influence current real money holdings, see Darby and Stockman (1983).

17. It is possible that there could be an element of double counting in the effects being measured by the transitory income term and the unanticipated money supply variable. In econometric terms, this would create a multicollinearity problem in the estimated regressions, which might help to explain the poor statistical performance of the transitory income term.

18. This problem arises because m_t appears on both sides of equation (7.17). Given $\tilde{m} = m - p$, we can assert that u_t determines m_t. Also, m_t^e is predetermined, so that u_t and $(m - m^e)_t$ are correlated. Carr and Darby attempt to allow for any simultaneity in their estimated equation, but here also their approach is criticised by MacKinnon and Milbourne.

19. MacKinnon and Milbourne use a different set of explanatory variables to those tested by Carr and Darby; they exclude the transitory income variable from the equation explaining money holdings and use current, rather than permanent, income.

20. Boughton and Tavlas (1991) argue that simultaneity problems may still be evident in the amended formulations, given in equations (7.19) and (7.21); this is because p_t, which now appears on the right-hand side of these equations, is correlated with the error term through the dependent variable of the equations.

21. We can illustrate the nature of the 'rationality' restrictions using a two-equation model, involving (7.20) and an expectations generating mechanism for the money supply of the form

$$m_t = \psi z_{t-1} + v_t \tag{A.1}$$

where ψ is a coefficient vector, z is a vector of variables which has a systematic influence upon the money supply and v is the non-systematic component of the money supply process. In the two-stage approach, the predictions from equation (A.1) yield a set of values for m_t^e for use in the estimation of equation (7.20). Alternatively, the vector of variables, which determine the expected money supply, can be substituted directly into equation (7.20) to produce the relation

$$\tilde{m}_t = bx_t + \varphi(m_t - \psi^0 z_{t-1}) + \lambda\psi^0 z_{t-1} + u_t \tag{A.2}$$

where ψ^0 is a coefficient vector. The cross-equation or 'rationality' restrictions require $\psi = \psi^0$ in the system formed from (A.1) and (A.2), and are implicitly imposed by the two-step procedure of substituting the predictions from equation (A.1) into equation (7.20). Cuthbertson and Taylor (1986) argue that a correct test of the buffer stock hypothesis should consider the validity of the cross-equation restrictions, as well as the significance of the estimated φ and λ coefficients. Joint estimation of the system formed from equations (A.1) and (A.2) enables this to be done, so that we can test for both neutrality ($\lambda = 0$) and rationality ($\psi = \psi^0$).

22. The Kalman filter may be viewed as a form of adaptive expectations, in which the expectations parameter is updated each period as new information becomes available. This method of forecasting is probably closer to that undertaken by agents in practice. In comparison, fixed-coefficient models generate forecasts for the early part of the data set, using information which was not available at the time the forecasts were made. This is because the estimated parameters used to generate the forecasts are based upon the entire set of observations. The Kalman filter technique is described more fully in Harvey (1981, pp. 101–19) and Cuthbertson (1988b).

23. In effect, if m is endogenous, we have two equations in only one endogenous variable.

24. A similar interpretation is given to a variant of the Carr–Darby model by Darby and Stockman (1983), Gandolfi and Lothian (1983) and Lothian *et al.* (1990).

25. There is, of course, an inconsistency in justifying adjustment lags in this way when the derivation of the long-run function is based partly upon transfer costs.

26. The form given in relation (7.26) is a multi-period generalisation of the one-period quadratic cost function outlined in (5.5), which is the basis of the simple partial adjustment mechanism.

27. A vector autoregressive scheme is one in which the expectations generating mechanism for each variable involves not only its own lagged values, but also the lagged values of all the other variables for which expectations are being generated within the model.

28. Nickell (1985), Domowitz and Hakkio (1990) and Cuthbertson and Taylor (1990b) show that a dynamic cost-minimising forward-looking model can be represented as a backward-looking model incorporating an error-correction mechanism. More generally, given forecasting equations for the regressors, it is obvious that a forward-looking model may be

re-specified as a general distributed lag equation containing only past values of prices, income and interest rates.

29. Hendry and Ericsson (1991b) reiterate this view, while the issue is also considered by Cuthbertson (1991).

30. Similar implications follow from the target-threshold models of Akerlof (1979) and Akerlof and Milbourne (1980), which we considered in Chapter 3. Davidson and Ireland (1990) also consider some of the issues raised by the association between target-threshold models and the concept of buffer stock money.

31. It is likely that empirical investigators have carried out such tests, but have not published their findings because of their inability to obtain meaningful results. For example, Davidson and Ireland (1987) report on a largely unsuccessful attempt to estimate a buffer stock equation for UK data on $M3$.

8 Bank Lending Equations

1. The use of the differential between the two rates, as an important determining factor of bank lending, follows the model of Sprenkle and Miller (1980), which we discussed in Chapter 3.

2. Sales receipts from higher output prices do not materialise immediately and, in the meantime, firms must meet higher costs by either increasing their bank borrowing or running-down their liquid asset holdings.

3. Stiglitz and Weiss (1981) develop the notion of 'equilibrium rationing' as an alternative theoretical justification for the existence of credit rationing in the advances market. They argue that the rate of interest which maximises bank profits is likely to be associated with credit rationing. Higher interest rates, which would remove the excess demand, are not favoured by the banks, since the higher cost of borrowing is likely to discourage the relatively safe, low-return, projects and encourage those involving a more speculative use of funds, which can offer greater potential returns, albeit with more risk. A rise in interest rates would therefore increase the overall riskiness of the banks' loan portfolio, and with it the probability of loan default, so reducing expected bank profits. In effect, this situation arises because the level of the interest rate affects the quality of the loan. Under such a scenario, it is in the banks' interest to keep lending rates at a level lower than that which clears the market, so that credit rationing can be viewed as an equilibrium phenomenon. Furthermore, because banks do not have enough information on potential borrowers and their plans to be able to identify a 'good' loan, advances are refused to borrowers who are observationally indistinguishable from those who receive them. Goodhart (1989b, pp. 156–75) offers a more extensive discussion of the role of credit rationing in the loans market.

4. The technique used involves separating the data sample into periods of excess demand and periods of excess supply. The supply function is estimated over periods of excess demand and the demand function is estimated over periods of excess supply. The direction of movement in the market rate of interest can be used to determine whether a demand or

supply observation occurs. If the observed rate exceeds the market clearing level, then the rate falls and the observed quantity presumably lies on the demand curve. On the other hand, if the rate is below the equilibrium value, then the rate will rise and the observed quantity can be taken to lie on the supply curve.

5. The modelling of bank advances in the Treasury model is considered in more detail in Chapter 10.

9 The Demand for Long-term Government Securities

1. In practice, the series is dominated by the capital gains term.
2. The available data can be realistically assumed to represent a set of observations on the demand curve because the authorities, over the data period, typically sold as many gilts as the market would bear.

10 Multi-asset Portfolio Models

1. Using the adding-up restrictions embodied in (10.3), and the fact that the own rate of return coefficients should be positive, it can be shown that at least some of the cross rate terms must be negative. In other words, some assets have to be substitutes for each other.
2. The theoretical validity of this restriction is often closely linked to the particular model used and, as we noted in Chapter 2, the symmetry of the variance–covariance matrix of asset returns means that the restriction is often particularly appropriate in mean–variance models.
3. Smith (1975) has shown that if only own lags are included in a system of demand equations, we must implicitly accept that all assets adjust at the same rate.
4. The adjustment mechanism, outlined in (10.6), is independent of whether we consider switches in the composition of a given stock of wealth, or revaluations of existing assets, or the allocation of new savings. In an extension to the adjustment mechanism, Brainard and Tobin also allow for the possibility that changes in the composition of a sector's portfolio may be affected, in the short run, by the flow of new funds arising from savings and capital gains. Such increases in net wealth may be allocated, in the first instance, in a way which depends upon the source of the funds. For example, changes in a company's cash flow are likely to be reflected initially in its holdings of liquid financial assets or short-term borrowing, and only later in its operating assets. Similarly, an increase in asset portfolios, resulting from a revaluation of existing equity shares or bond holdings, is likely to continue to be held in this form for some time.
5. The stability of the system, outlined in (10.6), has been investigated by Nadiri and Rosen (1969) in a study of factor demand equations. They show that such a system will converge if, and only if, the absolute values of the characteristic roots of the matrix $(I - \theta)$ (formed from the identity matrix, I, and the adjustment matrix, θ) are less than unity. It can also be shown that, if all the elements of $(I - \theta)$ lie between zero and unity, a

sufficient condition for stability exists if, for each column of the matrix, the own adjustment coefficient is greater than the sum of the cross adjustment coefficients. Since the column sum of all the coefficients is unity, this in turn implies that the own adjustment coefficient itself should be greater than one-half.

6. The relation outlined in (10.8) is a multi-asset generalisation of the quadratic cost function given in expression (5.5), which underlies the simple partial adjustment mechanism.

7. This result makes use of the conditions outlined in (10.3) and (10.7), and is explained in Sharpe (1973, p. 531). Since the column sums of the θ_{ik} sum to unity, and the column sums of the f_{kj} add up to zero, we can state that the column sums of the η_{ij}, formed from the θ_{ik} and the f_{kj}, must sum to zero. Similarly, since the column sum of the c_k adds to unity, the column sum of the ϕ_i, formed from the θ_{ik} and the c_k, must sum to unity.

8. For example, banks often act as rate-setters in loan markets, adjusting their rate-setting function in the light of the rates available on alternative assets and their own liquidity position. They must, however, act as a price-taker in at least one asset market, in order to maintain the balance sheet identity.

9. The controls imposed upon bank lending in the period up to 1971 are an example of such a policy directive.

10. The practice of liability management became more important in the UK after the Competition and Credit Control reforms of 1971. Since this time the clearing banks have actively engaged in bidding for deposits in the wholesale money market.

11. This result follows from a theorem outlined in Prais and Houthakker (1971, p. 84).

12. Similarly, if there are m sectoral financial models, only $(m - 1)$ equations need to be specified for each financial market; the mth sector's demand for the asset can be determined residually in order to ensure market clearing.

13. The validity of the symmetry restriction is viewed as a test of the mean–variance model used by Parkin, which is based upon a negative exponential utility function and the assumption of normally distributed asset returns. As we saw in Chapter 2, such a model predicts that the interest rate parameters in the demand equations will be functions of the variance–covariance matrix of asset returns, which is itself symmetric.

14. The exclusion of deposits from the choice set means that the banks are not assumed to be engaged in liability management and is a legitimate assumption in the pre-Competition and Credit Control era covered by the data period of these studies. The level of deposits is, in effect, demand determined by the private sector.

15. The basis of the general equilibrium accounting framework used in this study is described in Tobin (1969).

16. Such an approach removes the theoretical inconsistency of using a pure mean–variance model to analyse the choices among a set of non-risky assets.

17. A critique of the model and the empirical results obtained is provided by Courakis (1988).

18. For a detailed discussion of the principles underlying the development of the main monetary relations in the early versions of the Treasury model, the reader is also referred to Spencer (1986).
19. A definition which included personal sector holdings of notes and coin was tried, but was found to give less satisfactory results in estimation.
20. This approach is based upon the work outlined in Johnston (1985) and Hood (1987).
21. Further discussion of the nature of this equation is to be found in Westaway and Walton (1991).

Bibliography

Adam, C.S. (1991) 'Financial innovation and the demand for sterling M3 in the UK 1975–86', *Oxford Bulletin of Economics and Statistics*, 53, 401–24.

Ahmad, S. (1977) 'Transactions demand for money and the quantity theory', *Quarterly Journal of Economics*, 91, 327–35.

Aigner, D.J. (1973) 'On estimation of an econometric model of short-run bank behaviour', *Journal of Econometrics*, 1, 201–28.

Aigner, D.J. and Bryan, W.R. (1971) 'A model of short-run bank behaviour', *Quarterly Journal of Economics*, 85, 97–118.

Akerlof, G.A. (1979) 'Irving Fisher on his head: the consequences of constant target-threshold monitoring of money holdings', *Quarterly Journal of Economics*, 93, 169–87.

Akerlof, G.A. and Milbourne, R. (1980) 'The short-run demand for money', *Economic Journal*, 90, 885–900.

Allen, D.E. (1983) *Finance: A Theoretical Introduction*, Oxford: Martin Robertson.

Anderson, G.J. and Hendry, D.F. (1984) 'An econometric model of UK building societies', *Oxford Bulletin of Economics and Statistics*, 46, 185–210.

Arango, S. and Nadiri, M.I. (1981) 'Demand for money in open economies', *Journal of Monetary Economics*, 7, 69–83.

Arrow, K.J. (1965) *Aspects of the Theory of Risk-Bearing*, Yrjo Jahnsson Lectures, Helsinki.

Artis, M.J. (1978) 'Monetary policy – part 2', pp. 258–303, in Blackaby, F.T. (ed.), *British Economic Policy 1960–74*, Cambridge: Cambridge University Press.

Artis, M.J. and Lewis, M.K. (1974) 'The demand for money: stable or unstable?', *The Banker*, 124, 239–47.

—— (1976) 'The demand for money in the UK: 1963–73', *Manchester School*, 44, 147–81.

—— (1981) *Monetary Control in the United Kingdom*, Oxford: Philip Allan.

—— (1984) 'How unstable is the demand for money in the UK?' *Economica*, 51, 473–6.

Baba, Y., Hendry, D.F. and Starr, R.M. (1992) 'The demand for M1 in the USA 1960–88', *Review of Economic Studies*, 59, 25–61.

Backus, D., Brainard, W.C., Smith, G. and Tobin, J. (1980) 'A model of US financial and non-financial economic behaviour', *Journal of Money, Credit and Banking*, 12, 259–93.

Backus, D. and Purvis, D. (1980) 'An integrated model of household flow of funds allocations', *Journal of Money, Credit and Banking*, 12, 400–25.

Bain, A.D. and McGregor, P.G. (1985) 'Buffer stock monetarism and the theory of financial buffers', *Manchester School*, 53, 385–403.

Bar-Ilan, A. (1990) 'Overdrafts and the demand for money', *American Economic Review*, 80, 1201–16.

Barnett, W.A. (1980) 'Economic monetary aggregates: an application of index numbers and aggregation theory', *Journal of Econometrics*, 14, 11–48.

–––––– (1982) 'The optimal level of monetary aggregation', *Journal of Money, Credit and Banking*, 14, 687–710.

–––––– (1990) 'Developments in monetary aggregation theory', *Journal of Policy Modelling*, 12, 205–57.

Barnett, W.A., Offenbacher, E.K. and Spindt, P.A. (1981) 'New concepts of aggregated money', *Journal of Finance*, 36, 479–505.

–––––– (1984) 'The new divisia monetary aggregates', *Journal of Political Economy*, 92, 1049–85.

Barr, D.G. and Cuthbertson, K. (1990) 'Modelling the flow of funds with an application to the demand for liquid assets by the UK personal sector', pp. 223–46, in Henry, S.G.B. and Patterson, K.D. (eds), *Economic Modelling at the Bank of England*, London: Chapman & Hall.

–––––– (1991) 'Neoclassical consumer demand theory and the demand for money', *Economic Journal*, 101, 855–76.

Barrett, R.J., Gray, M.R. and Parkin, J.M. (1975) 'The demand for financial assets by the personal sector of the UK economy', pp. 500–32, in Renton, G.A. (ed.), *Modelling the Economy*, London: Heinemann.

Barro, R.J. (1978) 'Unanticipated money, output and the price level in the US', *Journal of Political Economy*, 86, 549–81.

Barro, R.J. and Santomero, A.M. (1972) 'Household money holdings and the demand deposit rate', *Journal of Money, Credit and Banking*, 4, 397–413.

Baumol, W.J. (1952) 'The transactions demand for cash: an inventory-theoretic approach', *Quarterly Journal of Economics*, 66, 545–56.

Beckman, S.R. and Foreman, J.N. (1988) 'An experimental test of the Baumol-Tobin transactions demand for money', *Journal of Money, Credit and Banking*, 20, 291–305.

Beenstock, M. (1989) 'The determinants of the money multiplier in the UK', *Journal of Money, Credit and Banking*, 21, 464–80.

Belongia, M.T. and Chrystal, K.A. (1991) 'An admissible monetary aggregate for the United Kingdom', *Review of Economics and Statistics*, 73, 497–503.

Berndt, E.R., McCurdy, T.H. and Rose, D.E. (1980) 'On testing theories of financial intermediary portfolio selection', *Review of Economic Studies*, 47, 861–73.

Bewley, R.A. (1981) 'The portfolio behaviour of the London Clearing Banks: 1963–71', *Manchester School*, 49, 191–210.

Boonekamp, C.F.J. (1978) 'Inflation, hedging and the demand for money', *American Economic Review*, 68, 821–33.

Bordo, M.D. and Jonung, L. (1981) 'The long-run behaviour of the income velocity of money in five advanced countries 1879–1975: an institutional approach', *Economic Inquiry*, 19, 96–116.

–––––– (1987) *The Long-run Behaviour of the Velocity of Circulation*, Cambridge: Cambridge University Press.

–––––– (1990) 'The long-run behaviour of velocity: the institutional approach revisited', *Journal of Policy Modelling*, 12, 165–97.

Boughton, J.M. (1979) 'The demand for money in major OECD countries', *OECD Economic Outlook: Occasional Studies*, January, 35–57.

—————— (1981) 'Recent instability of the demand for money: an international perspective', *Southern Economic Journal*, 47, 579–97.

—————— (1991a) 'Long-run money demand in large industrial countries', *IMF Staff Papers*, 38, 1–32.

—————— (1991b) 'Money demand in five major industrialised countries: estimating and interpreting error-correction models', pp. 109–29, in Taylor, M.P. (ed.), *Money and Financial Markets*, Oxford: Basil Blackwell.

Boughton, J.M. and Tavlas, G.S. (1990) 'Modelling money demand in large industrial countries: buffer stock and error-correction approaches', *Journal of Policy Modelling*, 12, 433–61.

—————— (1991) 'What have we learned about estimating the demand for money? A multi-country evaluation of some new approaches', *IMF Working Paper*.

Brainard, W.C. and Tobin, J. (1968) 'Pitfalls in financial model building', *American Economic Review*, 58 (Papers and Proceedings), 99–122.

Bronfenbrenner, M. and Mayer, T. (1960) 'Liquidity functions in the American economy', *Econometrica*, 28, 810–34.

Brookes, M., Hall, S., Henry, B. and Hoggarth, G. (1991) 'Modelling broad and narrow money: a study using cointegration', pp. 130–48, in Taylor, M.P. (ed.), *Money and Financial Markets*, Oxford: Basil Blackwell.

Browne, F.X. (1989) 'A new test of the buffer stock money hypothesis', *Manchester School*, 57, 154–71.

Brunner, K. and Meltzer, A.H. (1963) 'Predicting velocity: implications for theory and policy', *Journal of Finance*, 18, 319–54.

—————— (1964) 'Some further investigations of demand and supply functions for money', *Journal of Finance*, 19, 240–83.

—————— (1967) 'Economies of scale in cash balances reconsidered', *Quarterly Journal of Economics*, 81, 422–36.

—————— (1976) 'An aggregative theory for a closed economy', pp. 69–103, in Stein, J.L. (ed.), *Monetarism*, Amsterdam: North-Holland.

Budd, A. and Holly, S. (1986) 'Economic viewpoint: does broad money matter?', *London Business School Economic Outlook 1985–89*, 10, 16–22.

Buiter, W.H. and Armstrong, C.A. (1978) 'A didactic note on the transactions demand for money and behaviour towards risk', *Journal of Money, Credit and Banking*, 10, 529–38.

Buse, A. (1975) 'Testing a simple portfolio model of interest rates', *Oxford Economic Papers*, 27, 82–93.

Cagan, R. (1956) 'The monetary dynamics of hyperinflation', pp. 25–57, in Friedman, M. (ed.), *Studies in the Quantity Theory of Money*, Chicago: University of Chicago Press.

Carr, J. and Darby, M.R. (1981) 'The role of money supply shocks in the short-run demand for money', *Journal of Monetary Economics*, 8, 183–99.

Carr, J., Darby, M.R. and Thornton, D.L. (1985) 'Monetary anticipations and the demand for money: reply', *Journal of Monetary Economics*, 16, 251–7.

Chang, W.W., Hamberg, D. and Hirata, J. (1983) 'Liquidity preference as behaviour towards risk in a demand for short-term securities – not money', *American Economic Review*, 73, 420–7.

—————— (1984) 'On liquidity preference – again: reply', *American Economic Review*, 74, 812–13.

Chant, J.F. (1976) 'Dynamic adjustments in simple models of the transactions demand for money', *Journal of Monetary Economics*, 2, 351–66.

Chow, G. (1966) 'On the long-run and short-run demand for money', *Journal of Political Economy*, 74, 111–31.

Christofides, L.N. (1976) 'Quadratic costs and multi-asset partial adjustment equations', *Applied Economics*, 8, 301–5.

Clayton, G., Dodds, J.C., Ford, J.L. and Ghosh, D. (1974) 'An econometric model of the UK financial sector: some preliminary findings', pp. 323–61, in Johnson, H.G. and Nobay, A.R. (eds), *Issues in Monetary Economics*, London: Oxford University Press.

Coats, W.L. (1982) 'Modelling the short-run demand for money with exogenous supply', *Economic Inquiry*, 20, 222–39.

Coghlan, R.T. (1978) 'A transactions demand for money', *Bank of England Quarterly Bulletin*, 18, 48–60.

Cooley, T.F. and LeRoy, S.F. (1981) 'Identification and estimation of money demand', *American Economic Review*, 71, 825–44.

Courakis, A.S. (1974) 'Clearing bank asset choice behaviour: a mean-variance treatment', *Oxford Bulletin of Economics and Statistics*, 36, 173–201.

——— (1975) 'Testing theories of discount house portfolio selection', *Review of Economic Studies*, 42, 643–8.

——— (1978) 'Serial correlation and a Bank of England study of the demand for money: an exercise in measurement without theory', *Economic Journal*, 88, 537–48.

——— (1980) 'In search of an explanation of commercial bank short-run portfolio selection', *Oxford Bulletin of Economics and Statistics*, 42, 305–35.

——— (1988) 'Modelling portfolio selection', *Economic Journal*, 98, 619–42.

Cover, J.P. and Keeler, J.P. (1988) 'Estimating money demand in log-first-difference form', *Southern Economic Journal*, 55, 751–67.

Cuthbertson, K. (1985a) *The Supply and Demand for Money*, Oxford: Basil Blackwell.

——— (1985b) 'Sterling bank lending to UK industrial and commercial companies', *Oxford Bulletin of Economics and Statistics*, 47, 91–118.

——— (1986a) 'Monetary anticipations and the demand for money: some UK evidence', *Bulletin of Economic Research*, 38, 257–70.

——— (1986b) 'Price expectations and lags in the demand for money', *Scottish Journal of Political Economy*, 33, 334–54.

——— (1988a) 'The demand for M1: a forward-looking buffer stock model', *Oxford Economic Papers*, 40, 110–31.

——— (1988b) 'Expectations, learning and the Kalman filter', *Manchester School*, 56, 223–46.

——— (1991) 'The encompassing implications of feedforward versus feedback mechanisms: a reply to Hendry', *Oxford Economic Papers*, 43, 344–50.

Cuthbertson, K. and Barlow, D. (1990) 'The determination of liquid asset holdings of the UK personal sector', *Manchester School*, 58, 348–60.

Cuthbertson, K. and Foster, N. (1982) 'Bank lending to industrial and commercial companies in three models of the UK economy', *National Institute Economic Review*, 102, 63–77.

Cuthbertson, K., Hall, S.G. and Taylor, M.P. (1992) *Applied Econometric Techniques*, London: Philip Allan.

Cuthbertson, K. and Taylor, M.P. (1986) 'Monetary anticipation and the demand for money in the UK: testing rationality in the shock-absorber hypothesis', *Journal of Applied Econometrics*, 1, 355–65.

—— (1987a) 'Buffer stock money: an appraisal', pp. 103–24, in Currie, D.A., Goodhart, C.A.E. and Llewellyn, D.T. (eds), *The Operation and Regulation of Financial Markets*, London: Macmillan.

—— (1987b) 'The demand for money: a dynamic rational expectations model', *Economic Journal*, 97 (Supplement), 65–76.

—— (1987c) 'Monetary anticipations and the demand for money: some evidence for the UK', *Weltwirtschaftliches Archiv*, 123, 509–20.

—— (1988) 'Monetary anticipations and the demand for money in the US: further results', *Southern Economic Journal*, 55, 326–35.

—— (1989) 'Anticipated and unanticipated variables in the demand for M1 in the UK', *Manchester School*, 57, 319–39.

—— (1990a) 'The case of the missing money and the Lucas critique', *Journal of Macroeconomics*, 12, 437–54.

—— (1990b) 'Money demand, expectations and the forward-looking model', *Journal of Policy Modelling*, 12, 289–315.

Darby, M. (1972) 'The allocation of transitory income among consumers' assets', *American Economic Review*, 62, 928–41.

Darby, M.R. and Stockman, A.C. (1983) 'The mark III international transmission model: specification and estimates', pp. 85–161, in Darby, M.R. and Lothian, J.R. (eds), *The International Transmission of Inflation*, Chicago: University of Chicago Press.

Davidson, J. (1987) 'Disequilibrium money: some further results with a monetary model of the UK', pp. 125–49, in Currie, D.A., Goodhart, C.A.E. and Llewellyn, D.T. (eds), *The Operation and Regulation of Financial Markets*, London: Macmillan.

Davidson, J. and Ireland, J. (1987) 'Buffer stock models of the monetary sector', *National Institute Economic Review*, 121, 67–71.

—— (1990) 'Buffer stocks, credit and aggregation effects in the demand for broad money: theory and an application to the UK personal sector', *Journal of Policy Modelling*, 12, 349–76.

Domowitz, I. and Hakkio, C.S. (1990) 'Interpreting an error-correction model: partial adjustment, forward-looking behaviour and dynamic international money demand', *Journal of Applied Econometrics*, 5, 29–46.

Dotsey, M. (1988) 'The demand for currency in the US', *Journal of Money, Credit and Banking*, 20, 22–40.

Dowd, K. (1990a) 'The value of time and the transactions demand for money', *Journal of Money, Credit and Banking*, 22, 51–64.

—— (1990b) 'The value of time hypothesis and the demand for money: some new evidence for the UK', *Applied Economics*, 22, 599–603.

Dutkowsky, D.H. and Foote, W.G. (1988) 'The demand for money: a rational expectations approach', *Review of Economics and Statistics*, 70, 83–92.

Dutton, D.S. and Gramm, W.P. (1973) 'Transactions costs, the wage rate and the demand for money', *American Economic Review*, 63, 652–65.

Eisner, R. (1971) 'Non-linear estimates of the liquidity trap', *Econometrica*, 39, 861–4.

Engle, R.F. and Granger, C.W.J. (1987) 'Cointegration and error-correction: representation, estimation and testing', *Econometrica*, 55, 251–76.

Enzler, J., Johnson, L. and Paulus, J. (1976) 'Some problems of money demand', *Brookings Papers on Economic Activity*, 1, 261–80.

Eppen, G.D. and Fama, E.F. (1969) 'Cash balance and simple portfolio problems with proportional costs', *International Economic Review*, 10, 119–33.

Fair, R.C. (1987) 'International evidence on the demand for money', *Review of Economics and Statistics*, 69, 473–80.

Fair, R.C. and Jaffee, D.M. (1972) 'Methods of estimation for markets in disequilibrium', *Econometrica*, 40, 497–514.

Feige, E.L. (1967) 'Expectations and adjustments in the monetary sector', *American Economic Review*, 57 (Papers and proceedings), 462–73.

Feige, E.L. and Parkin, J.M. (1971) 'The optimal quantity of money, bonds, commodity inventories and capital', *American Economic Review*, 61, 335–49.

Fisher, D. and Serletis, A. (1989) 'Velocity and the growth of money in the United States 1970–85', *Journal of Macroeconomics*, 11, 323–32.

Fisher, I. (1911) *The Purchasing Power of Money*, New York: Macmillan.

Foster, J. (1975) 'The demand for building society shares and deposits 1961–73', *Oxford Bulletin of Economics and Statistics*, 37, 319–41.

Frenkel, J.A. and Jovanovic, B. (1980) 'On transactions and precautionary demand for money', *Quarterly Journal of Economics*, 94, 25–43.

Freund, R.J. (1956) 'The introduction of risk into a programming model', *Econometrica*, 24, 253–63.

Friedman, B.M. (1978) 'Crowding out or crowding in? The economic consequences of financing government deficits', *Brookings Papers on Economic Activity*, 3, 593–641.

Friedman, B.M. and Roley, V.V. (1979) 'Investors' portfolio behaviour under alternative models of long-term interest rate expectations: unitary, rational or autoregressive', *Econometrica*, 47, 1475–97.

Friedman, M. (1956) 'The quantity theory of money: a restatement', pp. 3–21, in Friedman, M. (ed.), *Studies in the Quantity Theory of Money*, Chicago: University of Chicago Press.

———— (1983) 'Monetary variability: United States and Japan', *Journal of Money, Credit and Banking*, 15, 339–43.

———— (1984) 'Lessons from the 1979–82 monetary policy experiment', *American Economic Review*, 74, 397–400.

———— (1988) 'Money and the stock market', *Journal of Political Economy*, 96, 221–45.

Friedman, M. and Schwartz, A.J. (1982) *Monetary Trends in the United States and the United Kingdom: Their Relation to Income, Prices and Interest Rates 1867–1975*, Chicago: University of Chicago Press.

Gandolfi, A.E. and Lothian, J.R. (1983) 'International price behaviour and the demand for money', pp. 421–61, in Darby, M.R. and Lothian, J.R. (eds), *The International Transmission of Inflation*, Chicago: University of Chicago Press.

Garcia, G. and Pak, S. (1979) 'Some clues in the case of the missing money', *American Economic Review*, 69, 330–4.

Ghosh, D. and Parkin, M. (1972) 'A theoretical and empirical analysis of the portfolio, debt and interest rate behaviour of building societies', *Manchester School*, 40, 231–44.

Gilbert, C.L. (1986) 'Professor Hendry's econometric methodology', *Oxford Bulletin of Economics and Statistics*, 48, 283–307.

Goldfeld, S.M. (1973) 'The demand for money revisited', *Brookings Papers on Economic Activity*, 3, 577–638.

—— (1976) 'The case of the missing money', *Brookings Papers on Economic Activity*, 3, 683–739.

Goldfeld, S.M. and Sichel, D.E. (1987) 'Money demand: the effects of inflation and alternative adjustment mechanisms', *Review of Economics and Statistics*, 69, 511–15.

—— (1990) 'The demand for money', pp. 299–356, in Friedman, B.M. and Hahn, F.H. (eds), *Handbook of Monetary Economics, Vol. I*, Amsterdam: North-Holland.

Goodfriend, M. (1985) 'Reinterpreting money demand regressions', pp. 207–42, in Brunner, K. and Meltzer, A.H. (eds), *Understanding Monetary Regimes*, Amsterdam: North-Holland.

Goodhart, C.A.E. (1981) 'Problems of monetary management: the UK experience', pp. 111–43, in Courakis, A.S. (ed.), *Inflation, Depression and Economic Policy in the West*, London: Mansell.

—— (1984) 'Disequilibrium money – a note', pp. 254–76, in Goodhart, C.A.E., *Monetary Theory and Practice: the UK Experience*, London: Macmillan.

—— (1989a) 'The conduct of monetary policy', *Economic Journal*, 99, 293–346.

—— (1989b) *Money, Information and Uncertainty*, London: Macmillan, 2nd edn.

Goodhart, C.A.E. and Crockett, A.D. (1970) 'The importance of money', *Bank of England Quarterly Bulletin*, 10, 159–98.

Gordon, R.J. (1984) 'The short-run demand for money: a reconsideration', *Journal of Money, Credit and Banking*, 16, 403–34.

Granger, C.W.J. (1986) 'Developments in the study of cointegrated economic variables', *Oxford Bulletin of Economics and Statistics*, 48, 213–28.

Graves, P.E. (1980) 'The velocity of money: evidence for the UK 1911–66', *Economic Inquiry*, 18, 631–9.

Gray, M.R. and Parkin, J.M. (1973) 'Portfolio diversification as optimal precautionary behaviour', pp. 301–15, in Morishima, M. and others, *Theory of Demand: Real and Monetary*, London: Oxford University Press.

Green, C.J. (1984) 'Preliminary results from a five-sector flow of funds model of the UK 1972–77', *Economic Modelling*, 1, 304–26.

Grice, J. and Bennett, A. (1984) 'Wealth and the demand for £M3 in the UK 1963–78', *Manchester School*, 52, 239–71.

Grossman, H.I. and Policano, A.J. (1975) 'Money balances, commodity inventories and inflationary expectations', *Journal of Political Economy*, 83, 1093–1112.

Gupta, K.L. (1980) 'Some controversial aspects of the demand for money', *Journal of Money, Credit and Banking*, 12, 660–5.

Hacche, G. (1974) 'The demand for money in the UK: experience since 1971', *Bank of England Quarterly Bulletin*, 14, 284–305.

Hafer, R.W. and Hein, S.E. (1979) 'Evidence on the temporal stability of the demand for money relationship in the US', *Federal Reserve Bank of St. Louis Review*, 61, 3–14.

——— (1980) 'The dynamics and estimation of short-run money demand', *Federal Reserve Bank of St. Louis Review*, 62, 26–35.

Hafer, R.W. and Jansen, D.W. (1991) 'The demand for money in the US: evidence from cointegration tests', *Journal of Money, Credit and Banking*, 23, 155–68.

Hafer, R.W. and Thornton, D.L. (1986) 'Price expectations and the demand for money: a comment', *Review of Economics and Statistics*, 68, 539–42.

Hall, S.G., Henry, S.G.B. and Wilcox, J.B. (1990) 'The long-run determination of UK monetary aggregates', pp. 127–66, in Henry, S.G.B. and Patterson, K.D. (eds), *Economic Modelling at the Bank of England*, London: Chapman & Hall.

Hall, T.E. and Noble, N.R. (1987) 'Velocity and the variability of money growth: evidence from Granger-causality tests', *Journal of Money, Credit and Banking*, 19, 112–16.

Hamburger, M.J. (1977a) 'The demand for money in an open economy: Germany and the UK', *Journal of Monetary Economics*, 3, 25–40.

——— (1977b) 'The behaviour of the money stock: is there a puzzle?', *Journal of Monetary Economics*, 3, 265–88.

——— (1983) 'Recent velocity behaviour, the demand for money and monetary policy', in Federal Reserve Bank of San Francisco, *Monetary Targeting and Velocity*.

——— (1987) 'A stable money demand function', *Contemporary Policy Issues*, 5, 34–40.

Harvey, A.C. (1981) *Time Series Models*, Oxford: Philip Allan.

Hendry, D.F. (1979) 'Predictive failure and econometric modelling in macro-economics: the transactions demand for money', pp. 217–42, in Ormerod, P. (ed.), *Economic Modelling*, London: Heinemann.

——— (1985) 'Monetary economic myth and econometric reality', *Oxford Review of Economic Policy*, 1, 72–84.

——— (1988) 'The encompassing implications of feedback versus feedforward mechanisms in econometrics', *Oxford Economic Papers*, 40, 132–49.

Hendry, D.F. and Ericsson, N.R. (1991a) 'An econometric analysis of UK money demand in *Monetary Trends in the United States and the United Kingdom*, by Milton Friedman and Anna J. Schwartz', *American Economic Review*, 81, 8–37.

——— (1991b) 'Modelling the demand for narrow money in the UK and the US', *European Economic Review*, 35, 887–932.

Hendry, D.F. and Mizon, G. (1978) 'Serial correlation as a convenient simplification, not a nuisance: a comment on a study of the demand for money by the Bank of England', *Economic Journal*, 88, 549–63.

Hendry, D.F., Pagan, A.R. and Sargan, J.D. (1984) 'Dynamic specification', pp. 1023–1100, in Griliches, Z. and Intriligator, M.D. (eds), *Handbook of Econometrics*, Vol. 2, Amsterdam: North-Holland.

Hicks, J.R. (1967) 'The pure theory of portfolio selection', pp. 103–25, in Hicks, J.R., *Critical Essays in Monetary Theory*, London: Oxford University Press.

Hoggarth, G. and Ormerod, P. (1985) 'The demand for long-term government securities in the UK by the non-bank private sector', pp. 171–91, in Currie, D. (ed.), *Advances in Monetary Economics*, London: Croom Helm.

Honohan, P. (1980) 'Testing a standard theory of portfolio selection', *Oxford Bulletin of Economics and Statistics*, 42, 17–35.

Hood, W. (1987) 'The allocation of UK personal sector liquid assets', *Treasury Working Paper*, 46.

Howard, D.H. and Johnson, K.H. (1983) 'The behaviour of monetary aggregates in major industrialised countries', *Journal of Money, Credit and Banking*, 15, 455–68.

Hwang, H. (1985) 'Tests of the adjustment process and linear homogeneity in a stock adjustment model of money demand', *Review of Economics and Statistics*, 67, 689–92.

Johansen, S. (1988) 'Statistical analysis of cointegrating vectors', *Journal of Economic Dynamics and Control*, 12, 231–54.

Johansen, S. and Juselius, K. (1990) 'Maximum likelihood estimation and inference on cointegration – with applications to the demand for money', *Oxford Bulletin of Economics and Statistics*, 52, 169–210.

Johnston, R.B. (1984) 'The demand for non-interest-bearing money in the UK', *Treasury Working Paper*, 28.

——— (1985) 'The demand for liquidity aggregates by the UK personal sector', *Treasury Working Paper*, 36.

Judd, J.P. and Scadding, J.L. (1982) 'The search for a stable money demand function: a survey of the post-1973 literature', *Journal of Economic Literature*, 20, 993–1023.

Kanniainen, V. and Tarkka, J. (1986) 'On the shock-absorption view of money: international evidence from the 1960s and 1970s', *Applied Economics*, 18, 1085–1101.

Karni, E. (1973) 'The transactions demand for cash: incorporation of the value of time into the inventory approach', *Journal of Political Economy*, 81, 1216–25.

——— (1974) 'The value of time and the demand for money', *Journal of Money, Credit and Banking*, 6, 45–64.

Kavanagh, N.J. and Walters, A.A. (1966) 'The demand for money in the UK 1877–1961: preliminary findings', *Bulletin of the Oxford University Institute of Economics and Statistics*, 28, 93–116.

Keating, G. (1985) 'The financial sector of the London Business School model', pp. 86–126, in Currie, D. (ed.), *Advances in Monetary Economics*, London: Croom Helm.

Kent, R.J. (1985) 'The demand for the services of money', *Applied Economics*, 17, 817–26.

Khan, M.S. (1973) 'A note on the secular behaviour of velocity within the context of the inventory-theoretic model of demand for money', *Manchester School*, 41, 207–13.

Klein, B. (1974a) 'The competitive supply of money', *Journal of Money, Credit and Banking*, 6, 423–54.

———— (1974b) ¦Competitive interest payments on bank deposits and the long-run demand for money', *American Economic Review*, 64, 931–49.

———— (1977) 'The demand for quality adjusted cash balances: price uncertainty in the US demand for money function', *Journal of Political Economy*, 85, 691–716.

Knight, M.D. and Wymer, C.R. (1978) 'A macroeconomic model of the UK', *IMF Staff Papers*, 25, 742–78.

Knoester, A. (1984) 'Theoretical principles of the buffer mechanism, monetary quasi-equilibrium and its spillover effects', *Kredit und Kapital*, 17, 243–60.

Kohn, M. and Manchester, J. (1985) 'International evidence on misspecification of the standard money demand equation', *Journal of Monetary Economics*, 16, 87–94.

Koskela, E. and Viren, M. (1987) 'Inflation, hedging and the demand for money: some empirical evidence', *Economic Inquiry*, 25, 251–65.

Laffont, J.J. and Garcia, R. (1977) 'Disequilibrium econometrics for business loans', *Econometrica*, 45, 1187–1204.

Laidler, D.E.W. (1966a) 'Some evidence on the demand for money', *Journal of Political Economy*, 74, 55–68.

———— (1966b) 'The rate of interest and the demand for money – some empirical evidence', *Journal of Political Economy*, 74, 543–55.

———— (1971) 'The influence of money on economic activity: a survey of some current problems', pp. 75–135, in Clayton, G., Gilbert, J.C. and Sedgwick, R. (eds), *Monetary Theory and Monetary Policy in the 1970s*, London: Oxford University Press.

———— (1980) 'The demand for money in the US – yet again', pp. 219–71, in Brunner, K. and Meltzer, A.H. (eds), *On the State of Macroeconomics*, Amsterdam: North-Holland.

———— (1982) *Monetarist Perspectives*, Oxford: Philip Allan.

———— (1984) 'The buffer stock notion in monetary economics', *Economic Journal*, 94 (Supplement), 17–34.

———— (1985) *The Demand for Money: Theories, Evidence and Problems*, New York: Harper & Row, 3rd edn.

———— (1987) 'Buffer stock money and the transmission mechanism', *Federal Reserve Bank of Atlanta Economic Review*, March/April, 11–23.

Laidler, D.E.W. and Bentley, B. (1983) 'A small macro-model of the post-war US', *Manchester School*, 51, 317–40.

Laidler, D.E.W. and O'Shea, P. (1980) 'An empirical macro-model of an open economy under fixed exchange rates: the UK 1954–70', *Economica*, 47, 141–58.

Laidler, D.E.W. and Parkin, J.M. (1970) 'The demand for money in the UK 1956–67: some preliminary estimates', *Manchester School*, 38, 187–208.

Lewis, K.A. (1974) 'A note on the interest elasticity of the transactions demand for cash', *Journal of Finance*, 29, 1149–52.

Lieberman, C. (1980) 'The long-run and short-run demand for money revisited', *Journal of Money, Credit and Banking*, 12, 43–57.

Lintner, J. (1965) 'The valuation of risk assets and the selection of risky investments in stock portfolios and capital budgets', *Review of Economics and Statistics*, 47, 13–37.

Litzenberger, R.H. (1971) 'The effect of credit on the interest elasticity of the transactions demand for cash: comment', *Journal of Finance*, 26, 1161–2.

Lothian, J.R., Darby, M.R. and Tindall, M. (1990) 'Buffer stock models of the demand for money and the conduct of monetary policy', *Journal of Policy Modelling*, 12, 325–45.

Lubrano, M., Pierse, R.G. and Richard, J.F. (1986) 'Stability of a UK money demand equation: a Bayesian approach to testing exogeneity', *Review of Economic Studies*, 53, 603–34.

Lucas, R.E. (1976) 'Econometric policy evaluation: a critique', pp. 19–46, in Brunner, K. and Meltzer, A.H. (eds), *The Phillips Curve and Labour Markets*, Amsterdam: North-Holland.

—— (1988) 'Money demand in the United States: a quantitative review', pp. 137–67, in Brunner, K. and Meltzer, A.H. (eds), *Money, Cycles and Exchange Rates: Essays in Honour of Allan H. Meltzer*, Amsterdam: North-Holland.

MacKinnon, J.G. and Milbourne, R. (1984) 'Monetary anticipations and the demand for money', *Journal of Monetary Economics*, 13, 263–74.

—— (1988) 'Are price equations really money demand equations on their heads?', *Journal of Applied Econometrics*, 3, 295–305.

Mankiw, N.G. and Summers, L.H. (1986) 'Money demand and the effects of fiscal policies', *Journal of Money, Credit and Banking*, 18, 415–29.

Markowitz, H.M. (1952) 'Portfolio selection', *Journal of Finance*, 7, 77–91.

—— (1959) *Portfolio Selection: efficient diversification of investments*, New York: Wiley.

Matthews, K.G.P. (1984) 'Private sector expenditure in the inter-war period: an integrated portfolio approach', *Manchester School*, 52, 33–44.

Matthews, K. and Minford, P. (1980) 'Private sector expenditure and financial asset accumulation in the UK', *Journal of Money, Credit and Banking*, 12, 644–53.

McCallum, B.T. (1976) 'Rational expectations and the estimation of econometric models: an alternative procedure', *International Economic Review*, 17, 484–90.

Melitz, J. and Sterdyniak, H. (1979) 'An econometric study of the British monetary system', *Economic Journal*, 89, 874–96.

Mellis, C., Meen, G., Pain, N. and Whittaker, R. (1989) 'The new Treasury model project', *Treasury Working Paper*, 54.

Meltzer, A.H. (1963) 'The demand for money: the evidence from the time series', *Journal of Political Economy*, 71, 219–46.

Meyer, P.A. and Neri, J.A. (1975) 'A Keynes-Friedman money demand function', *American Economic Review*, 65, 610–23.

Milbourne, R. (1983a) 'Optimal money holding under uncertainty', *International Economic Review*, 24, 685–98.

—— (1983b) 'Price expectations and the demand for money: resolution of a paradox', *Review of Economics and Statistics*, 65, 633–8.

———— (1986) 'Price expectations and the demand for money: reply', *Review of Economics and Statistics*, 68, 543–4.

———— (1987) 'Re-examining the buffer stock model of money', *Economic Journal*, 97 (Supplement), 130–42.

———— (1988) 'Disequilibrium buffer stock models: a survey', *Journal of Economic Surveys*, 2, 187–207.

Milbourne, R., Buckholtz, P. and Wasan, M.T. (1983) 'A theoretical derivation of the functional form of short-run money holdings', *Review of Economic Studies*, 50, 531–41.

Miller, M.H. and Orr, D. (1966) 'A model of the demand for money by firms', *Quarterly Journal of Economics*, 80, 413–35.

———— (1968) 'The demand for money by firms: extension of analytical results', *Journal of Finance*, 23, 735–59.

Miller, S.M. (1990) 'Disequilibrium macroeconomics, money as a buffer stock and the estimation of money demand', *Journal of Macroeconomics*, 12, 563–86.

———— (1991) 'Monetary dynamics: an application of cointegration and error-correction modelling', *Journal of Money, Credit and Banking*, 23, 139–53.

Mills, T.C. (1978) 'The functional form of the UK demand for money', *Applied Statistics*, 27, 52–7.

Mishkin, F.S. (1982) 'Does anticipated monetary policy matter? An econometric investigation', *Journal of Political Economy*, 90, 22–51.

———— (1983) *A Rational Expectations Approach to Macroeconomics*, Chicago: Chicago University Press.

Moore, B.J. and Threadgold, A.R. (1985) 'Corporate bank borrowing in the UK 1965–81', *Economica*, 52, 65–78.

Muscatelli, V.A. (1988) 'Alternative models of buffer stock money: an empirical investigation', *Scottish Journal of Political Economy*, 35, 1–21.

———— (1989) 'A comparison of the rational expectations and general to specific approaches to modelling the demand for M1', *Oxford Bulletin of Economics and Statistics*, 51, 353–75.

———— (1990) 'Monetary targets, buffer stock money and money market dynamics', *Scottish Journal of Political Economy*, 37, 166–83.

Nadiri, M.I. and Rosen, S. (1969) 'Interrelated factor demand functions', *American Economic Review*, 59, 457–71.

Nelson, C.R. (1975) 'Rational expectations and the estimation of econometric models', *International Economic Review*, 16, 555–61.

Nickell, S.J. (1985) 'Error-correction, partial adjustment and all that: an expository note', *Oxford Bulletin of Economics and Statistics*, 47, 119–30.

Norton, W.E. (1969) 'Debt management and monetary policy in the UK', *Economic Journal*, 79, 475–94.

O'Herlihy, C. St J. and Spencer, J.E. (1972) 'Building societies' behaviour 1955–70', *National Institute Economic Review*, 61, 40–52.

Orr, D. (1970) *Cash Management and the Demand for Money*, New York: Praeger.

Owen, P.D. (1981) 'Dynamic models of portfolio behaviour: a general integrated model incorporating sequencing effects', *American Economic Review*, 71, 231–8.

——— (1985) 'Systems testing of wealth-aggregation restrictions in an integrated model of expenditure and asset behaviour', *Applied Economics*, 17, 1099–1115.

——— (1986) 'Wealth-composition and cross-equation effects in the UK personal sector's expenditure and portfolio behaviour', *Manchester School*, 54, 65–98.

Parkin, J.M. (1970) 'Discount house portfolio and debt selection', *Review of Economic Studies*, 37, 469–97.

Parkin, J.M., Gray, M.R. and Barrett, R.J. (1970) 'The portfolio behaviour of commercial banks', pp. 229–51, in Hilton, K. and Heathfield, D.F. (eds), *The Econometric Study of the UK*, London: Macmillan.

Paroush, J. and Ruthenberg, D. (1986) 'Automated teller machines and the share of demand deposits in the money supply', *European Economic Review*, 30, 1207–15.

Patterson, K.D. (1987) 'The specification and stability of the demand for money in the UK', *Economica*, 54, 41–55.

Pigou, A.C. (1917) 'The value of money', *Quarterly Journal of Economics*, 32, 38–65.

Prais, S.J. and Houthakker, H.S. (1971) *The Analysis of Family Budgets*, London: Cambridge University Press.

Pratt, J.W. (1964) 'Risk aversion in the small and the large', *Econometrica*, 32, 122–36.

Price, L.D.D. (1972) 'The demand for money in the UK: a further investigation', *Bank of England Quarterly Bulletin*, 12, 43–55.

Purvis, D.D. (1978) 'Dynamic models of portfolio behaviour: more on pitfalls in financial model building', *American Economic Review*, 68, 403–9.

Radecki, L.J. and Wenninger, J. (1985) 'Recent instability in M1's velocity', *Federal Reserve Bank of New York Quarterly Review*, Autumn, 16–22.

Rama Sastry, A.S. (1970) 'The effect of credit on transactions demand for cash', *Journal of Finance*, 25, 777–81.

——— (1971) 'The effect of credit on the interest elasticity of the transaction demand for cash: reply', *Journal of Finance*, 26, 1163–5.

Roley, V.V. (1985) 'Money demand predictability', *Journal of Money, Credit and Banking*, 17, 611–41.

Romer, D. (1986) 'A simple general equilibrium version of the Baumol-Tobin model', *Quarterly Journal of Economics*, 101, 663–85.

Rose, A.K. (1985) 'An alternative approach to the American demand for money', *Journal of Money, Credit and Banking*, 17, 439–55.

Ryan, T.M. (1973) 'The demand for financial assets by the British life funds', *Oxford Bulletin of Economics and Statistics*, 35, 61–7.

Santomero, A.M. (1974) 'A model of the demand for money by households', *Journal of Finance*, 29, 89–102.

——— (1979) 'The role of transactions costs and rates of return on the demand deposit decision', *Journal of Monetary Economics*, 5, 343–64.

Santomero, A.M. and Seater, J.J. (1981) 'Partial adjustment in the demand for money: theory and empirics', *American Economic Review*, 71, 566–78.

Saving, T.R. (1971) 'Transactions costs and the demand for money', *American Economic Review*, 61, 407–20.

Serletis, A. (1987a) 'On the demand for money in the United States', *Empirical Economics*, 12, 249–55.

—— (1987b) 'The demand for Divisia M1, M2 and M3 in the United States', *Journal of Macroeconomics*, 9, 567–91.

—— (1991) 'The demand for Divisia money in the United States: a dynamic flexible demand system', *Journal of Money, Credit and Banking*, 23, 35–52.

Sharpe, I. (1973) 'A quarterly econometric model of portfolio choice – part 1: specification and estimation problems', *Economic Record*, 49, 518–33.

Sharpe, W.F. (1964) 'Capital asset prices: a theory of market equilibrium under conditions of risk', *Journal of Finance*, 19, 425–42.

Slovin, M.B. and Sushka, M.E. (1983) 'Money, interest rates and risk', *Journal of Monetary Economics*, 12, 475–82.

Smirlock, M. (1982) 'Inflation uncertainty and the demand for money', *Economic Inquiry*, 20, 355–64.

Smith, G. (1975) 'Pitfalls in financial model building: a clarification', *American Economic Review*, 65, 510–16.

—— (1978) 'Dynamic models of portfolio behaviour: comment on Purvis', *American Economic Review*, 68, 410–16.

Smith, G. and Brainard, W. (1976) 'The value of a priori information in estimating a financial model', *Journal of Finance*, 31, 1299–1322.

Smith, G.W. (1986) 'A dynamic Baumol-Tobin model of money demand', *Review of Economic Studies*, 53, 465–9.

Spencer, D.E. (1985) 'Money demand and the price level', *Review of Economics and Statistics*, 67, 490–6.

Spencer, P.D. (1981) 'A model of the demand for British Government stocks by non-bank residents 1967–77', *Economic Journal*, 91, 938–60.

—— (1984) 'Precautionary and speculative aspects of the behaviour of banks in the UK under Competition and Credit Control 1972–80', *Economic Journal*, 94, 554–68.

—— (1986) *Financial Innovation, Efficiency and Disequilibrium*, Oxford: Oxford University Press.

Spencer, P.D. and Mowl, C. (1978) 'A financial sector for the Treasury model: part 1, the model of the domestic monetary system', *Treasury Working Paper*, 8.

Spindt, P.A. (1985) 'Money is what money does: monetary aggregates and the equation of exchange', *Journal of Political Economy*, 93, 175–204.

Spitzer, J.J. (1976) 'The demand for money, the liquidity trap and functional forms', *International Economic Review*, 17, 220–7.

Sprenkle, C.M. (1966) 'Large economic units, banks and the transactions demand for money', *Quarterly Journal of Economics*, 80, 436–42.

—— (1969) 'The uselessness of transactions demand models', *Journal of Finance*, 24, 835–47.

—— (1972) 'On the observed transactions demand for money', *Manchester School*, 40, 261–7.

—— (1974) 'An overdue note on some "ancient but popular" literature', *Journal of Finance*, 29, 1577–80.

—— (1984) 'On liquidity preference – again: comment', *American Economic Review*, 74, 809–11.

Sprenkle, C.M. and Miller, M.H. (1980) 'The precautionary demand for narrow and broad money', *Economica*, 47, 407–21.

Starleaf, D.R. (1970) 'The specification of money demand-supply models which involve the use of distributed lags', *Journal of Finance*, 25, 743–60.

Starleaf, D.R. and Reimer, R. (1967) 'The Keynesian demand function for money: some statistical tests', *Journal of Finance*, 22, 71–6.

Startz, R. (1979) 'Implicit interest on demand deposits', *Journal of Monetary Economics*, 5, 515–34.

Stiglitz, J.E. and Weiss, A. (1981) 'Credit rationing in markets with imperfect information', *American Economic Review*, 71, 393–410.

Swamy, P.A.V.B. and Tavlas, G.S. (1989) 'Modelling buffer stock money: an appraisal', *Journal of Policy Modelling*, 11, 593–612.

Taylor, M.P. (1987) 'Financial innovation, inflation and the stability of the demand for broad money in the UK', *Bulletin of Economic Research*, 39, 225–33.

Teigen, R. (1964) 'Demand and supply functions for money in the US', *Econometrica*, 32, 477–509.

Thomas, R.L. (1985) *Introductory Econometrics*, London: Longman.

Thompson, W.N. (1984) 'Money in UK macro models', pp. 100–68, in Demery, D., Duck, N.W., Sumner, M.T., Thomas, R.L. and Thompson, W.N., *Macroeconomics*, London: Longman.

Thornton, D.L. (1982) 'Maximum likelihood estimates of a partial adjustment-adaptive expectations model of the demand for money', *Review of Economics and Statistics*, 64, 325–9.

Tobin, J. (1956) 'The interest elasticity of transactions demand for cash', *Review of Economics and Statistics*, 38, 241–7.

—— (1958) 'Liquidity preference as behaviour towards risk', *Review of Economic Studies*, 25, 65–86.

—— (1965) 'The theory of portfolio selection', pp. 3–51, in Hahn, F. and Brechling, F.P.R. (eds), *The Theory of Interest Rates*, London: Macmillan.

—— (1969) 'A general equilibrium approach to monetary theory', *Journal of Money, Credit and Banking*, 1, 15–29.

Tucker, D.P. (1966) 'Dynamic income adjustment to money supply changes', *American Economic Review*, 56, 433–49.

—— (1971) 'Macroeconomic models and the demand for money under market disequilibrium', *Journal of Money, Credit and Banking*, 3, 57–83.

Walters, A.A. (1965) 'Professor Friedman on the demand for money', *Journal of Political Economy*, 73, 545–51.

—— (1967) 'The demand for money – the dynamic properties of the multiplier', *Journal of Political Economy*, 75, 293–8.

Weale, M. (1986) 'The structure of personal sector short-term asset holdings', *Manchester School*, 54, 141–61.

Weinrobe, M.D. (1972) 'A simple model of the precautionary demand for money', *Southern Economic Journal*, 39, 11–18.

Wenninger, J. (1988) 'Money demand – some long-run properties', *Federal Reserve Bank of New York Quarterly Review*, Spring, 23–40.

Westaway, P. and Walton, D. (1991) 'Endogenous financial innovation and the demand for M0', pp. 149–70, in Taylor, M.P. (ed.), *Money and Financial Markets*, Oxford: Basil Blackwell.

Whalen, E.L. (1966) 'A rationalisation of the precautionary demand for cash', *Quarterly Journal of Economics*, 80, 314–24.

White, W.R. (1975) 'Some econometric models of deposit bank portfolio behaviour in the UK 1963–70', pp. 457–99, in Renton, G.A. (ed.), *Modelling the Economy*, London: Heinemann.

White, W.H. (1981) 'The case for and against disequilibrium money', *IMF Staff Papers*, 28, 534–72.

Wrightsman, D. and Terniko, J. (1971) 'On the measurement of opportunity cost in transactions demand models', *Journal of Finance*, 26, 947–50.

Index